ASEFF
THE SPY

RUSSIAN TERRORIST AND POLICE STOOL

ASEFF
THE SPY
RUSSIAN TERRORIST
AND POLICE STOOL

BORIS NIKOLAEJEWSKY

ACADEMIC INTERNATIONAL / orbis academicus

1969

THE RUSSIAN SERIES / Volume 14

Boris Nikolajewsky

ASEFF THE SPY

$3 23.2$
$N58a$
88580 *april 1974*

Reprint of the 1934 edition

Library of Congress Catalog Number: 73-98133
SBN 87569 - 011 - 4

Printed in the United States of America

Academic International / orbis academicus
Box 666 Hattiesburg, Mississippi 39401

PREFACE

PROVOCATION as a means of combatting revolutionary movements in countries where there exists little or no political freedom is not confined to Russia. Italy under Austrian rule, France in the time of Louis Philippe and Napoleon III, even Prussia in the reign of Frederick William IV, knew provocation on a much wider scale than contemporary Russia. It was also extensively used at different periods in many other countries. But whereas in all other countries it has only been used at specific periods and has consequently never become traditional, in Russia, on the contrary, the continuous and increasingly bitter struggle between the

Government and the growing revolutionary movement throughout the nineteenth century resulted in provocation being established as a system, to the development of which the best brains of the police were applied. There is nothing surprising, therefore, in that Russia has given the world a *classical* example of provocation.

The history of Aseff is undoubtedly such an example. Aseff served the police for over fifteen years as a secret agent and was, at the same time, for over five of those years the head of the largest and most important terrorist organizations known to history. He not only betrayed hundreds of revolutionaries to the police, but also organized a series of terrorist attempts, the success of which focussed on him the eyes of the world. Among such attempts may be mentioned the assassinations of Plehve, the Minister of the Interior, the Grand Duke Sergei and a number of other representative personages. He organized, too, an attempt against the Czar, the failure of which cannot be laid at his door. Aseff is therefore a perfect example of the logical conclusion of provocation applied as a system.

Acting in two worlds, in that of the secret police on the one hand, and in that of the revolutionaries on the other, Aseff never identified himself wholly with either of them, and, following his own ends, now betrayed revolutionaries, now the police. His activities left a lasting mark on both of these worlds. He was not, however, behind every action taken either by the Battle Organization of the Social Revolutionary Party, whose leader he was for so long, or by the Political Police, whose great hope he was in the struggle with the revolutionary organizations. And it is important to distinguish between the real character of the Battle Organization, its problems and its other members, and the personality of him who was accounted its leader. Nevertheless, Aseff's rôle in both these worlds was so important that, without understanding it, the student will be unable to grasp many things in the history of the first Russian Revolution of 1905 and the years that followed it.

It is this which makes Aseff's biography of interest to the historian, however much he may disapprove of him as a type. To present such a biography on the basis of ascertained facts, and to paint a historically true picture of his activities in both the revolutionary and the police worlds,—this is the task which the author has set himself.

In composing this book the author has had the opportunity of referring not only to all the literature on this subject published since the Revolution, but also to hitherto unpublished documents and memoirs. Of the documents we must first make mention of the archives of the Aseff affair, which are as follows:

The Police Department papers relating to Aseff for the years 1893–1902.

The Police Department papers 1909–1910, which were the basis of the Government's reply to questions asked in the Duma about Aseff.

The papers of the Examining Magistrate who conducted the inquiry into the Lopuhin affair.

The papers of the Extraordinary Commission of Inquiry set up by the Provisional Government in 1917 to investigate the Aseff case.

All these documents are of extreme importance in the history of Aseff, but have hitherto been almost entirely ignored in the literature upon the subject (the only references to them are to be found in the article of

M. A. Aldanoff). The author was able to gain access to them in the copies which had been made of them by Professor V. K. Agafonoff, the authority on the activities of the Russian Police abroad. For permission to examine these copies, without which it would have been impossible to throw light on a number of incidents, I express my deepest gratitude to V. K. Agafonoff and to S. G. Svatikoff.

For the hitherto unpublished material, I have availed myself of the verbal and written information given to me by the following people, who have for various reasons been in contact with Aseff: A. A. Argunoff, V. L. Burtzeff, R. D. and V. A. Buchgoltz, the engineer Zauer, V. M. Zenzinoff, F. Cursky-Blumin, E. E. Lazareff, V. I. Lebedeff, the former Moscow Rabbi Maze, I. I. Maisner, P. N. Milliukoff, O. C. Minor, C. P. Postnikoff, V. V. Sukhomlin, V. M. Tchernoff, and many others.

But undoubtedly the most important information of this type is that of A. V. Gerassimoff, who was the head of the Petersburg *Ochrana* from 1905–9 and Aseff's police chief from April, 1906, until his exposure. He not only gave me the opportunity of acquainting myself with some of the chapters of his unpublished memoirs, but he has also always been ready to reply in the many conversations we have had upon the subject to any questions which arose in the course of working on the material. This is the source upon which are principally based those parts of the book which deal with Aseff's relations with the police from 1906 to 1908.

As to the latter part of Aseff's life—that following his exposure—I have had the opportunity of consulting those documents which have been preserved by Madame N.: these consist of their correspondence, her letters to her mother, Aseff's prison note-books, etc. (I have used this material in fuller detail in my brochure, *The End of Aseff*.) I have, besides, been able to acquaint myself with some of the papers which Aseff took with him on his flight from Paris in January, 1909.

In so far as it has been possible, all evidence has been carefully verified; for, as we know, individual testimony always tends to be subjective. But in a number of cases such verification has proved impossible owing to the absence of those who could give corroborative evidence. In any case, the source of all such evidence has always been indicated. It is scarcely necessary to add that information of this kind is treated only as *factual material* and that all judgments and conclusions are made entirely on the author's responsibility.

I should like to express my deep gratitude to all those who have been so kind as to help me in my work.

In composing this book, the author had largely in mind the non-Russian reader, and this could not help being reflected in the presentation of the book. The reader must also keep in view the fact that all the dates are given in the *new style*.

BERLIN, *October* 15, 1931.

CONTENTS

LIST
OF
ILLUSTRATIONS

THE LAST PHOTOGRAPH OF ASEFF. TAKEN IN 1918.

ASEFF
THE SPY

RUSSIAN TERRORIST AND POLICE STOOL

CHAPTER I

A Conversation in a
Train

THE EASTERN EXPRESS had scarcely had time to leave Cologne station when an unexpected visitor, V. L. Burtzeff, entered the compartment occupied by the former director of the Police Department, A. A. Lopuhin.

They were already acquainted: Burtzeff in his capacity of editor of the historical review, *Byloye* (*The Past*), appearing in St. Petersburg in 1906–07, had on several occasions approached Lopuhin with the suggestion that he should write his memoirs for that paper. Lopuhin had declined these offers, as he did not care to embark upon the revelation of any of the secrets which had

come into his possession in the course of his former
official position.

But Burtzeff was now especially interested in the
bringing to light of these secrets. He was a pioneer in
the study of the history of the Russian revolutionary
movement, having begun work in this field at a time
when it attracted very little attention. Even before
then he had been interested in history, though not for
its own sake or through pure love of knowledge. The
revolutionary and publicist in him always triumphed
over the historian and investigator, and he always approached the study with a desire above all to draw from
it useful lessons for the political struggles of the day.
In the period following the revolution of 1905, he devoted himself to the discovery of the secrets of the Russian political police and to the exposure of those of its
agents who had penetrated into the ranks of revolutionary organizations in order to betray their plans.
With the object of obtaining the necessary material, he
established a series of acquaintanceships with police
officials, through whom he obtained a great deal of
valuable and important information, among which the
most important was the indication of the existence of a
traitor in the very heart of the Social Revolutionary
party. The name of this traitor was not revealed to
him—his informants were not aware of it themselves
—but it was known that he stood very close to the
Battle Organization of the party, that he had betrayed
a whole series of terrorist undertakings, and that he
was known in police circles under the pseudonym of
"Raskin." Several trifling details served as a guiding
thread in Burtzeff's researches. He followed up these
clues and arrived at the conclusion, very surprising to
himself, that this traitor was none other than the head

of the Battle Organization and an old member of the Central Committee of the Social Revolutionary party, E. F. Aseff.

From that moment began his fight to expose Aseff.

It was a hard struggle. None of the members of the inner councils of the party and, in particular, none of the leaders of the Battle Organization, who had for years worked side by side with Aseff, would listen to Burtzeff's conclusions. They better than others knew Aseff's rôle in the life of these organizations, and they knew, too, how much he could have betrayed, had he chosen, to the police, but had not done so. And Burtzeff, with his proofs drawn for the most part from police sources, appeared to them as a ridiculous and harmful maniac who was being used by the police to bring disintegration into the revolutionary movement by trying to discredit its leading and most formidable terrorist. They attempted to dissuade him and advised him to abandon his campaign; he was warned and almost threatened. It was all of no avail. With the obstinacy of a fanatic convinced that he was right, he was prepared to go to the end—even though he stood alone against all.

Then he was brought to trial. The issue was of the gravest importance to him: if condemned, he would be morally discredited for the rest of his life, which would be worse than death. Physical death, indeed, would not have been slow in following moral death; for Burtzeff had decided not to survive the latter. And the possibility of such a judgment was by no means remote. In such cases *documentary* proofs are practically never obtainable. Everything turns on indirect evidence. But in view of the confidence in which Aseff was held by his party colleagues, nobody was prepared to credit such indirect evidence. And Burtzeff searched hard for new, weightier, and more convincing proofs of Aseff's treachery.

These proofs he was to obtain from Lopuhin, who, by virtue of his former official position, could not but be exactly informed of the part played by Aseff. The whole problem lay in how to draw him into conversation and how to make him divulge the truth.

The meeting with Lopuhin in the train had been carefully contrived by Burtzeff, but he managed to give it the appearance of a chance encounter. They began to chat, as they did formerly in St. Petersburg, upon neutral subjects of history and literature. At that time Burtzeff had transferred the publication of his historical review to Paris, and he counted now on being able to write freely about all those subjects of which the censorship in St. Petersburg forbade mention. He was full of plans and hopes, and talked eagerly about them to Lopuhin. These general topics were only a natural prelude to the theme of Aseff, which was of such all-absorbing interest to Burtzeff. Going over the material which he was preparing for publication, he announced that in the coming number of *Byloye* he was going to expose the activities of a very important police agent who was at the head of the Social Revolutionary Battle Organization. "Lopuhin," Burtzeff recalls, "at first seemed not to pay any attention to my words. . . . But I sensed that he had suddenly become wary and had grown reserved, as if he were expecting indiscreet inquiries on my part."

He was right: the indiscreet questions were not long in following. Burtzeff put his question directly.

"Will you allow me, Alexei Alexandrovitch," he said, turning to him, "to tell you everything that I know about this *agent provocateur*, about his activities in both revolutionary and police circles? I shall give you proofs of the double rôle he is playing. I shall mention the name by which he is known to the Ochrana[1] as a spy in revolutionary circles, and also his real name. I know everything about him. I have worked long and laboriously over his exposure, and can now say with confidence that my task is finished. The exposure is complete. It only remains now for me to break down the obstinacy of his comrades, but that will not take long."

Lopuhin replied with great reserve, but not without curiosity.

"Please go on, Vladimir Lvovitch, I am listening."

And Burtzeff began his account.

He did not mention Aseff's real name, but only the pseudonym, "Raskin," by which he was known in the police world. But from his very first words Lopuhin understood to whom he referred. Burtzeff's account in part coincided with the knowledge Lopuhin had acquired in his former position, and he was astonished by the exactitude of the data collected by Burtzeff. "Above all," he afterwards told the examining magistrate, "I was amazed at the knowledge Burtzeff displayed of Aseff's various official police names as a secret agent, and of the place where he used to meet officials of the political police in St. Petersburg. . . : All this was perfectly correct." And this exactitude of the one part of Burtzeff's account which Lopuhin could check would inevitably inspire confidence in that other in which Burtzeff spoke of the mysterious "Raskin" as he was seen by the revolutionaries; of his rôle in the revolutionary camp—in the Central Committee and in the Battle Organization.

Lopuhin was no longer young, he was about forty-

[1] The Secret Police Department.

five. In his time he had managed to see many things; he had heard even more, and it probably seemed to him that nothing could astonish him any longer. But Burtzeff's story not only amazed him, it was like the opening of an old wound. Burtzeff did not suspect how much significance his story was to assume in the light of his hearer's memory. For Lopuhin saw his whole life rise up before him—all his vain hopes of the past and all the bitterness of his present disillusionment.

He was the eldest son of an old and distinguished family. The Lopuhins claimed descent from the half-legendary Kassog prince, Rededy; and the Czaritza Jevdokia, the wife of Peter the Great, the last Czaritza to come from an original Russian family, bore the name of Lopuhin. Like most of these families, the Lopuhins could not boast of any particular wealth. But they could not really be described as poor, for A. A. Lopuhin had inherited an estate of over a thousand acres in the Orlovsky and Smolensky provinces. Furthermore, they stood above the impoverished aristocracy by virtue of their ability, intelligence, and determination to succeed. They all had their share of ambition, particularly Alexei Alexandrovitch. Having taken his degree at the Moscow University at the age of twenty-two, he was appointed in 1886 to the department of the Ministry of Justice and at once began to mount rapidly in the service.

Through his university and personal ties Lopuhin found himself close to the moderate liberal circles of young men of good family; he approved of their political program and was on intimate terms with many of them, especially with the professor, Prince S. N. Troubetzkoy. But these liberal sympathies in no way prevented Lopuhin from building his career upon political cases, the development of which he had to watch in his capacity of representative of the public prosecutor. He was first appointed to this work in Moscow in the summer of 1890, and on that occasion he was entrusted with the task of supervising the activities of the Moscow branch of the Ochrana. There was usually internal friction between the Ochrana and the public prosecutor's department: the latter in one way or another opposed the attempts of the various Ochrana branches to exceed the bounds of their jurisdiction. This time, the head of the Moscow Ochrana, the famous Zubatoff, of whom more will be said later, adopted a different policy. Instead of latent opposition and attempts to prevent him from learning the working methods of the political police, Lopuhin encountered on Zubatoff's part a readiness to initiate him into all the secrets of the department work, into the means employed for fighting the revolutionary organizations, and so on. At that time Zubatoff adumbrated plans for the creation of legal workers' organizations under the control of the police, and he succeeded in winning over to his plans various professors and other public men. He found it still easier to win over the ambitious young prosecutor. Lopuhin went so far as to acquaint himself with the methods of the secret agents; there is even evidence that he had actually visited the secret rooms where Zubatoff used to meet his collaborators, and he became Zubatoff's enthusiastic supporter.

The young liberal prosecutor's bent for police work marked out his future career, the turning point of which he reached in May, 1902. By then Lopuhin was already public prosecutor in Kharkov. The newly appointed Minister of the Interior, V. K. Plehve, came to Kharkov in order to acquaint himself on the spot with

the extent and character of the waves of peasant unrest
which not long before had swept over the south of
Russia—the first portents of the coming storm of
agrarian revolution. Lopuhin had met Plehve before, at
the house of mutual friends in St. Petersburg. In Kharkov, Plehve asked Lopuhin to draw up a report for him
on the causes of the peasant unrest, insisting that he
should give his opinion with the utmost frankness. "My
opinion," Lopuhin said later, describing the conversation, "amounted to this: that the pogroms on the
estates in the Poltava and Kharkov provinces could not
be considered as accidental phenomena, that they were,
rather, the natural results of general conditions of
Russian life, of the ignorance of the peasant population,
of its terrible impoverishment, of the indifference of the
government to its spiritual and material interests, and,
finally, of the importunate administrative system, which
made no attempt at a legal protection of the interests
of the people." Plehve, according to Lopuhin's account,
agreed with his conclusions and informed him that he
himself recognized the necessity for reform and even
for the introduction into Russia of a substitute constitution by attracting the representatives of the public
organizations into the composition of the State Council.
In Plehve's opinion, only these reforms could save
Russia from revolution, the danger of which appeared
to him imminent. But Lopuhin does not tell of his
further conversation with Plehve, in which they discussed the use of repressive measures in the struggle
against revolution. Both Plehve and Lopuhin attached
the greatest significance to the struggle. To this end,
Lopuhin elaborated a whole plan of campaign in the
spirit of Zubatoff's policy and found in Plehve a warm
supporter of this program. That was why this conversa-

tion resulted in the offer to Lopuhin of the post of
director of the Police Department: he was to apply
to the whole of Russia those methods which until now
Zubatoff had tried only in Moscow.

This was a very tempting offer for Lopuhin: at the
age of thirty-eight he became the head of one of the
most important departments in the Empire and came
into close personal contact with the highest ruling
powers in the realm. It seemed to Lopuhin that, from
the point of view of a career, there opened before him a
most attractive prospect: from being the head of the
Police Department it was but a step to the post of Minister of the Interior. And the young liberal prosecutor,
whose conduct was largely governed by ambition, accepted the offer of a transfer from the Department of
Justice to the Police Department.

But in reality things turned out very differently from
what he had expected. The question of far-reaching reforms was never seriously considered. According to
Lopuhin's testimony, Plehve, it is true, demanded from
the archives all those projects for the reform of the State
Council, a whole series of which had been drawn up
during the reign of Alexander II, but without any
tangible results. Plehve told Lopuhin that he had
brought the question of the necessary reforms before
the Czar, but had come up against definite opposition.
It may be doubted whether he had really done so:
nothing has been found in the archives up to the present
to prove this, and a like reform was in its very essence so
contradictory to the whole trend of Plehve's policy
and to all his public declarations of that period that its
possibility seems more than remote.

Nor did anything come of the other proposed reforms, even of the plan to reform the police. The project

for the latter was drawn up by Lopuhin, but, as he sadly says, "Like all of Plehve's projects at that time, it never got beyond his office desk."

As the question of reform was more and more relegated to the background, so purely police questions assumed greater importance. Here Plehve felt himself at home, and Lopuhin's program was carried out to the letter. A clean sweep was made of all the leading officials of the Police Department, and it was finally converted into an "All-Russian Ochrana." Zubatoff was appointed the independent chief of the whole of the investigation department. A basic feature of the new policy was the introduction of secret agents into the revolutionary organizations. No expense was grudged. In the course of some two and a half years the whole of the reserve fund of the department, amounting to some five million roubles, which had accumulated during the previous decade of comparative tranquillity in the country, was exhausted.

To Lopuhin fell the task of exercising the principal supervision of this matter, and with the curiosity of a neophyte he entered into all the details. He did not make a good detective: he was too aristocratic and squeamish for such work. But at the same time, in his anxiety to make a career he did not avoid soiling himself with the mud which surrounded him. A liberal, given to dreams of a constitution, he directed the breaking up of the liberal *zemstvos* and signed the warrants for banishment to Siberia of a number of moderate liberals guilty only of similar thoughts of a constitution. Cultured, educated according to Western ideas, he yet set his seal on that anti-Semitic campaign which was being conducted by the Police Department at that time. Even if no credit can be given to the stories that he considered the anti-Semitic pogroms to be "a useful blood-letting,"[1] one fact at least remains indisputable: in a personal interview with N. F. Annensky, a representative of the Writers' Union, on the subject of the Kishenev pogrom, Lopuhin defended the reactionary writer, Krushevan, the ideological inspirer of that pogrom, calling him one of the few Russian writers who had not been "bought by the Jews." Only in private letters to his friend Prince Troubetzkoy did Lopuhin permit himself to give any expression to his liberal opinions. It was only after Plehve's death that he, the chief of the whole police of the Empire, learned, not without surprise, that the most minute police observation had been kept on his correspondence, reports on which were forwarded directly to the Minister. . . . Outwardly Lopuhin approved of everything that Plehve did, acting as a diligent and obedient executor of the latter's most reactionary commands. Plehve knew what he was doing when he appointed the young Liberal opportunist as his closest assistant: such people invariably placed the interests of their careers above all other sentiments.

Lopuhin left his mark upon the work of the department which controlled the activities of the *agents provocateurs*—work which blossomed into full flower during these years. It was he who in part helped Aseff in his career, although he was already aware that the latter's activities exceeded the bounds of even the very elastic police code of morals. It was he who, with Plehve's

[1]At one time a story got into the press that these words were used by Lopuhin about the Kishenev pogrom of 1903 in conversation with the Gendarme General Novitzky, and in support of it people quoted the latter's oral statement. But in Novitzky's published Memoirs there is no record of such a statement; they contain, however, a categoric assertion that Lopuhin had been forewarned of the projected Kishenev pogrom, but that he took no measures to prevent it.

direct approval, allowed Aseff, in the autumn of 1902, to become a member of the Battle Organization.

Both he and Plehve were, of course, convinced that they could control Aseff, and, through him, the whole of the Battle Organization. But now, six years later, on the journey between Cologne and Berlin, Lopuhin learned from Burtzeff's account what were the real consequences of that decision: their agent—the "Raskin" of Burtzeff's story—did not merely become, after Gershuni's arrest, a member of this organization, but he became its chief and planned all its notorious activities; it was he who organized the assassination of Plehve. . . .

The death of the latter was the first cruel blow in Lopuhin's official career: Plehve had been his chief support and protector. The death of Plehve meant also the death of all of Lopuhin's ambitious plans. If Plehve had remained alive, events would have taken another course. And now it was becoming clear that his death had been brought about by none other than his, Lopuhin's, agent —whose entry into the ranks of the terrorists had been connived at by both Plehve and himself. Was all this really true?

Till then Lopuhin had been listening quietly to his companion's story, though it was evident that he was becoming more and more interested. Thin, nervous, a typical Russian nihilist of the old school in both his dress and manner, Burtzeff betrayed considerable agitation. He gesticulated, was unable to sit still in his place, interrupted himself, repeated himself, went over again and again those episodes which seemed to him to be most significant, and all the time stared at Lopuhin with an eager questioning look, trying to catch his slightest reaction. But his face displayed nothing but a growing interest in the story. Lopuhin, who knew how to con-

trol himself, and who had, besides, the aloofness of his
class, sat there without losing a single word, and only
looked searchingly at his companion with his slightly
slanting eyes which showed the distant traces of Mon-
golian blood. But when Burtzeff came to the account of
Plehve's assassination, Lopuhin's sang-froid deserted
him.

"With the greatest amazement," Burtzeff recalls, "he
asked me, as if such a possibility were completely inadmissible:

"'Are you *sure* that this agent knew of the plans to
assassinate Plehve?'"

Burtzeff replied that not only did "Raskin" know
about them, but that he was the organizer of the assassination. And he went on to describe in full detail the
inner history of the preparations for it.

His account was very precise and clear, full of details
inspiring confidence, and yet to Lopuhin the story
sounded incredible.

Plehve's death was followed by a period of the greatest
difficulty for Lopuhin. The new Minister of the Interior,
Prince Sviatopolk-Mirsky, was well disposed towards
him, but the Minister's position was precarious, as he
was the object of intrigues on the side of the Court
reactionary party; an important feature of these attacks was the accusation of the lack of activity on the
part of the Police Department. This backstairs intrigue
was being hatched by Ratchkovsky, a prominent official
in the Secret Police who had powerful friends in the
Czar's court. Two years before, Plehve had summarily
dismissed him without taking into consideration all his
former services, and Lopuhin had, at that time, helped
to aggravate the injury. During Plehve's lifetime Ratchkovsky had been powerless, although he had been the

instigator of various intrigues. It was his turn now to pay off old scores. Ratchkovsky knew the technique of police work better than Lopuhin, and his blows struck true and hard. The decisive event in this struggle proved to be the assassination of the Grand Duke Sergei, the uncle and the influential counselor of the Czar. After the receipt in the Police Department of the telegram announcing the Grand Duke's murder, there dashed in Trepoff, the Governor General of St. Petersburg, who was at that moment the Czar's favorite, and who was under Ratchkovsky's influence. Without having himself announced, he burst into the chief's office, threw the word "Murderer" into the face of the disconcerted Lopuhin, and departed without uttering another syllable. And that very day, upon Trepoff's recommendation, Ratchkovsky was appointed the chief commissar of the Political Police in Petersburg, and the Czar, in the course of the report made soon afterwards by the Minister of the Interior, expressed his sharp discontent with the work of the Police Department. There was nothing left for Lopuhin but to hand in his resignation. All his hopes of a career were scattered to the winds. . . .

And now, from Burtzeff's further account, Lopuhin learned that this last blow had been struck against him by this very "Raskin": it was he who had worked out the plan for the assassination of the Grand Duke Sergei; it was he who had equipped the group of terrorists; it was he who had given the bomb to the assassin. . . . It was again difficult to credit the story, but it was impossible not to believe it; the information was so precise, and the references to living people invited confidence.

Burtzeff continued, dealing now with the later period of the activities of the mysterious "Raskin." The latter soon after made a complete change in his course of action, and from that moment an evil fate seemed to hang over all the undertakings of the Battle Organization. Every attempt was now doomed to failure. Even the most carefully laid plan, even the most cunningly concealed groups, were brought to light; the plotters were either arrested or forced to make their escape without having succeeded in attaining their ends.

Lopuhin was much less interested in all this. He had no sympathy to waste on revolutionaries. In his day, he had imprisoned and executed them without qualms. He had paid "Raskin" for the very purpose of betraying revolutionaries, and if this "Raskin" had served him, Lopuhin, honestly, then Burtzeff's account would have aroused no indignation in him. But now that he learned that "Raskin" had betrayed not only revolutionaries, but also those who paid him for those betrayals, Lopuhin, finding himself duped, felt almost sympathetic towards those revolutionaries whom "Raskin" had betrayed. He had never liked him, for he had been unable to overcome his finer scruples—the survival of the epoch in which the saying was current that "Traitors are paid, but not respected." To these scruples there was now added the irritation of a person who had been imposed upon. How could he have let himself be hoodwinked so easily? And by whom? By the very man whom he despised, whom he never really trusted, who he had always known was capable of treachery for money. He recalled now a whole series of incidents which had made him doubt and which had forced him to think that "Raskin" was not telling all he knew, particularly some of his reports during the winter of 1904–05, which tended to show that he played a much more important rôle in the party than he was usually prepared to admit.

Had not the advisability of demanding an explanation from "Raskin" occurred to Lopuhin even then? Would it not have been better to put an end to the policy which had been begun on Plehve's insistence? He had lacked the decision at the time to nip the affair in the bud: with all his faults "Raskin" was still very useful; from the police point of view the expenses of his salary were more than repaid. . . . And in spite of all his doubts, in spite of his realization of the dangers of that policy, Lopuhin had deliberately shut his eyes to the conduct of his agent.

And now, in addition, another question rose in his mind: Had "Raskin," in playing this bold game, acted solely on his own account? Lopuhin remembered Zubatoff's opinion of "Raskin," whom he knew thoroughly: he has always maintained that he was in the highest degree prudent, almost cowardly. Was this coward capable of playing such a bold game unaided? Had he not acted as a screen for some more powerful and influential person who was pursuing his own far-reaching aims and in whose hands he was but a pawn? The more Lopuhin thought over this question, the more surely did he favor an affirmative answer.

During the years in which he had occupied the post of director of the Police Department he had had the opportunity to gain an insight into the arcana of those Court intrigues and rivalries which seethed in immediate proximity to the very highest of the ruling powers, and he knew that, in the course of the savage struggle that was being waged, people were ready to stop short of nothing. This was not merely guesswork, not an arbitrary supposition. Lopuhin *knew* certain facts which confirmed his view. None other than C. U. Witte, the then president of the Imperial Cabinet, before he was made a "count," had approached Lopuhin with a suggestion which the latter would never have believed possible had it not come directly from the lips of Witte himself. Witte had just suffered a crushing reverse in his struggle against Plehve, and was irritated with the Czar, who, in his usual way, had played him false at the last moment by breaking all his former promises. A train of circumstances gave Witte to suppose that he could rely upon Lopuhin's support, and, in a confidential interview, in which he put all his cards on the table, he unfolded the plan of nothing less than the assassination of the Czar, to be carried out by the Police Department through the revolutionary organizations. Witte pointed out that Lopuhin, as director of the department and chief of the Secret Police throughout the Empire, having under his orders police agents who were members of the terrorist groups, could, through these agents, suggest to the revolutionaries the necessity of the Czar's assassination and so direct police supervision as to bring the attempt to a successful conclusion. All traces would be covered up, and it would be necessary only to act wisely and circumspectly. When Nicholas II had been removed, his brother Michael, who was entirely under Witte's influence, would come to the throne. Witte's power would increase enormously, and Lopuhin's services would, of course, be generously rewarded.[1]

Lopuhin did not run the risk of taking the course which Witte had suggested to him. But now that he

[1] Lopuhin tells of this interview with Witte in his *Memoirs* (Moscow, Gosizdat, 1923). As Witte conducted his struggle against Plehve with the support, among others, of Lopuhin's closest associate and the independent chief of all the department's agents, Zubatoff, are we not justly entitled to ask the question: Was not the interview between Witte and Lopuhin the continuation of the conversations on the same theme between Witte and Zubatoff?

heard these accounts of the terrorist attempts organized by police agents he could not but recall his former interview with Witte. Was not this a case of the application of the means of fighting for power which Witte had recommended to him on that occasion? Was not some other person making use of "Raskin" to advance his career by the employment of those means which he, Lopuhin, was too timid and too scrupulous to use?

The more Lopuhin thought over this question, the more feasible did his surmise seem. He began even to think that he could guess who was the secret influence behind "Raskin": in his opinion it could only be Ratchkovsky.

Lopuhin knew Ratchkovsky as a man capable of absolutely anything. Had he not organized the "anarchist" explosion in Liége Cathedral? Lopuhin had, as documentary proof of this fact, the testimony of the actual perpetrator of the explosion, a certain Yagolovsky, an agent of Ratchkovsky, who gave a full account of the whole affair to the public prosecutor of the St. Petersburg courts, when he had been handed over to the Russian authorities after his arrest in Belgium. Lopuhin knew, too, that Ratchkovsky was bound to Witte by secret ties: he had proofs that the theft of a packet of documents, compromising Witte, from Professor Tzion, the opponent of Witte's financial measures, was organized on the latter's request by Ratchkovsky. Ratchkovsky himself bore a grudge against both Plehve and Lopuhin, and the various terrorist attempts directed by "Raskin" were undoubtedly to his advantage; they paved the way for his return to power in the Police Department. Looking at things from this angle, Lopuhin thought he could see an explanation of the change in "Raskin's" conduct: the terrorist attempts organized by the latter ceased to have any successful results immediately after Lopuhin's removal from the department, when Ratchkovsky was entrusted with the control of the Secret Police. The latter, of course, could not possibly wish now to organize successful attempts which would only bring discredit on himself.

Finally, this surmise explained Witte's attachment to Ratchkovsky, which was most evident in the winter of 1905–06, and the reasons for which at that time were not clear to Lopuhin. During this period, when Witte had once more come into power, Lopuhin made an attempt to settle old scores with Ratchkovsky. Through his former associates in the department, he received data as to the organization by Ratchkovsky and his lieutenants of a secret printing press on the premises of the Police Department, which was used to print posters inciting the people to Jewish pogroms. The collected material was absolutely damning: it showed that the reactionary pogroms towards the end of 1905 had been directly organized by the department. Lopuhin brought this material to the notice of Witte. Witte could not question the truth of the facts laid before him; a number of prominent Ministers strongly urged Ratchkovsky's dismissal; and politically, Ratchkovsky was only a hindrance to Witte—but Ratchkovsky remained at his post.

All these facts taken together formed a harmonious pattern, and Lopuhin, almost to the end of his life, remained convinced that "Raskin" had acted under Ratchkovsky's orders. Lopuhin thus began to connect the exposure of "Raskin" with that of Ratchkovsky, the exposure, too, of the whole of that shadowy and sinister clique by whom the latter was surrounded. Lopuhin was intelligent enough to realize that this exposure could not now be of any use to him personally. Every door to a bureaucratic career was now closed against him. The exposure, however, would bring him moral satisfaction; it would balance the account of his long struggle with Ratchkovsky. . . .

By that time Burtzeff was finishing his story. He had as yet no precise idea of the real causes of "Raskin's" behavior. He realized that it was criminal from whatever point of view it might be regarded, and he used every effort to overcome Lopuhin's hesitation and to make him see the necessity of bringing about his exposure. He said that "Raskin" was still continuing his double dealing, on the one hand organizing terrorist attempts, and on the other, betraying the terrorists who acted on his instructions. Burtzeff had received definite proof from a trustworthy source that, only a short time before, "'Raskin' had planned an attempt against the Czar himself." If this attempt did not take place, it would be in no way due to "Raskin's" goodwill. There was no doubt that "Raskin" would continue to play his double game in the future, if he were not brought to book, and Burtzeff declared that all the future victims of the terror, all the executions of the terrorists betrayed by "Raskin," would be laid at his, Lopuhin's, door, if he still shielded his former agent and refrained from telling the truth about him.

"You, as director of the department," Burtzeff concluded, "could not but know of the existence of this *agent provocateur*. As you see, I have now completely exposed him, and I should like to beg you once more, Alexei Alexandrovitch, to allow me to tell you now who hides under the pseudonym of 'Raskin.' And it will only remain for you to say whether I am right or wrong!"

Only then did Lopuhin make up his mind.

"I know nobody of the name of 'Raskin,'" he declared, "but I have seen the engineer, Ievno Aseff, several times."

Thus for the first time in the course of this long interview was this name pronounced. . . .

"Of course," Burtzeff recalls later, "the name was less than ever of a surprise to me. For over a year it had been running through my head every moment. But when I heard it from Lopuhin's lips, it struck me like a thunderbolt. . . ." Lopuhin's statement proved, in fact, the decisive factor leading to Aseff's final exposure. . . .

The conversation continued for a long time—until the train got into Berlin. It was Lopuhin who did most of the talking now. Having taken the first step, he now began to put forward his theories as to the real motives underlying Aseff's conduct. It was he who, in the course of this conversation, first advanced the theory, and gave reasons in support of it, that Ratchkovsky was acting behind Aseff at the time of the assassinations of Plehve and the Grand Duke Sergei. This explanation left a lasting mark on the later literature about Aseff, but it in no way corresponds to reality. The real motives of Aseff's conduct were entirely different, and Lopuhin's version did nothing to elucidate them. And only now—a quarter of a century after this train interview, on the journey from Cologne to Berlin—when almost all the documents of the secret archives and a vast amount of other important material have been made accessible, has it become possible to give the correct answer to every question arising in Aseff's case. . . .

CHAPTER II

The Dawn of a
"Clouded Youth"

IEVNO ASEFF was born in 1869 in the district town of Lyskovo, in the Grodnensky province, the son of a very poor tailor, Fischel Aseff. The family, of which Ievno was the second child, was large: three sons and four daughters. Their lives were full of hardship, and for every bite of food there were many hungry mouths. Those who could, strove to get away from the "confines" which were imposed upon the Jews by the government at that time. When young Aseff was five years of age, his father broke away from the "confine" in an attempt to improve his fortune. The family settled down in Rostov on the Don, which in those years was developing rapidly as an industrial and commercial center of southeastern Russia. Enterprising people flocked from all parts to this region, rich in wheat and coal. Capital was quickly and easily found: to get it one had only to be resourceful and unscrupulous.

Aseff's father was, apparently, made of the wrong clay. He went in for trade and opened a cheap drapery shop, but failed to make his fortune. "A poor family"— such was the local police report on the Aseff family two decades after they had settled in Rostov. This Rostov atmosphere of hunting for quick and easy profits left, however, an ineffaceable mark on. at least one of the sons—on Ievno Aseff. Love of money and unscrupulousness as to the means of getting it became second nature to him at an early age.

With the greatest difficulty, and by the expenditure of all his resources, Aseff's father gave his children the opportunity of an education: he sent his sons to a gymnasium, where Aseff finished about 1890. He had, however, no means of doing anything further for his sons. For several years Ievno Aseff lived by working at odd trades: he gave lessons, was a reporter on a small local paper, *Donskaya Ptchela* (*The Don Bee*), and did clerical work in an office; eventually he got a job as a commercial traveler. This, of course, could not satisfy the young Aseff, especially as he knew of the existence of another and fuller life, not only from the flashy bustle of the large town, but also from the revolutionary-minded young men with whom he had mixed at the gymnasium and whose society he still frequented.

At the beginning of 1892, suspicion fell on him of having distributed a revolutionary manifesto. The question of his arrest was considered. He evidently guessed this, for a number of his acquaintances had already been arrested. The threat of arrest would seem to have been the deciding factor in forcing him to go abroad, where he was already drawn by his thirst for knowledge, without which a "better life" seemed impossible to him. Aseff's greatest obstacle was lack of money, but this he overcame. He was never noted for his scrupulousness regarding other people's money, a trait that had already shown itself in small ways while he was at the gymnasium. Now he took only a greater step. As a traveling salesman he had received a consignment of butter from a merchant; he sold it for eight hundred roubles and in the spring of 1892 absconded with the money to Karlsruhe, in Germany, where he entered the Polytechnic.

There was already a small colony of Russian students in Karlsruhe. Among them were a number of Aseff's Rostov acquaintances. Aseff became one of the group and shared rooms with the student Kozin, on the fourth floor of No. 30 Wertherstrasse. He joined the Russian Social Democratic group and also applied himself to the study of electrostatics. But very soon he was faced with a practical difficulty. Eight hundred roubles was at that time a large enough sum, but it could not last indefinitely—especially as, it appears, it did not all remain in Aseff's hands.

The opportunities for earning were few and far between. He could not hope for assistance from his family. Aseff knew want and gave those he met the impression of a man who was "literally suffering from hunger and cold." He could not long live in that way; and with great ease he stepped over another moral barrier: he began to trade in those secrets of his comrades' revolutionary activities which were known to him. These secrets were of no great importance; but the times were quiet, there was an absence of stirring revolutionary events, and Aseff, not without reason, hoped to interest the police with these trifles.

On April 4, 1893, he wrote his first letter to the Police Department. This letter was something in the nature of a feeler. "I have the honor to inform Your Highness," he wrote, "that two months ago a circle of revolutionaries was formed here whose aim is . . ." and so forth. There followed a list of names, and certain facts were cited to show that the writer of the letter was in a position to give information not only about the revolutionary temper of Russian students abroad, but also about the propaganda that was going on in Rostov. The letter contained no concrete suggestions about the future. The writer only begged that a registered letter should be sent to him at a given address if the police thought his information of any use to them. He did not mention his real name. The procedure of admitting a new agent into the Police Department was very complicated. Aseff's letter was brought to the notice of the vice-director of the department, and from him it went to the chief of the branch concerned. A number of marginal notes are still to be seen on this letter. Consultations were held, and information about him collected.

It was not till May 16th that an answer was sent. This was couched in the terms of a business man anxious to do a deal but who is at the same time afraid to betray any eagerness. "We know of the Karlsruhe group," wrote the department (in reality they knew scarcely anything about it), "and we are not very interested in it; therefore you are not of a such great value to us; nevertheless, we are prepared to pay you —on condition, however, that you reveal your name, for we have strict principles and will have no dealings with certain people."

Aseff replied without delay, and the price he demanded was "delightfully low"—only some fifty roubles a month, but he still hesitated to reveal his name. He feared lest the revolutionaries might intercept his letters and expose his secret without any real profit to him.

But his attempt to "play hide-and-seek" with the department was doomed to early failure, and he had only himself to blame, for, owing to his youth and lack of experience, he gave the department a clue to his identity. Simultaneously with his offer to the department, he had addressed a letter in almost the same terms to the Gendarmerie in Rostov, and it proved easy enough for them to identify the writer: the number of Rostov people living in Karlsruhe was very limited, and their names were known. It was the simplest matter to trace the author of the letter by the handwriting. Thus, by the time Aseff's second letter reached the department, information from Rostov had already revealed his identity. But the report of the Rostov police on Aseff's personal character satisfied all the demands which the department made on its agents. "Ievno Aseff," they wrote, "is intelligent and a clever intriguer; he is in close touch with the young Jewish students living abroad, and he could thus be of real use as an agent. It can also be assumed that his covetousness and his present state of need will make him zealous in his duty."

Such a recommendation made the department hasten to come to a decision. A few days after their receipt of his second letter a special memorandum was hurriedly drawn up, pointing out that Aseff could be "very useful" and that the price he demanded was quite moderate. On June 10, 1893, the assistant to the Minister of the Interior set the seal of his approval on this memorandum. Aseff's future was now determined. . . .

Aseff received his first salary from the department in June, 1893. His material situation improved as a result, but he had to be prudent in the spending of this money, for otherwise the suspicions of his comrades might have been aroused: they were well aware of the difficulties of earning money locally, and they knew, too, of the financial straits of the Aseff family.

Aseff continued, therefore, for some time to give the outward appearance of a poverty-stricken student and wrote appeal after appeal to every charitable institution he knew, especially the Jewish ones. He showed these appeals to his comrades on the pretext of wishing them to correct his bad German, and they helped to spread the legend of this source of his income. Not till a long time afterwards did Aseff cease to disguise the fact that his material position had very much improved.

The change in Aseff's circumstances produced an even more rapid change in his political ideology. In the first months of his stay in Karlsruhe he adopted a moderate attitude, spoke out against extreme revolutionary methods, and tended to side with the Marxists. But once he had become an informer for the department he quickly veered to the Left, and by 1894 he had acquired the reputation of a logical advocate of terrorist methods. He gradually made his influence felt in student circles. Claiming to be a "man of action" and not a "theorist," he professed dislike of speaking at gatherings but willingly undertook the execution of various technical jobs. He cleverly widened the circle of his acquaintances, and made a series of trips to neighboring towns in Germany and Switzerland, where he attended the more important revolutionary lectures and meetings.

As early as August, 1893, he went to Zürich and attended not only the public meetings of the International Socialist Congress, but also the gatherings of the Russian representatives and *émigrés*. In 1894 he visited Berne, where he made the acquaintance—which was to play such an important part in his career—of the couple Zhitlovsky, the founders of the "Union of Russian Social Revolutionaries Abroad." This "union" was as yet small and uninfluential. Its founders were, therefore, all the more eager to welcome adherents. Aseff judged rightly that he might profit by it, and he joined the "Union," which was to help him to become one of the founders of the Social Revolutionary party.

At about the same time, in Berne, Aseff made the acquaintance of another person who was to play an important part in his life, his future wife, then a student at Berne University. She was a sincere and convinced revolutionary and was making her way in life with great energy and self-denial. Aseff seemed to her to be a man with the same aims and ideals as herself. . . . She had, of course, no suspicions of his connection with the police.

It cannot be said that Aseff's path was strewn only with roses. He was very careful and circumspect, yet, even so, unpleasant rumors began to spread about him. He was far from commanding the complete confidence of everybody in Rostov, for by nature he did not belong to the category of good and faithful friends; he liked to jeer at other people's failings; he never forgot an injury and was revengeful. Even at that time many considered him to be capable of anything which might bring him profit. His very appearance did not inspire confidence. Unprepossessing and heavily built, with a puffy yellow face, large stuck-out ears, a low forehead narrowing towards the top, thick lips, and a flattened nose, he

repelled many people physically, and this prepared the
ground for suspicion towards him.

Soon after his first reports to the department people
in Karlsruhe were already speaking badly of him. News
was received from Rostov that the late arrests there had
been made on the strength of information received by
the Gendarmerie from abroad. Suspicion fell on Aseff,
and a fellow student of his, an Odessa man called Peters
(his name occurs frequently in Aseff's reports), declared
later in print that, after this incident, people in his
circle definitely distrusted Aseff. But, as often happens,
nobody made any serious investigation of these rumors,
the accusation was left unformulated, and the matter
went no further than local talk. The original members
of the circle, who knew all the details of this incident,
soon scattered on completing their college courses.
The newcomers knew nothing of it, and thus, when a few
years later one of the students, a certain Korobotchkin,
having heard somewhere of these early accusations,
publicly called Aseff a spy, the general sympathy went
to the "unjustly accused" Aseff, and Korobotchkin,
who could in no way substantiate his accusation, was
expelled from the circle as a slanderer.

By the end of his university course Aseff was firmly
established in the Russian student circles and enjoyed
general respect. At this time he was also the possessor
of a well-selected library of illegal publications, which
he allowed the students to use on payment of a small
subscription. He was usually elected chairman of the
student gatherings. In his views he was a "convinced"
Social Revolutionary, an upholder of the terror, and
Burtzeff recalls that when he published the first number
of his *Narodovoletz* (*The Freeman*), calling for the assassination of the Czar, Aseff's was the only sympathetic

response which he received from his readers. Aseff
steadily refused to address public meetings: "Silence is
Golden" was his guiding principle throughout life. This
gave added authority to the few words which he thought
fit to pronounce from time to time.

Several contemporary letters give us an idea of the
impressions which Aseff produced on the youth of that
period: in them he is spoken of as a "leading personality," who stood out among the students by his devotion
to the Revolution and its ideals. He evidently talked in
the same spirit in which he constantly wrote to his wife:
these letters, according to the testimony of a person who
read them, were "full of . . . the deep sorrow of a 'popular bard,' and at the same time of the ardor of a fighter
burning with the fire of idealism."

The police authorities were also satisfied with Aseff.
He sent his reports in regularly, supplying them with
valuable information about the activities of revolutionary circles abroad, and about their relations with their
sympathizers in Russia. For this he was paid fifty
roubles a month, with an additional bonus every New
Year. In 1899, in recompense for the amount of important information supplied, his salary was raised to a hundred roubles a month, and he was granted a bonus at
Easter as well as at New Year.

In 1899 he received the diploma of electrical engineer
at Darmstadt, where he had gone from Karlsruhe to
specialize in the subject. At one time he evidently toyed
with the idea of settling down abroad, and he even got a
post as an engineer in the firm of Schukert in Nurem-
berg. But the Ochrana had other plans for him: the
revolutionary movement was making ground, and there
was a great demand for adroit and "covetous" agents.
It was suggested that Aseff should go to Moscow, and

he was promised the necessary influence to obtain a post as an engineer and also a raise in his salary. Aseff naturally had no objection to embarking on such an enticing career.

In the autumn of 1899 he left for Russia, provided with the best possible recommendations. The Zhitlovskys recommended him warmly to their friends and sympathizers in Moscow, while the Police Department no less warmly recommended him to the careful attention of Zubatoff, the famous chief of the Moscow Ochrana.

CHAPTER III

The Makings of a Career

IN MOSCOW Aseff quickly got in touch with the leaders of the local "Union of Social Revolutionaries," which was one of the most important organizations of its kind at the time.

Aseff's introduction into that circle took place at the home of a woman writer, E. A. Niemtchinova, who from time to time held soirées at which the different shades of the revolutionary intelligentsia met and exchanged opinions. On that occasion, as usual, the room was noisy and filled with the smoke of innumerable cigarettes. The discussion turned on the theories of Mikhailovsky, whose influence was at that time supreme with the populists. All those present knew each other well, since

they were regular frequenters of these soirées and had
had time to sum each other up. They were, therefore,
all the more interested in the newcomer—a stout man
with high cheekbones and an unintellectual face, who
vigorously defended Mikhailovsky from the critical attacks of the Marxists. He held that Mikhailovsky's
theory of the "fight for individuality" was of particular
value. "He spoke long enough," says a memoir writer
who was present, "and impressed the gathering by his
sincerity and knowledge of the subject." The speaker
was Aseff.

A few days after this soirée the leaders of the Moscow
"Union" themselves met Aseff. He called at the house of
the founder and head of the "Union," A. A. Argunoff;
and it thereupon transpired that he was the very man
whom the Zhitlovskys had warned Argunoff to expect.
As he was, moreover, the personal friend of Tchepik,
another member of the "Union," whom he had met
abroad the year before, he was naturally enough at
once admitted into their confidence.

But before calling on the leaders of the "Union,"
Aseff had, of course, got into touch with Zubatoff, his
new police chief. The latter was undoubtedly the most
outstanding personality among those whom the Czarist
government had in the last decades of its existence entrusted with the task of fighting the revolutionary movement. And he was destined to play a very important
part in Aseff's life.

A man of medium build and of commonplace appearance, with chestnut hair brushed back, a small beard,
and always wearing tinted glasses, "a typical Russian
intellectual" in both manner and habit, Zubatoff was a
stranger in the world of bright-uniformed generals and
state councilors attached to the Police Department.

In his youth, while attending one of the Moscow gymnasiums about the middle of the 'eighties, he had mixed in revolutionary circles, but very soon "reformed" himself and, getting into touch with the Ochrana, he, to use his own phrase, began to undermine the revolutionary conspiracies with counterplots, or, to put it plainly, he became a Secret Police agent. On his denunciation a number of arrests were affected. But his double-dealing was soon discovered, and then he openly entered the service of the Ochrana.

Police investigation at that time was run on purely routine lines: ill-educated officials, who took but little interest in their work, merely carried on the system which they had learned from their predecessors. Zubatoff, who was a capable man, quickly able to grasp the essentials of a problem and to orientate himself in the tangled situation, and who was, besides, a convincing writer and speaker and a good organizer, and who, above all, had an interest in and a liking for the work of police investigation, soon rose above his obtuse official colleagues. Within ten years he became the head of the Moscow Ochrana, in whose hands was concentrated the business of political investigation over a good half of the Empire. With boldness and energy he introduced a series of reforms of a technical nature, such as the system of photographing all arrested persons and of taking their fingerprints, and that of keeping suspects under observation, creating thus for the first time in Russia a body of expert detectives. He was the first to raise the technique of police investigation in Russia to the level which it had already reached in western Europe. These years were for the Russian political police a period of real reform.

But Zubatoff's plans went considerably further than

the mere "trapping" of revolutionaries. In the years which saw the beginnings of the mass labor movement, he regarded the struggle with the revolutionaries as a political question. A believer in autocracy, he saw that the fundamental danger to it lay in the revolutionaries winning the laboring masses to their side. In so far as the movement had become a mass one, he thought it impossible to defeat it by purely repressive measures. The strategic problem of the government in its struggle with the revolutionary movement was, in his opinion, how to split its opponents' forces by sowing dissension between the revolutionary intelligentsia, whose political aims were of a republican character, and the working masses, who were supporting the revolutionaries only because the latter were aiding them in their struggle to improve material conditions.

Accordingly, Zubatoff pursued a dual policy. On the one hand, he actively supported labor legislation, not infrequently taking the part of the workers in their disputes with their employers, provided that these disputes were of a purely economic character, and he succeeded in getting permission for the workers to form lawful societies under the control of the police for the protection of their economic interests. On the other hand, he favored and even fostered the growth of an extreme revolutionary temper among the intelligentsia. "We shall provoke you to acts of terror and then crush you," he declared boastfully in moments of frankness. This plan was distinguished by its complete lack of understanding of social processes, but it cannot be denied that it was very bold. Vain and domineering, full of far-reaching ambitions, Zubatoff was extremely self-confident; he liked to play with fire but very soon burnt his fingers.

In the pursuance of this policy, Zubatoff paid considerable attention to the development of a "secret agency" within the revolutionary organizations. This was the side of police work which most attracted him. After he had retired he is said to have declared: "My connection with the 'secret agency' is my most precious remembrance." He knew how to recruit such agents, how to control them, how to "keep their tracks covered," and how to teach them the art of reaching the topmost rungs of the revolutionary hierarchy.

Zubatoff inspired a similar attitude in those of his assistants—young gendarme officers and Ochrana officials—whom he allowed to have direct dealings with the secret agents.

"Gentlemen, you must look upon your collaborators as you would upon a woman whom you love and with whom you are conducting a secret intrigue. Watch over her as the apple of your eye. One rash step, and you have dishonored her in the eyes of the world." That is how Zubatoff instructed his young gendarmes.

Of all the "loved women" of this very original "lover," Aseff became the most "beloved." Alas! it was through him, too, that Zubatoff was fated to convince himself of the risk of relying upon the "heart of a beauty"—even if she were enrolled in the Ochrana. Later, after Aseff's exposure, Zubatoff, in a private letter, gave this true summary of his character: "Aseff's," he wrote, "was a purely mercenary nature . . . looking at everything from the point of view of profit, working for the Revolution for the sake of personal gain, and for the government out of no conviction but also for the sake of personal profit." But this knowledge, like the bitter after effects of a drunken orgy, came too late. During these years, however,

Zubatoff, knowing well the covetousness of his "ubiquitous" agent, carefully primed him with the mysteries of Ochrana wisdom and gradually insinuated him into the heart of the revolutionary organizations. Aseff was a very apt pupil, and, under such expert direction, steered his way skillfully and avoided accidents.

It was doubtlessly with Zubatoff's help that Aseff obtained a good position as an engineer in the Moscow office of the General Electrical Company. He also became a member of the "Intellectual Aid Society," whose members included the flower of the Moscow intelligentsia. At the same time he contributed to the paper published by the society. He formed a large circle of acquaintances and attended the various meetings and banquets which were organized from time to time.

In his reports to Zubatoff, Aseff described minutely everything of interest that he learned in the revolutionary world. His reports were not limited to any one particular party: from him Zubatoff received information about the leaders of the then Moscow Committee of Social Democrats, of the Villensky printing press, of the "Social Democrat Library" publishing group, and so on. But his attention, of course, was principally directed to the Moscow "Union of Social Revolutionaries." This "Union" was rapidly extending the sphere of its activity and had begun to publish its own paper, *Revolutzionaya Rossiya (Revolutionary Russia)*, which soon became the central organ of the entire Social Revolutionary party. A printing press was set up in Finland, in the vicinity of the Taly station, on the estate of a woman landowner who sympathized with the views of the party. Two important populist writers, Nyakotin and Peshehonoff, were persuaded to join the editorial board. The first number was published in

January, 1901, but was dated December, 1900, as the printing was slightly delayed. A second number followed soon after. They were both fairly widely circulated through Russia. The interest towards them of the populist-minded intelligentsia was growing, and Zubatoff's interest in this group correspondingly increased. He knew now who were the members of the "Union," and he would not have had the slightest difficulty in affecting the arrest of its principal adherents. But he looked further ahead. As a rule he did not like to have individual revolutionaries arrested. Usually he gave organizations time to "mature," got to know in detail all their ramifications, and then affected arrests on a large scale, taking good care that his "agent" should not be "shown up," but that, on the contrary, he should have the possibility of mounting higher on the rungs of revolutionary hierarchy. It was better policy to let several prominent revolutionaries go free than to lose one of his useful agents—such was Zubatoff's fundamental principle.

Guided by Zubatoff, Aseff was circumspect and cautious in his relations with the leaders of the "Union." He declared himself a sympathizer, but in no way forced his acquaintanceship upon them; he never questioned them about anything and exhibited no suspicious curiosity. In general conversation he did not conceal the fact that he was skeptical about the possibility of founding large organizations and of setting up revolutionary publications on a solid basis inside Russia: the forces of police repression, according to him, were too strong. It was much more reasonable to do such publishing abroad; and from the very beginning he advocated this policy in relation to the organ of the "Union." He admitted only one way of fighting—the terror. While the Muscovites, who were terrorists in theory, took no practical steps in this direction, regarding it as a matter of the future, Aseff constantly showed himself a supporter of an immediate recourse to terrorist methods. All other forms of revolutionary activity seemed to him to be "trifling." "Terror is the only way!" he used to declare. And when, in the spring of 1901, Karpovitch's shot rang out, Aseff joyfully declared: "Well, it seems the terror has begun!" In making such pronouncements, Aseff was following the line which he had adopted while living abroad. Now it was no longer his own personal line: behind him undoubtedly stood Zubatoff.

Though Aseff did not value highly the nonterrorist activities of the revolutionaries, yet he never refused his aid when it was sought. When, for example, Argunoff had need of a "solid but not too unwieldy roller" for the printing press, Aseff willingly undertook to procure it: he let it be known that he had a trustworthy friend, an engineer, who worked in a factory and who could make it. Little by little he gained the reputation of a cautious and prudent but not cowardly man, whose advice might prove useful on practical questions, and his counsel was more and more frequently sought. That the "solid but not too unwieldy roller" was made with the help of the Ochrana, and that it served as one of the principal clues leading to the detection of the "Union's" printing press, became known only later. . . .

Zubatoff, for various reasons, considered it inadvisable to close down the printing press in Finland. It was therefore decided to "frighten" the revolutionaries and to compel them to transfer their press elsewhere. A special watch was now kept on all revolutionaries going to Finland. Detectives literally "hung on their heels." The conviction grew that a raid would be made any day, and it was decided to transfer the press. A suitable place was found in Siberia. Dr. Pavloff, a brother of Argunoff's wife, had got the post of director of the emigration center in Tomsk. This center was situated outside the town in a lonely spot in the forest. The personnel of the officials was made up exclusively of revolutionaries. It would have been difficult to find a better place. The press itself was brought over in parts, with every precaution. In order to escape observation, the workers made a wide detour through Russia. C. N. Barikoff, for example, went from Moscow to Tomsk via Tiflis. This, however, did not save him from being followed by detectives as far as Tomsk. Zubatoff, however, learned of the transfer of the printing press in a more direct way: he asked Aseff to locate it.

In September, 1901, the printing press had been set up again, and it began work on the third number of *Revolutzionaya Rossiya*. Going minutely into the question with Aseff, Zubatoff came to the conclusion that its suppression would not endanger his agent. A gendarme officer, Spiridovitch, was specially sent to carry out the arrests and to institute an inquiry. But action was taken before his arrival: detectives had given information from Tomsk that there was every indication that a new number was already in the press, and Zubatoff therefore ordered the Tomsk police to act immediately. But the inquiry was afterwards conducted by Spiridovitch, who skillfully concealed from those arrested the extent of the authorities' knowledge. Not a shadow of suspicion fell upon Aseff. On the contrary, it was just at this time that his position in revolutionary circles was consolidated.

After the Tomsk raid the Moscow leaders of the "Union" did not doubt that their turn was close at hand. They had no fear for themselves: psychologically they had long been prepared for arrest. They had only one preoccupation: that was to save what remnants of the organization they could—and to this end it was necessary to put at the head of affairs some man who was not as yet compromised and therefore in no danger of arrest. Such a savior was found in Aseff, who of late had become particularly intimate with Argunoff. "Aseff," the latter recalls, "wholeheartedly shared our sorrow. It might have been his own grief. His attitude changed. From a passive collaborator he became an active member of our 'Union.' There was no formal entry into the 'Union': it all happened quite naturally."

At first it was necessary to take the greatest precautions. Argunoff tells of one meeting in the Sundunovsky Public Baths, where the revolutionaries discussed their affairs while washing. Later it grew easier to meet; for, as soon as it became clear that Argunoff intended Aseff to be his successor, Zubatoff ordered the observation to be relaxed. Aseff had already told Argunoff that he would have to go abroad on personal affairs; but this was the plan of the Police Department, which had decided that Aseff would be of more use abroad. This trip appeared now more than ever timely. Aseff offered his services to Argunoff for the arrangement abroad of all necessary affairs. He failed to persuade Argunoff to accompany him, but Maria Seliuk, another member of the "Union," decided to follow him.

"Like a dying man, we entrusted everything to Aseff," Argunoff continues his account. "We told him all our passwords, all our connections (literary and organizational), the names and addresses of our associates, and we recommended him warmly to all our friends. He was to arrive abroad together with Seliuk, enjoying our full confidence as the representative of the 'Union.' We looked upon him as a comrade, even, perhaps, as a friend. In those days of misfortune his active participation drew him closer to us."

The success of Zubatoff's policy was complete. All the ramifications of the "Union" were now known to him. He was in a position to suppress the Social Revolutionary groups throughout Russia. This, however, was no part of his plan. He wished to continue his game and to insinuate his agent into the very heart of the All-Russian organization. To this end, Aseff, when abroad, was to take part in the negotiations for the union of all the populist groups in Russia.

Aseff's funds were rapidly increasing, and his salary had also been raised. In January, 1900, he was receiving a hundred and fifty roubles a month, but after the Tomsk raid, and in consideration of his journey abroad, his salary was at once increased to five hundred roubles a month, a figure undreamed of till then.

At the end of November, 1901, Aseff left Russia with his family. Shortly before, Seliuk had also set out. Her activities were well known to the Ochrana, but Zubatoff decided to leave her alone, as she might be of use to Aseff. And this was the case, for in the beginning Aseff found her presence of great help when figuring as the representative of the Moscow "Union."

The police waited till Aseff had departed before arresting Argunoff. They did so a fortnight later. After two and a half years in prison, he was exiled to Siberia, from which he only managed to escape in 1905.

CHAPTER IV

The Foundation of the Social Revolutionary Party

THE PRINCIPAL COMMISSION given to Aseff by Argunoff was that of concluding the negotiations for the fusion of the scattered populist groups into one large "Socialist Revolutionary" party. The ground for this fusion had already been prepared, and the negotiations had been begun before the Tomsk raid. The two numbers of *Revolutzionaya Rossiya* published by Argunoff had been sympathetically received by all the populists, and they had inspired confidence in the promoters of the negotiations. The more important populist groups had already agreed in principle to this fusion. The most difficult part of the negotiations had thus been sur-

43

mounted. To Aseff's share fell the easier and more profitable task of formally concluding the union, negotiating with *émigré* sympathizers, and arranging for the future publication abroad of *Revolutzionaya Rossiya*, which was to be the organ of the new party. The Moscow representatives, Aseff and Seliuk, were helped in this work by G. A. Gershuni, who represented the organizations of the south and northwest. They came to a rapid understanding, and, in all ensuing negotiations conducted in Berlin, Berne, and Paris, they mutually supported each other. In some two months the negotiations were brought to a successful conclusion, an agreement being reached on all questions of program and tactics. Until the meeting of the Congress, the direction of the party work was temporarily entrusted to the Saratov group, led by E. K. Breshkovskaya, the Rakitnikoffs, and others.

It was decided to publish *Revolutzionaya Rossiya* in Switzerland, and M. R. Gotz and V. M. Tchernoff were appointed editors.

Gotz, Gershuni, and Tchernoff likewise acted as the executive members and, though men of different character, they complemented each other very well.

Tchernoff was from the very beginning the chief literary and theoretical influence in the young party. Though under thirty at that time, he had, before becoming one of the editors of *Revolutzionaya Rossiya*, already drawn attention to himself by a series of articles in both the lawful and clandestine press: in these he strove to construct a new ideological foundation for the old populist conception, and to this end he had recourse to the theories of western European Socialism—for the most part of the so-called revisionist camp. His individual outlook, as it was expressed in *Revolutzionaya Rossiya*, inevitably stamped both in its weak and in its strong points the whole program of the Social Revolutionary party.

The functions of the chief practical organizer fell to Gershuni. Until his arrest in May, 1903, he was constantly traveling round Russia, sharing his work with Breshkovskaya. There existed a kind of division of labor between them: Breshkovskaya, like a "Holy Ghost of the Revolution," flitted about the country, proselytizing and inciting everywhere the revolutionary temper of the youth; Gershuni usually followed in her tracks and turned to practical account the enthusiasm which she aroused, consolidating it into organizations affiliated to the Social Revolutionary party.

There was a personal element in Gershuni's attitude towards the old régime: when a young man and still politically undecided, he was imprisoned, fell into the hands of Zubatoff, and had personal experience of the methods employed to break the wills of the opponents of absolutism. Gershuni had given way at the time and had written a "recantation" of his "errors." But he did not mention any names or betray anyone to the police; this we know from the documents of the case which have all been published. The course taken by Gershuni on this occasion would not have been thought admissible by a logical revolutionary. Gershuni was well aware of this, and there was an element of personal hate in his attitude towards the old order. It was just this subjective shade which made of Gershuni a particularly passionate apostle and propagandist for the renewal of terrorist methods.

An enthusiast, whole-heartedly devoted to a single idea, Gershuni was possessed of an extraordinary power of influencing those with whom he came in contact. In the eyes of a stranger or a skeptical observer there was not infrequently a theatrical element in his conduct. It is enough to recall his gesture when he was put into chains after his arrest in Kiev: he bent down and silently kissed the iron chains. It would have been difficult to think of a more artificial and deliberately theatrical gesture. It made, nevertheless, an unforgettable impression on those who witnessed it—and these, prison guards and gendarmes, were not by the nature of their profession people who might be called particularly impressionable. His genuine inner passion compelled people to overlook what in others would have seemed a deliberate pose.

It was natural that Gershuni's influence on the youth of his time should have been still more marked: it was he who inspired many of the future terrorists. Less obvious, but of still deeper significance to the fate of the young party, was the influence of Gotz. Of the triumvirate referred to above, he was the oldest in years and experience. The son of a Moscow millionaire, he entered the revolutionary movement in the middle of the 'eighties, was arrested, and sent to Siberia, where, in 1889, he took part in the protest of the Yakutsk political prisoners against the very severe conditions imposed upon them by the administration. Harsh measures were taken to subdue the demonstrators.

Several were killed, and the others were beaten and handed over for trial, with the result that three of them were executed and some twenty others condemned to penal servitude. Gotz was among these latter. He regained his freedom in 1899, and soon after went abroad, principally for reasons of health; for at the time of the Yakutsk beating he had been struck on the spine by the butt of a rifle and had ever after suffered from mysterious pains. Not until 1904 was their cause discovered:

a tumor had affected his brain, causing him unbearable agony and threatening him with paralysis. The tumor could be removed only by an operation which might easily prove fatal. Gotz decided to risk the operation, and died in 1906 under the surgeon's knife.

But this was later: in 1902 Gotz, though suffering from ill health, was still full of energy. He had no great literary talent, but he could write simply and clearly and outline his fundamental thought with precision. The readers of his articles always knew what the author was driving at. Gotz brought this power of defining his fundamental thoughts to bear upon the political organization of the new party. From the very beginning he became its leading politician and organizer. He devoted all his inexhaustible mental energy to the task, and his part in the "political" development of the party was enormous.

Aseff, who had soon gained a reputation for sober practical judgment and for his ability to cope with the details of all projected undertakings, was in closest touch with this "triumvirate." His qualities particularly impressed Gershuni. According to Tchernoff's testimony, Gershuni was already at that time on such intimate terms with Aseff that together they decoded the secret correspondence from Russia. This intimacy was of particular interest to Aseff, since Gershuni was the first to advocate the adoption of terrorist methods. The discussion of this theme was confined to a very narrow circle, containing scarcely anybody outside of the four already mentioned.

There was no objection in principle to the terror, but it was decided to countenance it openly only after a terrorist act of the first importance had been committed. The party would then assume responsibility for the act and would give the group which had carried it out the right to become the Battle Organization of the party. Gershuni declared that he would undertake the organization of this act, and did not conceal that the first attempt, for which he claimed already to have volunteers, would be directed against the Minister of the Interior, Sipyagin. There is no doubt that Aseff was kept fully informed of the projected attempt. Its details, however, were not known to anybody, as they were largely worked out later by Gershuni on the spot.

During these months Aseff wrote frequent detailed reports to the Police Department. His letters breathe the satisfaction of the spy who has penetrated into the very heart of the enemy's camp. "In Berlin and in Paris I have penetrated into the very heart of things," he wrote. His reports about Gershuni were particularly full, and he made a point of stressing the leading part taken by the latter in all parleys abroad and in all the undertakings of the newly created party generally.

When, at the end of January, 1902, Gershuni was setting out on a tour of the local groups to advise them of the fusion that had taken place, Aseff informed the department both of the date of his departure from Berlin and of his proposed itinerary. But Aseff accompanied his information with an insistent demand that Gershuni should not be arrested. "He must not be arrested yet under any circumstances; bear this in mind." Thus the department had every opportunity to arrest Gershuni, but they took Aseff's advice. "Gershuni will not escape us now," the department wrote confidently to Zubatoff. "Since he is in such close contact with our agent, his immediate arrest would leave us in the dark as to his plans and furthermore might compromise the agent." It was therefore decided to allow Gershuni to complete his "very interesting trip," as the department put it, through Russia; but note was to be taken of all whom he met, and this was to pave the way for mass arrests later on.

The plan was not at all a bad one, but it took too little account of Gershuni: an experienced conspirator, he soon discovered that he was being watched and quickly shook off his pursuers. The police were unable to track him to any of his appointments, and Sipyagin, the Minister of the Interior, paid with his life for their over-confidence.

As soon as he arrived in Russia, Gershuni concentrated all his energy on the attempt against Sipyagin. A young Kiev student, Balmasheff, volunteered. The direct preparations were made by Gershuni, together with P. P. Kraft and M. M. Melnikoff, members of the Saratov executive of the Social Revolutionary party. According to the plan, if he failed to kill Sipyagin, Balmasheff was to assassinate Pobiedonostzeff, the head of the Synod, one of the inspirers of extreme reaction.

All the preparations were made in Finland, whence Balmasheff set out on April 15, 1902, wearing the uniform of an aide-de-camp. At the last moment the attempt was almost frustrated, for it was only in the train that the "officer" realized that he had left behind in his hotel that essential part of an officer's uniform, his sword. A new one had to be bought on the way. Balmasheff called on the Minister a little before the reception hour, hoping to meet him in the anteroom. The calculation was accurate: "The aide-de-camp of the Grand Duke Sergei," as Balmasheff called himself, was admitted to the anteroom and, when the Minister appeared, somewhat surprised at the visit of a special messenger from the Grand Duke, Balmasheff handed him a sealed packet containing the sentence of the Battle Organization and, at the same time, killed him outright with two shots.

That was the first act of the Battle Organization. Balmasheff paid for it with his life: he was condemned to death by court-martial and, on May 16th, hanged in Schlüsselburg.

For a few days after the assassination Gershuni remained in St. Petersburg. He was hoping to follow up this first blow with a second and then a third. At Sipyagin's funeral, Grigorieff, an officer and terrorist, was to kill Pobiedonostzeff, while, in the confusion, his fiancée, Iurkovskaya, was to assassinate Kleygels, the Governor General of St. Petersburg who had become notorious for his cruel measures against student demonstrators. These plans came to nothing, as Pobiedonostzeff was prudent enough not to attend the funeral. Only after this did Gershuni safely leave St. Petersburg. The police failed to get on his track, although they were aware of his presence in the capital and guessed at his complicity in the assassination.

The assassination of Sipyagin made a tremendous impression on the country. A feeling of elation was experienced, naturally enough, by Gershuni and the Social Revolutionaries, who were now introducing the terror as a new weapon into the arsenal of the Revolution. Sletoff, a party comrade of Gershuni's, who met him by chance at a railway station, described his state of mind at the time. "He was cheerful and gay and full of his first important success. 'It is only the beginning,' he said. 'The Gordian knot has been cut; the terror has justified itself. It has begun; all discussion is now superfluous.'" A new and decisive period of struggle had begun: it was the moment to take every risk and to pay no heed to the cruellest repressions. "It is time for the youth to come forward. Time does not wait; we must act at once."

He was right. Sipyagin's assassination had really opened a new chapter in the struggle against Russian absolutism—the chapter of terror. The real existence of the Battle Organization dates from this moment. The resources at its disposal were as yet very slender. When Gershuni wanted to reply to the execution of Balmasheff by a proclamation from Kiev, he was unable to do so because the Kiev Social Revolutionaries had no printing press. He had to content himself with a substitute. A poem of the Revolutionary poet, Lentzevitch, was reprinted by means of a hectograph, and the chief of the Battle Organization was himself obliged not only to write out the text but to prepare the ink.

But this lack of resources was counterbalanced by the optimistic temper which now reigned everywhere. The badly printed and almost illegible words of the poem fell on a particularly sympathetic audience:

> *A comrade has gone to his death,*
> *And given his life in the night.*
> *His corpse freshly strewn with the earth*
> *Lies buried in ominous night.*
>
> *Remember and find a true friend,*
> *Then sharpen the keen dagger bright.*
> *It's time not to cry, but avenge,*
> *—Avenge the lives lost in the night.*

Those eager to "avenge" were not wanting. Dozens, even hundreds, of new volunteers were ready to take the place of every one who fell.

CHAPTER V

Aseff and the Battle Organization in Gershuni's Time

ASEFF, IN THE MEANTIME, was living in Berlin; he explained that the General Electrical Company had sent him there in order to perfect his technical knowledge. In reality, he was there at the orders of the Police Department. Documents show that he worked in the Berlin factories without payment, merely to disguise the real reason of his presence.

To all appearances Aseff worked with great zeal for the police at that time. His letters to the department were packed with names and facts. They were written in the tone of a man who had wholly identified himself with the police interests. He very often referred to the

police and himself as "us": "My trip to Paris and
Switzerland was very useful to us." Sometimes his
letters display a strain of jealousy towards the revolutionaries. Thus, when informing the department of
Gershuni's scheme for smuggling propaganda into
Russia, and pointing out how this could best be frustrated, he added: "Gershuni has been boasting a lot of
his marvelous scheme."

But this was only on the surface. In reality, his
double game dates from this time, and he begins to
conceal a large amount of important information from
the department. Comparing Aseff's reports to the
department with what we know about him from the
accounts of the revolutionaries, we can establish the
fact beyond doubt that Aseff at the time systematically
concealed from the police everything that had bearing
upon Gershuni's terrorist activities. First of all, his
reports make no mention of the fact that the question
of the terror had been raised during the negotiations
for the fusion of the revolutionary groups. Furthermore,
Tchernoff, now the only surviving negotiator, thinks
that Aseff could not but have known the details of
Gershuni's plan and his intention to strike his first blow
against Sipyagin. There is not a word of this in Aseff's
reports.

This policy of silence becomes still more evident
after the assassination of Sipyagin. According to Aseff's
own admission, he learned of Gershuni's rôle in the
affair from Gotz "a few days" after Balmasheff's deed.
As it is known that Gotz stayed with Aseff in Berlin
on April 17 and 18, 1902, there can be no doubt that
his admission refers to these dates. And yet, in the
course of the next five weeks, that is, during the time
that Gershuni remained in Russia, Aseff's reports tried

to convince the department that Gershuni was in no
way implicated in the affair. He insisted that Gershuni
was too much absorbed in the work of organizing the
party to risk his head in terrorist acts, and that the
assassination had been organized by an independent
terrorist group which had no connection with *émigrés*.
And only at the end of May, after Gershuni had left
Russia, did Aseff carefully prepare the department for
the news that Gershuni was involved in the Battle
Organization. He concocted a version according to
which he had offered five hundred roubles to Gotz for
the needs of the Battle Organization, and that Gotz,
in reply, had suggested that this money should be
given to Gershuni, who was expected from day to day.
This was followed by an account of his interview with
Gershuni, in which Aseff alleged that he had learned
the exact part played by Gershuni in the Battle Organization.

Ratayeff, who had supervised Aseff's work for a
number of years, concludes in his memoirs that the
treachery of Aseff—an old and trusted agent—was due
to his friendship with Gershuni. In Ratayeff's opinion,
the latter possessed the power of influencing people
almost to the point of hypnotism; and Aseff would
seem to have fallen under this spell. From Aseff's later
admissions we know that he was prepared to betray
Gershuni, but he could not come to terms with the
police about the price, a fact which it is difficult to
reconcile with the theory of hypnotic influence. The
explanation, however, was much more simple: at that
time Aseff's position in the party depended upon his
friendship with Gershuni. Gershuni's trust in him
inspired general confidence. His arrest might easily
have roused suspicion against Aseff, and such suspicions

would have deprived him of a very easy way of earning his living and would also have endangered his life. It can scarcely be doubted that these were the considerations leading Aseff to protect Gershuni.

Aseff met the latter several times in Switzerland in the first half of June. Gershuni was buoyed up by his success and was full of the most daring plans. He was now planning attempts against Plehve, the new Minister of the Interior, Obolensky, the Governor of Kharkov, who had just crushed a peasant rising by mass floggings, and also against Zubatoff. He invited both Gotz and Aseff to share in the discussion of these projects. He was steadily drawing Aseff into the work of the Battle Organization and also into a scheme for the construction of dynamite works in Switzerland. Aseff went into all these schemes and shared actively in the discussions. ... The situation in which he found himself obviously embarrassed him, for he was not yet accustomed to playing a double game. He wrote to the department: "We must have a personal conversation about my further work. My position has become somewhat dangerous. I am now playing a very active part among the revolutionaries. It would be unprofitable to retreat now, but any action calls for the greatest care."

He informed the department of many things that he learned from Gershuni, including the plans for the attempts against Plehve and Zubatoff and the proposals for the establishment of the dynamite workshop, and so on. But his information was far from complete. His reports made no mention of the project to assassinate Obolensky, although, as Aseff knew perfectly well, Gershuni had resolved to execute this attempt first, immediately upon leaving Switzerland for Kharkov and Kiev. Furthermore, though giving a detailed report

of the negotiations with Meysner about the establishment of the dynamite workshop, Aseff concealed the
fact that Meysner had, in the end, declined the proposition; and he did not mention the names of those who
now did this work under his supervision.

His reports about Gershuni are particularly characteristic. It had now become impossible to conceal the
latter's connection with the Battle Organization; for
too many people were aware of this. Aseff no longer
attempted to deny the fact, but he strove to convince
the department that Gershuni played but a secondary
part, such as collecting money and recruiting young
terrorists. According to his assertions, the Battle
Organization was directed by a group of outlaw revolutionaries unknown to him. The reasons for his attitude
are obvious. While safeguarding Gershuni as his chief
support within the party, Aseff wished to betray the less
important members of the Battle Organization, making
them out to be its leaders in the eyes of the department.

The department agreed with the reasons Aseff gave
for the necessity of a personal interview and, in July,
1902, Aseff arrived in St. Petersburg. Important changes
had meanwhile been made in the staff of the Police
Department. With Plehve's sanction, Lopuhin, the
newly appointed director of the department, entrusted
the political side of the work to Zubatoff and his closest
assistants, and it was decided to concentrate on the
development of a secret service. Aseff, who had opportunities to enter the very heart of the Battle Organization, was therefore a welcome guest. His case was
brought before Plehve himself, and the latter at once
ordered that Aseff, contrary to all the department's
regulations for secret agents, should try to penetrate
into the party center and the Battle Organization.

By this time the Battle Organization was already a
fully autonomous body as far as its organization was
concerned. As the necessity arose, Gershuni, the supreme chief, found collaborators for particular tasks.
His methods were simplicity itself. In the course of his
trips in Russia, undertaken on general party business,
he made a point of recruiting revolutionaries who
desired, and in his opinion were able, to take part in
the terror. He "took them in hand," sometimes leaving
them on the spot, sometimes requiring them to abandon
their general party work, and occasionally persuading
them to go abroad for their greater security. P. P.
Kraft and Melnikoff were at that time in closest touch
with the work of the Battle Organization; and Gotz was
its trusted representative abroad.

As a result of its organizational weakness, all the
acts of the Battle Organization were in the nature of
isolated blows. No elaborate preparations were made.
The terrorists acted with their revolvers. In the attempts a great deal depended on the improvisation of
the moment—for which Gershuni in particular had a
genius. Zubatoff afterwards said very rightly that
Gershuni was "an artist in terror" and that he often
acted without a preconceived plan, "according to
inspiration."

Such was Gershuni's real place in the Battle Organization; and Aseff, of course, was perfectly aware of it.
But in his reports to the department Aseff made Kraft
and Melnikoff out to be the most dangerous terrorists,
referring to Gershuni merely as their assistant. The
attention of the department was thus principally directed to discovering the identity and whereabouts of
Melnikoff and Kraft with a view to their arrest.

On receiving the permission of the department to

join the Battle Organization, Aseff persuaded Gershuni
to call a meeting of those most closely connected with
its work. This was the first and only consultation of the
sort before Gershuni's arrest. It was held in Kiev in
October, 1902. Those present were Kraft, Melnikoff,
Aseff, and Gershuni, who arrived a little late. None of
them left any record of this meeting in their memoirs,
and, as a result, we have no details of it. We know only
that they discussed a plan for an attempt against
Plehve: two mounted officers, Grigorieff (who was to
have assassinated Pobiedonostzeff at Sipyagin's funeral) and his friend Nadaroff, were to attack the
Minister's carriage, one of them killing the horses and
the other the Minister. It goes without saying that this
plan came to nothing, for, on Aseff's warning, the
department kept these officers under strict observation.

Aseff, of course, did not go to the Kiev meeting alone:
he was accompanied by several expert detectives to
whom he pointed out all those who took part in the
meeting. No arrests were made in Kiev; but a careful
watch was now kept on Kraft and Melnikoff, who were
eventually arrested a few months later. Gershuni was
also watched carefully; but, as less importance was
attached to his arrest, he succeeded in escaping the
detectives. Besides his trip to Kiev, Aseff made a number of other trips in the winter of 1902–03, to Moscow,
Kharkov, Saratov, and other places, accompanied
everywhere by detectives. And everywhere his visits
were followed by arrests.

St. Petersburg was Aseff's principal base of action.
Here, as representative of the General Party Executive,
he supervised the importation of propagandist literature
via Finland, was in touch with the populist writers,
Peshehonoff, Myakortin, Klemens, Ivantchin-Pissareff,

and others, who supplied material for *Revolutzionaya Rossiya*, and collected what information he could as to Plehve's mode of life. On his shoulders fell all the local work. Peshehonoff states that the St. Petersburg Social Revolutionary Committee was at that time entirely controlled by Aseff. In consequence, the latter had to engage in such minor work as keeping in touch with young students who were anxious to do propaganda work among the working classes. And this routine work almost brought about his downfall.

Among those whom Aseff met in this way was a very young student, a certain Kristianinoff. His ideas of revolution and revolutionaries were most naïve and romantic. He pictured revolutionaries as "elegant young people with pale noble faces." Fate willed it that Aseff should be the first revolutionary with whom this romantic young man came in contact. According to the law of contrasts, the impression he received was very striking. Aseff's appearance, as Kristianinoff says, remained indelibly imprinted on his memory: an angular, unintelligently shaped head with dark, close-cropped hair, which came down low over his narrow forehead, large protruding impenetrable eyes that glided from face to face—all this made a strange and somewhat unpleasant impression. "But from this ponderous figure, sitting heavily on a chair, with its dark and, as it seemed to me, immobile face, radiated strength and will-power . . ." Aseff advised Kristianinoff to engage in propaganda among the workers, the type of activity with which all young revolutionaries began at that time. But the workers' group to which he detailed Kristianinoff was entirely made up of Ochrana agents.

The Ochrana had found itself in a delicate position. While opposing the existence of groups in which the workers would be initiated into revolutionary ideas, it yet could not refuse to help Aseff, whose position in the party would be weakened if he did not succeed in setting up at least a few of these groups. But a solution was found. Such groups were to be made up of workers in the pay of the police, who were ordered to hand over to the authorities, without reading it, all the illegal literature which they received from the party propagandists. In this way the police sought both to protect the sheep and satisfy the wolves. The propagandist would duly arrive, give his lecture, and distribute various pamphlets; after the meeting the agents would report to the authorities and hand in all the literature they had received. The conviction grew among the propagandists that they were making progress with their work, and in his letters abroad Aseff underlined the success which he had achieved. At the same time, there were no foundations "shaken," and, from the point of view of the police, the activity of the propagandists was rendered harmless as long as it was kept within these bounds.

The scheme, for all its ingenuity, broke down in the case of Kristianinoff. One of the worker agents, Pavloff, felt well disposed towards the young propagandist. The dirty work of an *agent provocateur* disgusted him; and, moreover, the "chief detective" had in some way offended him. As a result, after Kristianinoff's very first visit to the group, Pavloff confessed to him that he was in the pay of the police, told him of the real nature of such groups and of his desire to lead an honest life. In the course of subsequent interviews, Pavloff gave him a number of other details which convinced him that there was a highly placed traitor within the party and that this could be none other than Aseff.

"The Ochrana knows all about your party, comrade," said Pavloff. "It must be one of your leaders who is giving all the information. Your people think that everything is aboveboard, but there is somebody laughing up his sleeve. . . . For example, I heard today that your party has a secret arsenal in an electrical appliance shop called 'Energy,' and there all your arms and literature are hidden. The Ochrana won't raid it because it has an agent there already; so neither your arms nor your literature can run away."

This arsenal, "Energy," had been organized by Aseff with the help of two of his old Darmstadt comrades, both of them devoted revolutionaries, and it was one of the chief arsenals of the Social Revolutionary party in St. Petersburg. This discovery might well have staggered even a more experienced revolutionary, and, naturally, the young Kristianinoff was completely overwhelmed. He felt that it would be hopeless for him to entangle himself in the nets spread out by *agents provocateurs*, and that he might be arrested at any moment. And yet he could do nothing at the time to expose this systematic provocation, as all treated his stories as the ravings of a neurasthenic. And in truth, he did fall ill and was tormented by nightmares. He succeeded, however, in having a small committee formed to investigate the truth of his information. Two leading writers belonging to the party, Peshehonoff and Gukovsky, were on this committee.

They heard Kristianinoff, whose account, as he himself admits, was somewhat confused, and who realized later that he had forgotten to mention certain important facts. This confused account was countered by Aseff's brief but absolutely lucid statement. It is now clear that this "lucid statement" would not have stood the test of a searching examination, but the judges had little experience in such matters and took a great deal on trust. On their recommendation, the party executive reported that Aseff stood "above suspicion." As a result, the judges felt almost guilty before the unjustly accused Aseff; and they accepted as their due the reproaches which, towards the end of the trial, began to appear in Aseff's speeches. "This young man may be forgiven for making a mistake, but you, men of experience . . ." Aseff said reproachfully, but did not finish the sentence. Aseff came out of the trial fully vindicated, but it was evident that his fate hung on a hair.

About the same time the danger of exposure came from another quarter. Aseff, it will be remembered, had betrayed the plans of the proposed attempt on Plehve by the two officers. A strict watch had been kept on these officers for the past six months, but with very little result. They were arrested on February 21, 1903; on that day the Czar was to hold a review in which these officers were to take part, and the police were afraid that they might make an attempt on the Czar's life. When examining them, the police guardedly hinted at the extent of their information. Grigorieff and his fiancée were completely taken aback, for the police were evidently aware of what had been planned by only a very few people. Within two or three days they had made a "full confession" and had given the names of all those with whom they had been working. The department could not keep those confessions secret: the examination was conducted in the presence of a representative of the public prosecutor, and the evidence would consequently become the basis for the prosecution of the Battle Organization. The persons implicated were naturally arrested, and among them were people such as the medical practitioner Remyanikova, who were closely connected with Aseff. The fact that Aseff remained untouched while many of his friends were arrested inevitably brought suspicion upon him; and he was very angry with the police for their carelessness.

But the police too were dissatisfied. Its chiefs, Zubatoff and Lopuhin, were certain by now that Aseff was not telling all he knew and that he was concealing, as Zubatoff wrote later, "very serious things." This is even an understatement, for Aseff was at that time hiding from them the *most important thing*—the part played by Gershuni in the Battle Organization and his own relations with him.

This fact became of the utmost importance to the department. From the statements of Grigorieff and Iurkovskaya the part played by Gershuni was made clear. On hearing the report of the Grigorieff affair the Czar promised a "handsome reward" to anyone who arrested Gershuni. Plehve was in a great rage. Summoning Zubatoff, he declared that he would keep Gershuni's index card on his desk until he was arrested, as a constant reminder of the importance of the matter. The photograph and description of Gershuni were circulated to all detective branches, and it was rumored that a reward of fifteen thousand roubles was being offered for his head. Searches were made all over Russia, and numerous persons who had the misfortune to resemble Gershuni were arrested. But Gershuni himself always succeeded in escaping.

Zubatoff naturally enough brought pressure to bear on Aseff. Aseff had every means of helping him. Later, he admitted to Burtzeff that he was prepared to betray Gershuni, but for not less than fifty thousand roubles.

He evidently knew of the Czar's offer of a handsome reward, but he preferred that this should go to him rather than to his superiors.

There is scarcely any doubt that this was the precise reason for the conflict between him and his chief, Zubatoff. The latter frankly told Lopuhin of his doubts as to the admissibility of the system of concealment practised by Aseff. With the object of forcing Aseff's hand, an interview between him and Lopuhin was arranged, but it did not help in any way. To the allegations of the department, Aseff replied with counter allegations and accused the department of not paying sufficient attention to his information. In the end, it was merely decided to send Aseff abroad again.

Failing to come to terms with Zubatoff about Gershuni's betrayal, Aseff went to Moscow to meet the latter. This interview took place at the end of March, in the house of the engineer Zauer, a Darmstadt friend of Aseff's, who now occupied the post of assistant director of the Moscow Electrical Station. Aseff made use of his house for particularly important meetings. The greatest secrecy was observed about the interview; the police apparently got no inkling of it; and Gershuni and Aseff stayed with Zauer for three days without leaving the house. It was here that Gershuni appointed Aseff as his successor in all party matters and in the affairs of the Battle Organization in particular. There can be no doubt that during this interview it was decided to make an attempt against the Ufa Governor Bogdanovitch, on whose orders some unarmed workers had recently been shot down. At all events, immediately after this interview Gershuni set out for Ufa. He had made Aseff his close associate in this attempt and had charged him to get in touch with the terrorists chosen for assassination who were living in the West and to send them to Ufa. Aseff fulfilled his mission faithfully; but, as it happened, the help of the new arrivals was not required. In Ufa, Gershuni learned that the local Social Revolutionaries, headed by V. V. Leonovitch, were not only already keeping observation on Bogdano-vitch, but had found two local volunteers for the deed, a railway worker, Dulebov, and the intellectual "Apos-tle," whose real name is still a mystery. Their plan was sanctioned by Gershuni and was then successfully carried out.

On May 19, 1903, about midday, two young men went up to Bogdanovitch, who, as was his custom, was strolling in a secluded corner of the cathedral garden, and, thrusting the sentence of the Battle Organization into his hand, riddled him with their Brownings; then, jumping over the low garden fence, they disappeared in the ravine which led from the town on the hillside to the river. All search proved fruitless. Many arrests were made, but no trace of the real perpetrators was found.

Gershuni, who had hitherto been so lucky in escaping from the nets spread for him, was at last caught almost by accident. He made his escape from Ufa without difficulty. He even had time to write and to send abroad a detailed account of the events in Ufa; and he also published an official manifesto about it in the name of the Battle Organization. He stopped in Saratov to see some party friends and was then making his way abroad, full of plans for the future. Unfortunately he decided to stop in Kiev on the way, although he knew that this town was particularly dangerous for him. He sent a prearranged telegram indicating the time of his arrival. The telegram came to the knowledge of a petty *agent provocateur*, the student Rosenberg, who did not even suspect whom it concerned. But it was enough for the local police. An ambush was arranged at the station indicated. When, on the evening of May 26th, the train pulled in, there descended from it a well-dressed man wearing an engineer's cap and carrying a portfolio under his arm. At first he walked the length of the train, pretending to look at the wheels, but really looking about him. The detectives did not move from their place. The train whistled and moved out. Gershuni went out into the street, stooped down, and pretended to tie his bootlace, looking out for any suspicious signs. Alas, there were plenty of them: the place was alive with detectives. They caught Gershuni's glance and from it guessed that he was the man they were seeking. "That's our man," jerked out the chief detective. "He's got slanting eyes."

Noticing that he was being watched, Gershuni went up to a fruit stall and ordered a glass of lemonade. The detectives saw that he was nervous and that his hand was trembling so much that he could scarcely hold his glass. Gershuni felt the noose tightening round his neck. Within a few minutes he was arrested, put in chains, and sent off to St. Petersburg, where there awaited him a fortress, a trial by court-martial, and a death sentence, which was afterwards commuted to penal servitude for life. . . .

In the meantime Aseff had gone abroad, for he was afraid that the police might suspect him of complicity in the assassination. Already in May he had sent to his chief, Ratayeff, an unimportant telegram from Berlin, which was to serve as an alibi in case of need.

CHAPTER VI

The Hunt after Plehve

AT THE TIME of his last visit abroad at the beginning of 1903, Gershuni left with Gotz, who was his confidant in all matters and especially in the affairs of the Battle Organization, as his last bequest, all the memoranda pertaining to the Battle Organization: these were the careful supervision of all its affiliations, addresses, secret correspondence, passwords, and so on, as well as a list of persons who had offered to work for it. According to this bequest, Aseff was to become the chief of the Battle Organization in case of Gershuni's arrest. Gotz fully approved of Gershuni's choice; and when Aseff appeared on the Geneva horizon in June,

1903, he was greeted by Gotz and his close associates
as the recognized new chief, who was to bring even
greater fame to the Battle Organization. And Aseff
applied himself to his task without haste.

The question of an attempt on Plehve became the
order of the day. The famous anti-Jewish pogrom in
Kishenev had taken place shortly before. For two days,
on April 19 and 20, 1903, an organized crowd had
plundered without impediment Jewish houses, pillaged
shops, violated women, and murdered without consideration of age or sex. Neither the police nor the
troops made any attempt to stop the pogrom. Indeed,
the rioters not infrequently heard words of encourage-
ment and praise from them. But when groups of Jews
attempted any resistance, the police made themselves
evident by scattering them, making arrests, and not
even hesitating to use firearms. Dozens were killed;
and the number of those who suffered could be reckoned
in hundreds. It was generally felt that the chief fault
lay with Plehve, who considered anti-Jewish pogroms a
useful means of fighting the revolutionary movement,
and who openly expressed this opinion in confidential
discussions with officials of the administration.

The Kishenev pogrom made a tremendous impression
both in Russia and abroad. It also made a deep impression on Aseff, though he was no Jewish nationalist;
but, nevertheless, he was at heart a Jew. The memory
of his childhood spent in a Jewish environment was
still with him, and one of the most painful episodes in
the Kishenev pogrom was the account of the brutal
slaughter of children and infants, whose heads were
dashed against walls.

Aseff also held Plehve responsible and did not conceal
his indignation. This he did not confine to revolutionary

circles; it was even a subject of his conversations with his police chiefs. Even before Aseff's departure abroad Zubatoff records that, in an interview with him, he "shook with fury and hate in speaking of Plehve, whom he considered responsible." And later, when abroad, Aseff expressed himself in the same spirit in conversations with his police chief, Ratayeff. There can be no doubt that this circumstance was the decisive factor in Plehve's fate. If, in other cases, Aseff, for reasons of greed, more or less passively acquiesced in the commission of terrorist acts, in Plehve's case he actively helped in bringing it to a successful conclusion.

But profit also played an important part in Aseff's conduct in the case of Plehve. Formerly, the Police Department had been his principal source of income. The revolutionary organizations brought him in nothing or a very little. He was a revolutionary only in so far as this was required of him by the police. And he sold the secrets of the revolutionaries with a "clear conscience." But the position had very much changed. The head of the Battle Organization now had absolute control of funds amounting to many thousands. These funds could provide an income much larger than the five hundred roubles a month paid him by the Police Department. Naturally enough, he was now very much concerned in strengthening his position in revolutionary circles, or, to put it simply, in obtaining unchecked control of the revolutionary funds. To achieve this, it was necessary that the Battle Organization should be successful in its undertakings, for continued failure would inevitably lead to his being superseded in leadership. And now a peculiarly favorable situation permitted economics to ally themselves with his own inclination. Thus the assassination became in every way desirable to him.

When Aseff assumed the leadership, the forces at the disposal of the Battle Organization were sufficiently large; there were both money and volunteers. Together with Gotz, his right-hand man now, Aseff worked out a plan of action against Plehve. It was known that the Minister drove regularly to report to the Czar; it was necessary only to study the route of these drives, to learn the days and the hours, and then to make a bomb attack on the carriage—an attack like that organized against Alexander II in 1881.

As a result of this plan, the attempt lost the character of an individual and isolated act; its success depended entirely upon a complex organization and the concerted action of a whole group of people. Revolutionaries disguised as cab drivers, newspaper vendors, and hawkers were to keep watch; specialists were to prepare the explosives; and the leaders were to coördinate the work of the various groups. The actual assassination thus became the last link in a carefully forged chain, and the perpetrator merely the more or less accidental actor representing a large organized body.

The plan was carefully thought out in all its details and then approved. The original group chosen to act against Plehve was composed of Sazonoff, Savinkoff, Schweitzer, Pokotiloff, and the two brothers Matzevsky, all young, and, for the most part, former students who had been expelled from the universities for participation in the student movements of 1899–1902. The government, on the whole, paid very dearly for the severity with which it had repressed what was originally a purely academic movement. During the revolutionary epoch of 1905, the leaders of all the revolutionary organizations, Social Revolutionary as well as Social Democratic, were almost entirely recruited from the former participants in this student movement.

The members of the terrorist group had no particular experience of such work; but this was compensated by their enthusiasm, devotion, and readiness to sacrifice their lives. Experience came only later, bringing with it the poison of skepticism; and only then did it become clear that youthful enthusiasm in such matters counts for more than well-founded experience. Aseff was the only person of experience, the only practical leader among these young enthusiasts. He served as a link between the separate parts of an organization, whose members, at the beginning, were only bound together by him.

Aseff personally acquainted himself with every member of the detachment and made them all undergo a searching test before sending them to their posts, where they were to do their share of the preparatory work. When sending them off, Aseff explained to them in a business-like manner the precise nature of their tasks and invariably added with conviction: "If there is no traitor among us, Plehve will be killed!"

His quiet assurance communicated itself to the other terrorists. Armed with it, they set out on their journey in the late autumn of 1903. The campaign against Plehve had begun. . . .

Everything went smoothly at first. But Savinkoff, who directed the work of the watchers in St. Petersburg, showed signs of nervousness. The terrorists soon picked out Plehve's carriage and discovered some of the streets through which he habitually drove. But Aseff, who had promised to be in St. Petersburg in the early part of December, gave no signs of life; he did not arrive, sent no news of himself, and did not even reply to letters. Savinkoff was perturbed and could not account for his chief's conduct. Moreover, there were indications that the police were on their guard; but as Savinkoff is the only authority for this, it may only have existed in his nervous imagination. In any case, it proved the drop which finally overflowed the cup of Savinkoff's impatience; he stopped his work of observation, dispersed the group, and hurriedly left St. Petersburg.

Confused and ill at ease, conscious, too, that he had violated the discipline of the Battle Organization, and yet not knowing what other course he could have taken, Savinkoff reported first of all to Tchernoff and then to Gotz. They received him almost as if he had deserted his post in battle. Aseff, they said, had not arrived because he was occupied with important party affairs; Savinkoff's letters had not reached their destination through his own fault, since he had given the wrong address. He must immediately return to Russia where decisive action was to be taken in the near future. These interviews restored Savinkoff's morale: he had already begun to lose confidence in himself and had asked to be given some less responsible task; but now, on receiving orders from Aseff to proceed to Moscow to discuss future plans, he set out once more taking with Gotz's consent his old friend Kalyaeff to help him in his work.

The explanation of Aseff's nonarrival in St. Petersburg was not so simple as it appeared from Tchernoff's and Gotz's accounts. Aseff had spent these months in studying the general situation in the Ochrana world. He wished to kill Plehve, but he was not prepared to risk both his life and his salary.

Arriving abroad in the summer of 1903, Aseff was

put under the orders of Ratayeff, who had shortly
before been appointed the chief of the Russian Political
Police abroad. Though far from stupid, Ratayeff was
not at all fitted for such a responsible post. A society
man, a Don Juan, a regular theatergoer, he did his
police work in a purely routine way. Over two decades
of service in the department in responsible positions had
given him a knowledge of the technique of police work
and, when he wished, he could hold his own successfully
in his complicated surroundings, but he rarely took the
trouble. His interest in the detective side of his work
was purely formal. This was perfectly obvious to those
who were at the head of the Police Department at the
time. Plehve openly said that Ratayeff was a "blot"
on the department. His appointment abroad was merely
a polite way of removing him from the department,
where he had directed the Special Branch, that is, the
Political Police. Ratayeff understood the real significance of his new appointment and felt himself aggrieved.

A man of this kind was naturally least of all capable
of controlling Aseff, although the necessity of such a
control had now made itself particularly felt. It may be
definitely stated that, throughout the period of Aseff's
work under Ratayeff (this lasted until Ratayeff's retirement in the summer of 1905), it was not Ratayeff who
controlled Aseff, but the latter who used him in his
own interests, deftly employing him as a screen for his
activities, learning from him the extent of the department's knowledge, and, with his help, getting rid of his
party enemies.

During his first months abroad, Aseff supplied Ratayeff with no information whatsoever, telling him that
"he had had no time to look round him or to consolidate
his position." Only at the end of September did he begin

to send in reports dealing for the most part with the life of the *émigré* groups, Social Revolutionary as well as Social Democratic. But in the late autumn, that is, after the departure of the terrorists to Russia, Aseff, according to Ratayeff's memoirs, showed himself a "little more lively." He had arrived in Paris and had called personally on Ratayeff. Aseff was "sprightly, energetic and talkative," but he talked of everything except the attempt against Plehve which he was preparing. Indeed, in so far as the latter was discussed, Aseff clearly tried to find out how much the police knew in this direction.

His efforts were far from fruitless. Ratayeff told him that the department knew that Sazonoff had gone abroad and that he had, in conversations with his friends, expressed his determination to kill Plehve. According to Ratayeff, Aseff said, without the flicker of an eyelid, that he did not know Igor Sazonoff, though he had once met his brother Izot; but that he could, if necessary, make an attempt to question him further. From this conversation Aseff could easily conclude that the police, or, at all events, the talkative Ratayeff, had no precise information. This information was of capital interest to him, since he had, it appears, dispatched Sazonoff to Russia only a few days before.

Shortly afterwards Aseff began to prepare for his departure to St. Petersburg. This trip was essential to him for two reasons: in the first place, to organize Plehve's assassination, and, in the second, to prevent another projected attempt. Not all of the party leaders were content that Aseff should have complete control of the Battle Organization. Thus S. Klitchoglu, a woman terrorist, who had helped the Battle Organization in various ways in Gershuni's time, had now, with the support of several influential party leaders in Russia such as Potapoff, founded a small terrorist group in the south, and had come to St. Petersburg to make an attempt of her own against Plehve. This was a direct challenge to Āseff. If her attempt were to succeed, he would probably lose control of the Battle Organization and, of course, of its funds. This made him anxious to destroy the Klitchoglu group; such a betrayal, too, would consolidate his position in the eyes of the police and would make it easier for him to carry out his own attempt.

Acting on this argument, Aseff informed Ratayeff about Klitchoglu's plans, and persuaded the latter to accompany him to St. Petersburg for the exposure of this terrorist plot. Ratayeff was all the more ready to fall in with this project, as he hoped to raise his prestige in the Minister's eyes by such an exposure. It was also to Aseff's advantage to have Ratayeff at hand now that he was engaged on this complicated double game; the police chief would serve as a most convenient screen.

They set out for St. Petersburg within a short time of each other. If we are to believe certain evidence, Aseff took with him not only his denunciation of the Klitchoglu group, but also a quantity of dynamite for the use of his own group. Thus he took full advantage of Ratayeff's protection!

The Klitchoglu group was quickly run to ground in St. Petersburg; but a serious difference now arose between Aseff and the department on the question of the arrests. Knowing that the arrests were imminent, Aseff wished to avoid meeting Klitchoglu, but the department insisted on this, promising that the arrests would not take place immediately afterwards. On this assurance Aseff met her and learned from her all the details as to the composition and the plans of the group. He passed on these details to the department, but the latter did not keep its word. The St. Petersburg Ochrana was at that time conducting an intrigue against Ratayeff, and, at its orders, Klitchoglu's arrest took place almost immediately after Aseff's interview with her. According to Ratayeff, this "disloyal" action on the part of the police affected Aseff in the most adverse way. He declared bluntly that under such circumstances it was becoming "difficult to work for the police." His immediate chief, Ratayeff, was in complete agreement and supported him in his discussions with the department chiefs. A close alliance was being knit between the "injured" Aseff and the "injured" Ratayeff against those who had broken their solemn promise: that is, the department and the St. Petersburg Ochrana. A particularly favorable situation was thus being created for Aseff's complex game. Ratayeff now held back part of Aseff's information from the department, while the latter in its turn withheld still more from the Ochrana.

At the very height of these official intrigues Aseff found time to visit Moscow, where he met Savinkoff, who had just returned from abroad, and several other members of the Battle Organization. Aseff rebuked Savinkoff stiffly for violating terrorist discipline. "Your duty was to wait for me and to keep watch on Plehve," said Aseff. A plan for future work was then drawn up. All the preparatory work was to be done by Savinkoff and Kalyaeff. Ratayeff, it is needless to add, was kept in ignorance of this Moscow meeting.

In the second half of February, 1904, the members of the Battle Organization began to assemble in St. Petersburg and to renew their watch on Plehve's movements. Aseff continued to control them, discussed the information gathered by them, and gave them directions. If the police had thought of watching him closely they would have had little difficulty in getting on the tracks of the Battle Organization. Aseff realized the danger he was running, and he maintained his relations with Ratayeff in such a way as to allow of his making a *volte face* at any moment and selling the Battle Organization. In his daily reports to Ratayeff he mingled the elements of truth and artifice in order that he might be able, in case of need, to interpret these reports in the most profitable way for himself; and he was always careful to make sure whether the police were keeping him under observation.

To this end he used to tell Ratayeff about mysterious terrorists who came to see him with passwords from abroad. He claimed not to know their names, but his descriptions of them corresponded exactly to those of the members of the Battle Organization. He gave the police, however, no concrete information which might have helped them in their researches. He did once tell them of an appointment he had with a leading terrorist in a public bath; and his description of him corresponded to that of Kalyaeff. This was brought to the notice of the director of the department, and E. P. Melnikoff, who was considered a talented detective and who was in charge of the department's Detective Branch, was sent specially to overhear this interview. But the police were no wiser for this public-bath watch: Aseff arrived and washed long and thoroughly, but nobody turned up. Thus the police failed to get on the tracks of the Battle Organization; and Aseff, by his daily meetings with Ratayeff, assured himself that the police had no suspicion of his double game.

* * *

In the meantime the members of the Battle Organization had found out the days and hours of Plehve's visits to the Czar. But the route taken had not yet been completely ascertained, and Aseff insisted on the work of observation being pursued. But the young revolutionaries had grown impatient, and they insisted on an immediate attempt. They suggested attacking the Minister's carriage on its departure from or its arrival at the Police Department building in which he lived. Aseff protested against this haste, pointing out that the police supervision in such a place would be much more intense. These arguments did not bear great weight with the young men, who had already seen the police guard and thought the attempt quite feasible. Aseff could do nothing but consent. "Very well," he said to them. "If you insist, we will try our luck!"

The details were gone into at a special meeting; and the attempt was decided on for March 31st, only a few days after the meetings. This fact was very embarrassing for Aseff. He had grounds to believe that the police might suspect something was wrong if the attempt took place so soon after his arrival in St. Petersburg. Ratayeff had already hurriedly left for Paris on business, leaving Aseff in the charge of Lopuhin, the director of the department. In keeping with his tactics, Aseff had called on the latter to feel the ground and to insure himself against future suspicions. Aseff's pretext was the disclosure of a supposed plot against Lopuhin.

There was an element of truth in Aseff's story: he described correctly all the organizational and technical details of the intended attempt, following the plan he had worked out against Plehve; and he even indicated the place of the attempt—near the department building on the Fontanka—and mentioned bombs as the means to be used. But he mentioned neither the names of the perpetrators nor the time of the attempt. Incidentally, Aseff raised the question of an increase of salary. It is possible that Aseff would have added further details had his request for an increase of salary been favorably received. This, however, was not the case. Whether Lopuhin suspected Aseff of an attempt at extortion, or whether he had really decided on economy in police expenditure, he treated Aseff's request coldly, promising to consult Ratayeff about it. Thus the visit ended.

Immediately after this interview Aseff left St. Petersburg. He had arranged to meet the members of the Battle Organization on April 4th in Dvinsk, after the attempt, but he went abroad instead. First of all, he informed Gotz of the intended attempt and of his own doubts as to its success, and then he called on Ratayeff in Paris. He thus insured himself against possible accusations from either side. If, profiting by his warning of an impending attack on Lopuhin, the police had kept a careful guard in the vicinity of the department building, they might well have come across the terrorists who were preparing the attempt against Plehve.

The credit for this arrest would have gone to Aseff: the terrorists could not possibly have suspected him, as he had been careful to point out the dangers of the plan; it would also have been made clear during the investigation of the case that the police were under the impression that they had to do with an attempt directed against Lopuhin and not against Plehve. If, on the other hand, the police were careless enough to allow the attempt to take place, Aseff's excuse was ready made: he had given his warning and had even indicated the exact spot of the attempt; if he did not know at whom the attempt was aimed it was because the terrorists had not initiated him into the full details of the plan, and even so, they might have changed their plans at the last moment when they found that they could assassinate Plehve instead of Lopuhin. In the eyes of the revolutionaries all the credit for the assassination of Plehve would go to Aseff, since they knew that without his authority the inexperienced revolutionaries would not have carried their work through. . . . The game was finely calculated and, whatever its issue, Aseff was bound to come out a winner.

Aseff told Ratayeff of his visit to Lopuhin and learned that his request for a raise of salary had not been referred to him. March 31st had already passed. The attempt, for some reason, did not take place, but there was no news either of arrests. The police clearly could not lay their hands on the young revolutionaries, who wandered in bands near the department building. It is not difficult to guess Aseff's mood at that time: there was no point in standing on ceremony with fools, who knew nothing of police work and who, furthermore, grudged him a raise in salary. And Aseff really did stop standing on ceremony.

A few days after his arrival in Paris Aseff told Ratayeff that his old mother had fallen seriously ill, and that he must go to Vladikavkaz to see her. Ratayeff was loth to let him go, but he was obliged to give way to Aseff's insistence. Aseff, of course, made a lot of promises, saying that he would lay his hands on those unknown terrorists whose activities he had brought to Ratayeff's notice in St. Petersburg. He saw Gotz before his departure; and he doubtlessly told him that the young terrorists had bungled and that he had to go and put things in order. . . .

Aseff arrived too late in Dvinsk to find the terrorists there; but he met one of them, Pokotiloff, by chance in the train on the way to St. Petersburg, and learned from him what had taken place during his absence.

On March 31st, the group took up their positions in the street according to plan. Three of them, Sazonoff, Pokotiloff, and Borishansky, had bombs; Kalyaeff and Matzevsky were to act as signalmen, while Savinkoff was in general command. They kept fairly close together, between the department building and the Neva. The Minister was cornered like a beast in its lair. But the attempt was not carried out. Either the Ochrana was particularly on its guard after Aseff's visit to Lopuhin, or the inexperienced terrorists were a little nervous; in any case, one of them, Borishansky, thought he was being surrounded by detectives and deemed it advisable to leave his post.

This disorganized the attackers, and the attempt did not take place, although it could easily have been carried out by the two remaining bomb throwers, who saw no signs of their being watched. After this failure Savinkoff and Pokotiloff went to Dvinsk, where they had their appointment with Aseff for April 4th. The latter was not there, nor was there any word from him. The young terrorists decided that Aseff had been arrested and that they were now thrown on their own resources, and Savinkoff once more lost his head.

The plan could still be easily carried out, as the terrorists remained untouched and as they still had their bombs. Pokotiloff insisted on this, but Savinkoff was of a different opinion; assuming that Aseff had been arrested, he thought the strength of the detachment without Aseff insufficient for an attack on Plehve. But he did not wish to give up the idea of a terrorist attempt altogether and suggested the less difficult task of assassinating Kleygels, the Governor General of Kiev. This was an easy enough matter, as Kleygels used to drive openly through the streets of Kiev, but it had no political significance. Some years before, Kleygels had drawn on himself the hatred of the St. Petersburg students by his cruelty to them, but so many events had taken place since then that few remembered him.

The terrorists held a meeting at which Savinkoff put forth his views. Kalyaeff and Schweitzer supported him, but the remainder insisted on the continuation of the original plan against Plehve. The decision arrived at was the worst possible: the terrorists were to be split up into two groups, one of which (Sazonoff, Pokotiloff, Borishansky, and Matzevsky) was to carry out the plan against Plehve, while the second (Savinkoff, Kalyaeff, and Schweitzer) was to deal with Kleygels. Thus Savinkoff's contention that the "whole" group was insufficient for an attack on Plehve merely resulted in the matter being entrusted to a part of the group. Under such conditions all attempts became hopeless.

When Aseff met Pokotiloff he was on his way to St. Petersburg to carry out the attempt. Borishansky and he had already waited in vain for Plehve on April 7th; and the next attempt had been fixed for the 14th. Aseff tried to dissuade him, but without success: Pokotiloff's nerves were too strung up to agree to any delay. His career as a terrorist was indeed extraordinary: he was an unsuccessful terrorist of a very special kind. He had already come to St. Petersburg in 1901 with the idea of killing the Minister of Education. But before his preparations were completed the Minister was killed by Karpovitch, who had acted quite independently. After this Pokotiloff met Gershuni and offered his

services for the assassination of Sipyagin, but Gershuni's
choice finally fell on Balmasheff. Pokotiloff then made
Gershuni promise that he would pick him to carry out
the next assassination undertaken by the Battle Organization. Gershuni had already entrusted him with
the task of killing Obolensky, when, at the last moment, Foma Katchura, a worker and native of the province where the peasants had been whipped by Obolensky, offered his services. As an assassination carried out
by Katchura would produce a far greater impression
than one carried out by a student, Gershuni once more
persuaded Pokotiloff to give way. Twice the latter had
waited for Plehve with bombs, and on both occasions
without success. He could wait no longer. He would
bring it off this time whatever happened. Pokotiloff
went to St. Petersburg and, on the eve of April 14th,
the day appointed for the attempt, he was accidentally
killed by the explosion of one of his own bombs. Thus
he remained an unsuccessful terrorist to the end. . . .

The news of his death naturally produced a very dis-
heartening impression on the remaining members of the
organization. Borishansky at once left for Kiev, where
it was decided to give up the attempt on Plehve and to
concentrate on Kleygels. Schweitzer set out for St.
Petersburg in order to persuade the two remaining
"cabmen," Sazonoff and Matzevsky, to sell at once
their coachmen's disguises and go abroad.

But then, almost immediately after Schweitzer's
departure, Aseff came on the scene. He had apparently
been to Odessa; at any rate, he had become aware of the
distrust which many of the leading party members felt
for the Battle Organization under his control. Sletoff,
who had met Savinkoff in Kiev at the time of the latter's
first flight from St. Petersburg, had been unfavorably

impressed by the organization in which Savinkoff was playing such an important part.

This impression was shared by other leading party members, and in 1904 they held a meeting in Odessa, at which they called for an inquiry into the state of the Battle Organization. They held that, if no satisfactory answer were given them, they would "consider themselves free to undertake the organization of future terrorist attempts." This was a direct threat of a party revolt against Aseff. His party career was now in jeopardy. Only a successful attempt on Plehve could right the situation. He therefore had to be all the more severe in dealing with Savinkoff. He at once attacked the latter: "What are you up to? What's the meaning of this attempt against Kleygels? Why aren't you in St. Petersburg? What right have you to alter the decisions of the Central Committee?"

And after listening attentively to all of Savinkoff's explanations, he forcefully refuted his arguments:

"Even if I had been arrested, you had no right to give up the attempt on Plehve. You say you weren't strong enough to kill Plehve? Pokotiloff's death? But you should have been prepared for the destruction of the whole organization down to the very last man. What prevented you? If you hadn't enough men, you should have found them. If you hadn't any dynamite, you should have made it. But you should never have given up the attempt. Plehve has to be killed in any case, and if we don't kill him, nobody will. . . ."

Aseff's unbending severity was, of course, a pose which came all the easier to him since he had assured his own safety on every side. This pretense of being an uncompromising terrorist succeeded in its object, and Savinkoff and his comrades could not but be impressed.

They hastened to agree with Aseff and decided once more to concentrate on an attempt on Plehve.

"Aseff's insistence, his coolness and assurance, restored the spirit of the terrorists," Savinkoff recalled later. "It may be said without exaggeration that Aseff recreated the organization. We went back to our task with faith and the determination to kill Plehve at any cost."

Aseff fanned the terrorists' ardor by telling them of the distrust in which the Battle Organization was held by many of the leading members of the party. This story sowed the first seeds of dissension between the "fighters" and the party executive; and this was in accordance with Aseff's calculations. For the moment it had the positive effect of making the young men wish to rehabilitate their honor by *action*.

By the beginning of May the vanguard of the terrorists was in St. Petersburg. A flat was taken for their secret meetings in the very center of the town, at 31 Zhukovsky Street. Savinkoff became its ostensible tenant in the guise of a rich Englishman, McCullough. The part of the lady of the house, his mistress, was played by Dora V. Brilliant, the daughter of a prosperous orthodox Jewish merchant who had run away from her family at an early age to devote herself to the revolutionary movement; later she went mad in the fortress of Peter and Paul and died in a lunatic asylum. They lived on a "grand scale," kept a "butler" and a "cook," the first being Sazonoff and the second P. C. Ivanovskaya, an old revolutionary and member of the executive committee of the "Narodnaya Volya" party. In her time she had taken part in plots to assassinate Alexander II and had been condemned to penal servitude for life, but had now, almost a quarter of a century later, escaped from Siberia to rejoin the ranks of the terrorists. The watch kept by the terrorists now began to give results: the watchers had grown more experienced, and some of them, especially Kalyaeff, played their parts like real artists.

In the middle of June Aseff arrived in St. Petersburg. He had spent the last six weeks traveling about Russia; he had taken his mother to watering places in the North Caucasus, and had also been to Samara and Ufa. In all these places he was busy carrying out Ratayeff's orders. In Samara he tried to "discover" the identity of the terrorist who had blown himself up in St. Petersburg. He visited Ufa specially to see Sazonoff and to find out his brother Igor's plans. These two individuals—the mysterious St. Petersburg terrorist and Igor Sazonoff—particularly interested Ratayeff; but Aseff, whom he had specially commissioned to find out about them, helped him very little. He was now organizing Plehve's assassination quite seriously, and was not prepared to betray the secrets of the Battle Organization to the police!

Only upon his return to St. Petersburg did Aseff think it possible to reveal the identity of the mysterious terrorist, Pokotiloff. Aseff stayed for over a week in the Zhukovsky street apartment. He reviewed the activity of the terrorists, once more rebuked Savinkoff for breaking the rules of the conspiracy, saw all the watchers, and again departed on "party affairs," appointing a general meeting of all the leading members for the beginning of July in Moscow. This meeting took place as arranged. The terrorists were finally chosen for the attempt; their parts were assigned, and the day was fixed. Four of them, two former students, Sazonoff and Kalyaeff, and two Bielostok workers, Borishansky and

THE REMAINS OF PLEHVE'S CARRIAGE AFTER SAZONOFF'S BOMB.

Sikorsky, were to act as bomb throwers. Aseff was to wait for news in Vilna.

The attempt was first fixed for July 21st; but it did not take place because Sazonoff arrived late at the appointed place. This time Aseff kept his word and waited with Ivanovskaya in Vilna. The appointed day came, but the prearranged telegram did not arrive. Aseff appeared to be very agitated, and he said frowningly, "This means a complete failure or a betrayal." He had staked a great deal on this card. In his last letters to Ratayeff he not only made no attempt to "safeguard" himself further, but, at the risk of drawing suspicion upon himself, he tried to lull the vigilance of the department by telling them that the Social Revolutionaries had decided to postpone the attempt on Plehve.

By next day the alarm had somewhat subsided. The bomb throwers themselves arrived, and Sazonoff, with a bitter smile, explained the reasons for the attempt not having taken place. Aseff was nervous, questioned them again and again, went over every seemingly insignificant detail in order to see if any change need be made in the plan. The terrorists stayed a week in Vilna, spending most of their time with Aseff and Ivanovskaya. Before leaving for St. Petersburg they sat up the whole night in a gloomy tavern. "In a small, dimly lit room," Ivanovskaya recalls, "sat thoughtful men, whose fate was already sealed, exchanging trivialities. Aseff alone seemed calm, attentive, and unusually kind." He kissed them all farewell.

Later, when he met Burtzeff in Frankfort after his exposure, Aseff said, referring to this leave-taking: "When I kissed Sazonoff it was not the kiss of a Judas."

On July 18th, the terrorists made a new attempt against Plehve. This time no one was late. The bombs were given out in time. At the appointed hour the bomb throwers moved up the Izmailovsky Prospect to meet Plehve's carriage. First came Borishansky: he was to let the carriage pass him and act only in case the others failed and Plehve turned his carriage back, when he was to make sure of him with his bomb. Behind him walked Sazonoff, the chief bomb thrower. If his aim were true, he would save the lives of those who followed him, for they would not have to act. The first of these was Kalyaeff, who had during these months become Sazonoff's intimate friend. Last came Sikorsky. Once in this net Plehve had but little chance of escaping with his life.

It was a clear sunny day. Plehve's carriage appeared as if by appointment, for he was always punctual in his reports to the Czar. As if by chance, the horses slowed up near Sazonoff, as they had to pass a slowly-moving droshky. Stepping quickly off the footpath, Sazonoff ran towards the carriage. Through the glass window he saw Plehve start back as the latter caught sight of him— and then a twelve-pound bomb struck against that very glass. There was the heavy shattering sound of an explosion. Plehve had settled his accounts on this earth.

. . . News of the assassination reached Switzerland that very evening. In Geneva, on the borders of the peaceful lake, a congress of the Social Revolutionaries living abroad was being held. At the climax of an important discussion a member burst in with a telegram in his hand. "For several minutes," as Sletoff later recalls, "pandemonium reigned. Several men and women became hysterical. Most of those present embraced each other. On every side there were shouts of joy. I can still see N.: he was standing a little apart; he dashed a glass of water on the floor and, gnashing his teeth, shouted, 'That's for Kishenev!'"

CHAPTER VII

The Battle Organization Embarks upon a Great Campaign

PLEHVE'S ASSASSINATION made an enormous impression upon all strata of Russian society. Peshehonoff, who on the day of the assassination wandered about the streets of St. Petersburg listening to fragments of conversation, came to the conclusion that this act of the Battle Organization "might be counted as one of the most successful acts of the revolutionary struggle." As far as terrorist acts are concerned this conclusion was undoubtedly true. But the opponents of the terror as a revolutionary weapon did not, of course, change their views on the subject. But the Izmailovsky Prospect bomb was accepted even by opponents of terror as a

telling blow against absolutism, against that system of
which Plehve was the incarnation.

The act was naturally greeted with particular enthusiasm by the Social Revolutionaries. They regarded
it as *their* victory and triumph. And Aseff's authority as
the chief "organizer" of this victory was now at its
height. He at once became the hero of the party and was
triumphantly received in Geneva. Old quarrels were
forgotten and hostile voices stilled. Breshkovskaya, the
old revolutionary and one of the founders of the party,
who had already served two terms of penal servitude
in Siberia, greeted him in the old Russian fashion by
bowing almost to the ground. She had instinctively
disliked Aseff: she could not understand why a man of
his cold nature was working with a band of young and
enthusiastic revolutionaries; but now she felt all the
more the necessity for showing her gratitude to him for
bringing the Plehve affair to such a successful termina-
tion.

Her bow was symbolic of the attitude of the party as
a whole towards Aseff. There still remained, of course,
those who had an antipathy towards him, and Breshkovskaya herself admitted to her intimate friends that
she did not like him personally, but everybody now
respected him as a terrorist organizer. The terror
now became the "holy of holies," and Aseff, as its
high priest, was placed on an even higher footing than
the greatest terrorists of the past, such as Zhelyaboff
and Gershuni. A legend gradually grew up about him:
he was represented as a man of iron will and inexhaustible initiative, an extraordinarily daring chief and organizer, and a remarkably exact "mathematical"
mind. "Formerly we were led by a romantic," said Gotz,
comparing Aseff to Gershuni; "now we have a realist.

He is not a talker, but he will carry out his plans with a ruthless energy which nothing can withstand."

The members of the Battle Organization were chiefly responsible for the creation of this legend: they idealized Aseff, were devoted to him and looked forward to further work under his leadership. His position as chief of the Battle Organization was now assured. But the "organizer of victory" did not feel very jubilant for the first few days after it. He had really wished to remove Plehve, and had even worked towards this end with unusual recklessness. Of late he paid little attention to his police chiefs. But now that Plehve was out of the way and he had fulfilled his promise to Gotz, Aseff was seized with alarm lest he had abused Ratayeff's confidence too much. He realized better than anyone how many possible clues he had left. In *their* place, he would have soon discovered this double game. And Aseff was fearful lest the suspicions of the department might fall on him.

Aseff and Ivanovskaya were waiting as arranged in Warsaw for the result of the attempt. On the eve of the attempt they met in a restaurant and went over the details of the plan till late in the night. They were probing to see if there were any weak spots in the arrangements. Their thoughts centered on one thing. "What is in store for us tomorrow?" said Aseff with a note of alarm in his voice as he said good-bye. They met again in the morning at the time when the news of the attempt was expected. They were walking down the Marshalkovskaya, one of the principal streets of the town, when near the Vienskaya station they were met by running newsboys with special editions announcing that a bomb had been thrown at Plehve. But the telegram did not give the result of the attempt. "Can it have failed?" Aseff asked in alarm. A few minutes afterward other newsboys rushed by with later news. "Aseff," Ivanovskaya recalls, "seized the new edition with trembling hands. 'Plehve assassinated,' he read out aloud, and suddenly went limp, letting his arms drop loosely by his sides. 'I feel all faint,' he exclaimed." He had good cause to feel so, for at that moment everything went out of his mind except the explanations he would have to make to his police chiefs.

As had been arranged, Aseff and Ivanovskaya were to await Savinkoff's arrival in Warsaw before deciding as to the further movements of the terrorists. At the appointed hour only Ivanovskaya was there to meet Savinkoff. Without warning her, Aseff had left for Vienna by express train the very day he learned the news of the assassination. He knew that it would be easy enough for him to find some excuse to give to the members of the Battle Organization. But his chief anxiety for the moment was the creation of a satisfactory alibi for the police. With this in view he sent a telegram to Ratayeff from Vienna immediately on his arrival there. Its contents were unimportant, but it was to serve as documentary evidence that he had only learned of Plehve's assassination in Vienna, and that the news was as much of a surprise to him as it was to Ratayeff. As future events showed, this precaution was far from superfluous; his fate, at that time, did really hang on a thread.

Plehve's assassination caught the department napping. The possibility of the assassination had long been foreseen: the exposure of a number of plots against Plehve clearly pointed to his being one of the first victims of the terror. The chiefs of the department and Plehve himself were, however, convinced that they would be able to frustrate this blow. R. F. Kony told his friends, soon after the assassination, of a meeting he had with Plehve. They had met by chance not long before while out for a morning walk on the Aptekarsky Island. Plehve was strolling along unguarded, and Kony asked him how he ventured to run such a risk, knowing that the revolutionaries were plotting against him. Plehve smiled with self-assurance and said: "I shall know about all these plans in good time." Plehve must have supposed that it was not in vain that he had allowed Aseff to join the Battle Organization, and he evidently thought himself safe from that quarter. All the more unexpected was the blow struck by Sazonoff. The department was quite at sea and indulged in the most varied speculations. "Things must be in a bad way if Aseff knew nothing about it," they said. At one time they even supposed that the assassination was the work of Polish Socialists.

When they were at last driven to believe that the bomb had been thrown by a member of the Battle Organization, the department recalled Ratayeff from Paris for an explanation. No doubt the latter saw Aseff before setting out for St. Petersburg, but there is no direct evidence as to this interview, and Ratayeff's *The History of Aseff's Treachery* closes with the assassination of Plehve. We have, however, Lopuhin's account of what Ratayeff said to him. According to the latter, "Aseff explained his lack of information in this particular case by the fact that the Police Department had not paid careful enough attention to his information, too often making ill-advised use of it and thus putting the Social Revolutionaries on their guard and in this way cutting off at this juncture his sources of information." It is clear that Aseff continued to play on Ratayeff's vanity, and that he did this as successfully as ever. In any case, Ratayeff shielded Aseff; Lopuhin accepted his explanation, or, at any rate, pretended to do so.

As a result, Aseff weathered the storm. No investigation was made of his activities, although such an inquiry would inevitably have been fraught with unpleasant consequences for him. We know that the department had in its hands sufficient facts to expose Aseff's game. The inquiry in Sazonoff's case established that his fellow conspirator, Sikorsky, had spent the few days preceding the assassination in Vilna. It was known, too, that Aseff had been there at the time, for one of his reports to Ratayeff was dispatched from Vilna. Finally, Sazonoff, who had been seriously injured in the explosion, had mentioned a number of names in his delirium—and among them were those of "Valentine" and "Auntie." This delirium was noted down and carefully studied by the department agents; and some of them knew that "Valentine" was Aseff's party pseudonym. It would not have been difficult to piece these clues together had there been any desire to clear up this side of the affair.

But the department had not the slightest desire to do so. The whole inquiry into Plehve's assassination was conducted in the most slipshod way. When perusing the documents connected with this case it is at times difficult not to feel that the investigators were pursuing their researches merely as a matter of form, and that in their hearts they were ready to condone the act. Hated during his lifetime, Plehve went to his grave deserted by all.

Aseff, of course, saw the danger of his position better than anybody. He knew of Sazonoff's delirium and also that the fact of Sikorsky's stay in Vilna had been established. That the police failed to piece these threads together was for him the best confirmation of his opinion of their chiefs. He was now finally convinced that they were very easy to dupe. His fears were allayed, and he pursued his double game with the greatest boldness. Police documents tend to regard the period following Plehve's assassination as one of the most brilliant in Aseff's police career.

This idea entered later into Stolypin's famous speech about Aseff in the Duma. "Immediately following this assassination," the Minister said, "Aseff sent in extremely important and valuable reports which led to the discovery of a whole series of criminal plots." This speech as a whole was full of gross errors—and the above is one of the grossest. As a matter of fact, it is during this period that Aseff makes use of his position of police agent more boldly, or, rather, more shamelessly, than ever to cover up the activities of the Battle Organization.

The members of this latter met in Geneva soon after Plehve's assassination. They reviewed their past work, received the congratulations on their achievement, and prepared for the future. Here, too, they learned for the first time of the friction which was taking place in the Central Committee, of the desire of some of the members to bring the Battle Organization under its direct control, and of the criticisms leveled at its chief. Although this was ancient history it affected the terrorists very strongly; there were signs among them of irritation against the Central Committee. Aseff cleverly made use of this. He fanned the discontent by quoting accidental remarks and unfavorable opinions he had overheard, and he did not even stop short of pure invention. He acted, however, very carefully. Outwardly, he made a pretense of smoothing things over, but in fact fanned the flames with his insinuations. He attained his end.

In order to frustrate even the possibility of any attempt on the part of the Central Committee to gain control over it, the Battle Organization drew up a constitution of its own, which made it completely independent of the party executive. In theory, a committee of three— Aseff, Savinkoff, and Schweitzer—was set up at its head; but, in fact, all decision was left to the chairman, and Aseff had been elected to that post. The treasury of the Battle Organization, into which donations were now pouring, and which, according to Savinkoff, amounted to many tens of thousands, was now also in his hands. The Central Committee had no control over it, and the Battle Organization Committee, which had the right, never thought of exercising it. Aseff used it as he liked. The department, on the other hand, was still paying him a "paltry" five hundred roubles a month, and was, moreover, never prompt in the payment of his expenses!

Aseff's strengthened position in the Battle Organization led to the consolidation of his position in the Central Committee. He had succeeded Gershuni as a member of the latter in 1903, but he had not felt himself at all secure there. If some doubted his fitness to control the Battle Organization, there were many more who questioned his presence in the executive body of the party. Aseff had never concealed his contempt for questions of theory and program. He had boasted openly that he was not a "theorist," and that he regarded theorizing as mere "idle chatter." He was no less skeptical in his view of Socialism, and he made no bones about it. According to Tchernoff, "he put Socialism into the distant future."

In a talk with Peshehonoff he said frankly, "Do you really believe in Socialism? It's necessary, of course, for the youth and the workers, but not for you and me . . ." And he differed on many other points from the program laid down by the Central Committee. "He had no belief whatsoever in the masses or mass movements as an independent revolutionary force," Tchernoff wrote about him. "His only immediate reality was the struggle for political freedom, and his only revolutionary means, the terror. He would seem to have regarded propaganda work, agitation, and mass organization with contempt as mere educational work, and recognized as 'Revolution' only the active fighting done by the few members of a secret organization."

The testimony of other contemporaries is even more definite: they assert rather than imply that Aseff did talk in this vein. They labeled him a "Liberal terrorist" —that is to say, a Liberal whom only the acceptance of terror as a means of fighting autocracy had brought into the Social Revolutionary party. Nor did Aseff deny this, he even declared later that he was but a "fellow traveler" and that he would leave the party as soon as political freedom had been achieved. It was not strange, therefore, that people should be found to doubt Aseff's fitness to be a member of the Central Committee. The really strange thing was his admission to the membership of this body.

The political success of the assassination strengthened the terrorist cause in the party, which now put all its hopes and threw all its energy into the terror. This had its influence on the successive slogans by the party, and on the direction taken by its practical activities. Work among the masses was to a large extent put into the background. The warm sympathy with which the

moderate Liberals greeted Plehve's assassination seemed
to create a sufficiently solid basis for the establishment
of a lasting agreement with them. And this agreement
was really consecrated at the "Conference of the Representatives of the Opposition and of the Revolutionary Organizations of Russia," which assembled in Paris
in October, 1904. This step was the logical outcome of
the new attitude towards political terror.

This also gave ground for important conflicts within
the party in which Aseff took a leading post. Though he
said little, yet, in his brief retorts, he formulated clearly
and forcibly the views of the terrorist wing. All other
speakers made reservations and tried to base the new
policy on Socialist hypotheses. But Aseff was not
interested in these things. A "Liberal terrorist," he
really *wished* his party to take up the position of
Liberalism allied to terrorism. And, as usually happens,
the logical clarity of his position lent special weight to
his words and thus drew particular attention to them.
From the technical chief of the Battle Organization he
was tending to become the practical leader of the terrorist wing of the party. The Battle Organization was, of
course, Aseff's chief support in the party. He realized
this and did everything in his power to make his position
in it secure. Most of his attention, efforts and energy
went to its work; and the part he played in its life was
indeed enormous. He did not, it is true, display any
particular initiative or scope.

The story which attributed to him the invention of
the new terrorist methods, which the Battle Organization applied during the years 1904–06, is but a myth.
The real initiative came from Gotz, who, as he pro-
gressively devoted more thought to the terror, was less
able to take a direct part in it on account of his illness.

The new ideas were generally his, and Aseff merely gave them shape, worked them out in detail, and applied them. But Aseff, as the chief of the staff, controlled all the members and the organizational work of the Battle Organization.

His influence began with the election of new members. These were selected usually by Aseff in person, and he was very careful to exercise this privilege, especially at the beginning. He was particular in his choice and made great demands upon the candidates. His methods were characteristic. His predecessor, Gershuni, had usually by his very sincerity inspired the new volunteers with some of his own enthusiasm for the terror. Aseff, on the contrary, first of all attempted to dissuade the candidate from his intention, emphasized all the hardships of terrorist work, and tried to induce him to take up some other form of party work. Even such a hostile critic as Sletoff has said that, at such moments, Aseff showed that he could "behave with a true spirit of comradeship."

Sometimes Aseff seemed to be consciously trying to put off a candidate, and the more emotion the latter displayed and the more glowingly he talked, the less desire Aseff had to admit him into the Battle Organization. He had no faith in enthusiastic professions; and only when the candidate proved that his decision to become a terrorist was well founded, that he had really thrashed out the issue in his own mind, and that his decision was not due to a momentary impulse or to the intoxication of fine phrases—only then were the doors of the organization opened to him.

There can be no doubt that Aseff's behavior was governed by his general distrust of people. It is also indisputable that his *professional* position had a great deal to do with it: he not only feared treachery in general, but he had to be especially on his guard lest his own treachery should be brought to light. Whatever his motives, the results were very telling for the Battle Organization. While the terrorists recruited by Gershuni included some who, like Grigorieff, Iurkovskaya, and Katchura, were not proof against the trials of imprisonment and the fear of execution, the Battle Organization in the time of Aseff knew no traitors except, of course, himself.

Once a new member was admitted Aseff, as a rule, showed the greatest solicitude for him, going into all his personal needs down to the smallest detail, giving advice and directions. He noticed and remembered everything. There is unanimous agreement on this point. "Aseff appeared to us to be extraordinarily attentive, tactful, and even kind-hearted," recalls Zenzinoff, one of the recruits. This was, of course, a pose: Aseff was much more his true self when expressing himself in his natural blunt and harsh manner. But those who had dealings with him were much more impressed by his habitually considerate manner, and they reciprocated it. "All his fellow terrorists not only respected him very highly, but loved him very warmly!"

There can be no doubt that Aseff's attitude was the result of a careful plan to attach the terrorists personally to him. By this means he would hold the organization the more securely in his hands. He attained his aim; the terrorists were the last to be convinced of his treachery.

While binding the members of the Battle Organization to himself, Aseff systematically isolated it from the other branches of the party. Isolation was natural enough to the Battle Organization by the character of its activities, but Aseff made this a principle, adding, furthermore, a certain element of psychological isolation. He systematically inculcated in its members a contempt for any other kind of party work, disbelief in the masses and mass movements, and indifference to questions of theory and program. And they came to regard these as unimportant trifles in comparison with their task of hunting down the representatives of authority.

It must, however, be noted that it was not all the members who fell under Aseff's influence. Nor, again, were all the members of equal value to him. It was only the *politically* influential "older officers," acting now as his assistants, who were of the first importance to him. Therefore, they and, above all, Savinkoff fell most under his influence.

In the late autumn of 1904 the Battle Organization, whose membership had greatly increased, began to prepare for a new campaign.

A meeting of the Battle Organization and of the members of the Central Committee was held in Paris. It was decided to strike a blow at the Court reactionary party, which was headed at that time by the Grand Dukes Sergei and Vladimir Alexandrovitch, the Czar's two eldest uncles and his closest and most influential counselors, who were opposed to all reform. Their assassination would serve as a warning to the Czar. The question of the assassination of Kleygels, the Governor General of Kiev, was again brought up. It was suggested that these three blows, at St. Petersburg, Moscow, and Kiev, should be struck more or less simultaneously. This would, of course, greatly add to their significance.

In accordance with this plan the Battle Organization sent out three separate detachments: the St. Petersburg detachment headed by Schweitzer, the Moscow by Savinkoff, and the Kiev by Borishansky. The detachments varied in size; only three terrorists were sent to Kiev and four to Moscow. The St. Petersburg detachment had the most difficult task. Besides the assassination of the Grand Duke Vladimir, it had to explore the possibilities of removing Durnoff, the assistant to the Minister of the Interior, and later Trepoff, the Governor General of St. Petersburg; the detachment therefore consisted of fifteen men. There was no lack of volunteers or material resources.

Aseff directed the working out of these plans, selected the men, and alloted them their tasks. Under his supervision a laboratory in Paris made the necessary dynamite; he also arranged for its importation into Russia. He provided passports for the terrorists going to Russia.

In the second half of November the terrorists set out. Aseff was to follow them later, when all the preliminary arrangements had been made, in order to make a final survey and to approve the plans of action. The Battle Organization consciously strove to reduce its leader's risks to a minimum. In the meantime Aseff had not been forgetting Ratayeff. In the second half of 1904 he sent in a series of reports which his police chiefs thought particularly valuable, and, in fact, they really were. He gave them full details of the congress of the representatives of the Social Revolutionary organizations abroad, of the International Socialist Congress in Amsterdam, of the parleys between the Social Revolutionaries and the Finnish revolutionary "Activist" party, of the Paris conference of the "Revolutionary and Opposition" parties, and of many others.

But these reports, though detailed, were no evidence that the information supplied by Aseff was either complete or even based on real facts. He speaks in detail and, apparently, with accuracy where the parleys of the Social Revolutionaries with the other parties are concerned. He had no motive for concealing the secrets of these other parties. But he puts a very definite interpretation on the events taking place within the Social Revolutionary party.

The department, as can easily be understood, was chiefly concerned with the party's terrorist activities. Aseff was bound to provide some information about these. But the information he provided was deliberately intended to put the police on a false trail and to divert suspicion from the real work of the Battle Organization.

According to his reports, the terrorists aimed primarily at the assassination of the Czar. This decision was taken, according to him, at the Congress of Social Revolutionary Organizations abroad in July, 1904. This, of course, was manifestly untrue; not only was no attempt against the Czar contemplated, but the question had not even been seriously raised. "The center of the Battle Organization's activity," he reported, "is in Odessa"—a town with which the organization had no connection, but where lived many former revolutionary exiles who had been involved in various trials in the 'seventies and 'eighties. Most of them had now become Social Revolutionaries, and many of them were hostile to Aseff. It was these "old men" whom Aseff now strove to represent as the members of the Central Committee and the leaders of the Battle Organization. He mentioned by name people such as V. I. Sukhomlin, who had never been members of the Central Committee, and who were in no way connected with the Battle Organization.

The most dangerous terrorists, according to Aseff,

were Sletoff and Seliuk; but they were really the most
decided opponents of Aseff's terrorist policy. He represented them to be members of the Central Committee sent to Russia to organize terrorist acts and, in
particular, the assassination of the Czar. This blatant
perversion of the truth may be attributed to Aseff's
desire to rid himself of his political opponents. He succeeded in this, for, on the strength of his reports, both
Sletoff and Seliuk were arrested, and they were only released after the amnesty of October, 1905.

Aseff's reports concerning his nearest collaborators,
the real members of the Battle Organization, had quite
a different character. His letters to Ratayeff displayed
his anxiety to divert suspicion from them. He did not
willingly refer to them. When obliged to answer
Ratayeff's questions, based on information received
from other sources, Aseff always tried either to plead
ignorance or to send him on a false trail. Only when the
police were absolutely certain of the truth of their evidence did Aseff confirm it. That was the course he took
in Savinkoff's case: to the first questions he replied
evasively, and only when Ratayeff sent him Savinkoff's
photograph did Aseff admit that he was the terrorist
known as "Pavel Ivanovitch." Not once did he give
any information which would lead to the arrest of any
member of the Battle Organization.

Such was the general character of Aseff's work for the
police at that time.

Aseff's careful covering up of the Battle Organization
enabled its members to reach their destinations in
safety.

At that time events were taking a critical turn in
Russia. Defeat followed defeat in the Far East. Unem-

ployment was on the increase. Only a spark was required to produce an explosion in this tense atmosphere.
This was not long in coming. Five workers were dismissed from a St. Petersburg factory for some trifling
offense, and the men working in the same shift went on
strike in protest. The entire factory supported them.
The news of this strike spread from factory to factory.
It answered so much to the general temper that everywhere the workers stopped their machines and poured
out into the street. Within a few days the whole town
was at a standstill; and on the following Sunday a crowd
of many thousands, with icons and portraits of the
Czar, made its way slowly towards the Winter Palace
in order to present to the Czar in person a petition
signed by tens of thousands, setting forth their grievances and their demands. But they were met with vol-
leys which killed many hundreds and which destroyed
forever an old and great illusion. Next morning, in the
workers' quarters, people were already singing:

> *Conquered in the East,*
> *Victor over Russia,*
> *Be accursed, cruel Czar,*
> *Steeped in blood!*

And, in keeping with this mood, the priest Gapon, the
adventurer and rascal, who had been carried by chance
on the crest of a popular wave, proclaimed: "We no
longer have a Czar. . . . Take bombs and dynamite. I
absolve you!"

Thus ended the "Bloody Sunday" of January 22,
1905—one of the most significant landmarks in the
history of Russia for the last hundred years.

These events could not but act as a spur to the mem-

bers of the Battle Organization. The moment was ripe
for action on their part. They were impatient and full of
plans. There was even the possibility of killing the
Czar himself, but they sadly missed the assurance and
direction which their chief would have given them.

The most urgent appeals were sent to Aseff. But he
was perfectly sure that he could not repeat successfully
the course he had adopted in Plehve's case. He knew
that this time the police could not fail to discover his
treachery. This "ruthless terrorist" was a coward at
heart and clung tenaciously to his life. The very thought
of going to Russia at that time made him almost hysterical. He was surprised in one of these moments by
Ivanovskaya, who had called at his flat in the hope of
seeing his wife. Not finding anybody in the outer room,
she went through, and, in the inner room, caught sight
of Aseff lying on a couch, trembling like an autumn leaf
and with his eyes looking as pitiful as those of a beaten
dog. His fear of going to Russia was so great that he was
prepared rather to throw up everything and to flee to
America with his wife. The young terrorists were therefore left to their own devices. From abroad they received
only directions urging the political importance of an
immediate attempt. This, of course, only heightened
their nervous tension, whereas all they needed was a
little method and coolness.

Only a part of the plan was realized. Kalyaeff's bomb,
thrown on February 17, 1905, killed the Grand Duke
Sergei in Moscow. The Kiev attempt was abandoned,
as it was thought too unimportant, and Borishansky
hurried to join the St. Petersburg group. It was here
that the chief blow was to be struck. This was intended
for March 14, 1905. On that day the leading members
of the government were to gather in the Peter and Paul

Cathedral for a memorial service to the Emperor Alexander II, who had been killed thirty-four years earlier. The Battle Organization hoped to station its members on all the roads leading to the Cathedral, and to throw bombs at the Grand Duke Vladimir, Trepoff, the Governor General of St. Petersburg, Bouligin, the Minister of the Interior, and his Assistant, Durnoff. That indeed would have been a crushing blow, a fitting tribute to the memory of those who had given their lives thirty-four years ago in the struggle against Alexander II.

Marc Schweitzer, the most talented and sympathetic of all the young revolutionaries, directed the work. He was one of the few terrorists whom Aseff could not inspire with contempt for the masses. A sincere Socialist, and interested in all European Socialist movements, he used to sing to himself, when engaged on dangerous work in the laboratory, the words of a Viennese workers' song:

> *Durch die Gassen*
> *Zu den Massen . . .*

He was young, daring, fearless, and full of initiative, and his one fault was too much self-reliance. In the present case he had clearly undertaken too great a task. He not only assumed the rôle of chief organizer and kept in direct contact with all the members of his detachment, but he also took on the technical work of charging the bombs. A trained chemist, he considered that in this task he would run less risk than anybody else. And he had, indeed, great experience in this matter. But the unexpected happened. He had obviously overtired himself when, on the evening of March 10th, he said goodbye to his comrades. This fatigue proved to be his doom.

On the night of March 11th, he was in his hotel room charging the bombs which were to be distributed the next day. A slip must have been responsible for the explosion. Schweitzer was blown to pieces. . . .

His death brought the work of the detachment to an abrupt end. To crown all, the police got on their tracks; an *agent provocateur* had succeeded in coming in contact with the group and had pointed out some of its members to the police. The members began to feel that a net was being drawn round them. Prudence demanded that they should disband and reorganize themselves in safety before returning to their task. But they felt it a pity to abandon an attempt on which they had already spent so much energy. The attempt for March 14th could not take place, but there was a chance that separate attempts on Trepoff and Bouligin might succeed. They were expecting Savinkoff's return from abroad, and they also hoped that Aseff might come with him. Their flight also might place them in difficulties, as they had lost touch with possible places of refuge.

It was therefore decided to await Savinkoff's arrival before undertaking the necessary reorganization. This was a mistake. Neither Savinkoff nor Aseff stirred. The police net meanwhile was tightening, and, on March 29th and 30th, all the remaining members of the detachment were arrested in St. Petersburg. Only Dora Brilliant succeeded in escaping. In the search, dynamite was discovered. The police were triumphant. The reactionary newspaper, *Novoye Vremya*, spoke of these arrests as "the Mukden of the Russian Revolution." Once more an absolutism which had been cruelly "defeated in the East" naïvely thought that it was saving itself by this small "victory over Russia."

CHAPTER VIII

Two Traitors

THE ARRESTS of March 29th–30th were not so much the "Mukden" of the Revolution as that of the Battle Organization. It was a political as well as an organizational defeat. The Battle Organization was never as strong again as it had been immediately after Plehve's assassination; and it was now disabled at the very moment which most revolutionaries thought ideal for decisive action.

In the days of success a theoretical conception of its rôle had been worked out: its terrorist deeds were to blaze a trail for the revolutionary movement and were to concentrate on it general attention and sympathy.

The mass movement was regarded merely as a background for the heroic struggle of the Battle Organization units. Mass demonstrations were to follow its various acts. This was one of the chief points of the concrete program of political action drawn up at the Paris Conference of the representatives of the Opposition and Revolutionary parties in October, 1904. The Russian atmosphere in the days of Plehve had indeed created the illusion of the possibility of a like conception, for the Minister's assassination had been an isolated act at a moment when the country was silent.

But the situation had fundamentally changed. The mass movement had made tremendous progress. The wave of strikes, demonstrations, peasant risings, and rebellions of all sorts steadily gained in volume. But, at that very moment, the instrument of organized terror ceased to function, and its heroic leaders, who should have directed the masses, all found themselves in the hands of the police. That sounded the death knell of those terrorist illusions which had flamed up in the days of Plehve. The heroic period of the Battle Organization was over.

The news of the events in St. Petersburg could not fail to make a tremendous impression on Aseff and Savinkoff. After the news of Schweitzer's death, it was clear to them that they ought to hurry to St. Petersburg, for there remained nobody qualified to carry out such a complex undertaking. According to Savinkoff, it was Aseff's unwillingness and procrastination which prevented their going. Savinkoff could, of course, have gone alone, but he preferred to wait for Aseff. A clever leader might, indeed, have been able to save the situation: documents show that the police got on the track of the other terrorists only after Schweitzer's death;

but Aseff and Savinkoff abandoned the St. Petersburg
terrorists to their fate, and they soon had the opportunity of reading telegrams giving them the details of their
arrests. St. Petersburg was now out of the question;
the Battle Organization had virtually ceased to exist,
and its reorganization had to be undertaken anew.

There was as yet no exact evidence as to the causes
leading to the St. Petersburg arrests. Only later did it
become clear that there was a traitor in the case. This
traitor was N. Tataroff. He was no novice in revolutionary movements. His first encounter with the police was
in 1892, when taking part in a student demonstration;
he was later arrested on three other occasions and was
finally sent to eastern Siberia in 1901. Here he came into
contact with several old exiles, the former leaders of the
Narodnaya Volya party, under whose influence he
joined the young Social Revolutionary party, and very
soon played a prominent part in the latter's Siberian
organization. It was he who organized the party's secret
printing press at Irkutsk. As this printing press remained undiscovered by the police, Tataroff got the
reputation of an experienced conspirator and a convinced revolutionary.

This, however, was far from being the case. A *poseur*,
and fond of all the good things of life, Tataroff entered
the revolutionary movement only because it gave him
the opportunity of playing a prominent part in student
circles. He had neither real convictions nor strength of
character. His exile had "cured" him of revolution,
while his connections held out the promise of money
and of a smart life. His father was the arch-priest of the
Warsaw Cathedral and had influential friends in the
administration and the police. He was acquainted with
Count Kutaisoff, the Governor General of eastern

Siberia, and one of the latter's sons had been at school with Tataroff. They renewed their friendship at Irkutsk, and the political exile and organizer of the revolutionary press was often a guest at the house of the Governor General. Old Count Kutaisoff tempted Tataroff to become an *agent provocateur* and, having won him over to the idea, introduced him to the Police Department, which eagerly welcomed the new recruit. The times were troubled, and Aseff, the only *agent provocateur* whom the police had in the Social Revolutionary party, was far from being entirely satisfactory. Thus, on January 17, 1905, the department telegraphed permission for Tataroff to go to St. Petersburg, the official excuse of his liberation being the illness of his old father.

On February 9th Tataroff left Irkutsk, and by the 20th he had arrived in St. Petersburg. Here he found a number of Social Revolutionaries, such as Freedenson, Tiutcheff, and others, whose acquaintance he had made at Irkutsk. They at once told him the latest party news: he learned from them that a Battle Organization detachment was in St. Petersburg, and that it included, among others, Ivanovskaya, whom Tataroff had met in Siberia. Somebody was so indiscreet as to give him her address. That was the starting point from which the police began their observations.

During the arrests of March 29th–30th, Tiutcheff was allowed to escape. This was done for the sake of "preserving the source of information," in order to give Tataroff the opportunity in the future of getting further information from him. This calculation was correct: Tiutcheff helped Tataroff to become a traveling agent of the Central Committee and, later, a member of it. He was not, of course, admitted into the inner councils of the Battle Organization, but he neverthless managed to get hold of a great deal of information. Thus the police had now two agents within the Central Committee. Aseff's monopoly had come to an end.

It is difficult to say when Aseff learned of this change in his position. It is most probable that his first suspicions came after the St. Petersburg arrests. He knew too much of arrests, which left hidden the agents responsible for them, not to suspect something of the kind in this case. He could not but guess at this from the department questionnaires. But these showed also that the information at the disposal of the department was not very full as far as it concerned the Battle Organization. Tataroff knew comparatively little about the real state of affairs, and his guesses only confused the department. Thus the first announcements included Savinkoff among those arrested; and the department believed this for a long time, confusing Moisenko with Savinkoff.

The department further failed to discover Schweitzer's real identity. Nor did they succeed in solving the assassinations of Plehve and the Grand Duke Sergei. All this went to prove that the department's source of information was limited and that the informer was not one of the leaders of the party or a member of the Battle Organization. Such were probably Aseff's conclusions during the first months following the St. Petersburg arrests. His behavior changed accordingly; he became more careful in his reports to Ratayeff and more suspicious of new recruits.

Meanwhile a change had taken place within the party. The influence of the purely terrorist wing declined with the growth of the mass movement. The party was now organizing a series of peasant risings for the summer. Aseff was a firm opponent of these plans.

He was still of the opinion that all the energies of the party should be concentrated on the terror. The Central Committee did not, of course, refuse to subsidize the Battle Organization, but Aseff thought these subsidies too small. The reëstablishment of the Battle Organization therefore became a most urgent necessity, and Aseff and Savinkoff now devoted all their energies to this task.

The task was more difficult than it might appear. The active revolutionaries were now devoting themselves chiefly to work among the masses, and for the first time in its history the Battle Organization experienced a lack of volunteers. This lack was so obvious that the idea of a big terrorist undertaking had to be abandoned. Instead, according to the new plan, Savinkoff and the terrorists set out for Kiev to organize an attempt against Kleygels. It was thought that his assassination would demonstrate that the St. Petersburg arrests had not disorganized the Battle Organization. Later, Aseff was to make a tour of the country with the object of enrolling fresh recruits.

Aseff did not go to Russia with a light heart, but the risk of the trip was now much smaller for him. He was obliged to take the risk, for new members could be found only in Russia. He had, of course, prepared his police chiefs for this visit. Dissatisfied with the increase in the numbers of revolutionaries favoring mass revolts, he took his own measures against them; his letters to Ratayeff are full of denouncements of them. Thus he denounced Vedenyapin and Troyitzsky as terrorists who were going to put their aims into execution in Russia. This fact, he argued, made his trip to Russia a necessity, and Ratayeff was in the end obliged, though unwillingly, to agree to this.

In spite of Savinkoff's efforts, the attempt against Kleygels did not take place. The terrorists chosen wavered at the last moment and did not carry out their instructions. They had to be expelled from the Battle Organization. But Aseff's trip gave good results; he succeeded in finding five volunteers answering his strict test. There were also many other people available for less important tasks. This made possible some more important undertaking. A general meeting of all the members of the Battle Organization was arranged to take place under Aseff and Savinkoff at Nijni-Novgorod at the beginning of August. By the new plan, which was now being given its final shape, the attempt against Trepoff was to come first.

The circumstances seemed very favorable, but not only did the Battle Organization not succeed in bringing the affair to a successful end, but they never even started it. The assembled members were awaiting the arrival of one more recruit, A. V. Jakimova, a leading member of the Narodnaya Volya party, who had already served a twenty-year sentence of penal servitude in Siberia for an attempt against the Czar, and who had now escaped to resume her terrorist work. As she delayed her arrival, Aseff went off to Moscow on party business. On his return, the first words he addressed to Savinkoff were: "We are being watched."

He went on to explain that, immediately after meeting Jakimova in Moscow, he noticed that he was being followed by detectives. Aseff was sure that Jakimova had been kept under observation and that the net had now spread to Nijni. He insisted on the necessity of leaving that town. Savinkoff and the other terrorists at first doubted the correctness of his assumption, but within a day or two they convinced themselves that they were really being watched. According to Aseff's plan, they left the town by different ways, and they were to meet again in St. Petersburg. Everything went off without a hitch: no one was arrested except Jakimova, whom the police apprehended some three weeks later when getting off a train in Vladimir.

From documents which came to light later, this Nijni episode had the following explanation. Jakimova had, before setting out for Nijni, met Tataroff in Minsk, and she told him as a member of the Central Committee that she was going to take part in a meeting of the Battle Organization, presided over by "Valentine" (Aseff) and "Pavel Ivanovitch" (Savinkoff). Tataroff immediately informed his police chief, and the best detectives were at once put on Jakimova's trail.

Aseff's experience made him conclude that this was no chance incident. It is possible, too, that he realized that he had to do not with local detectives but with those from the department. If so, it would be clear to him that this watch was the result of secret information which, by its knowledge of Jakimova's plans, emanated from the center of the party. In these circumstances, Aseff had to deal with a double problem: he was obliged to safeguard the newly formed Battle Organization, and he had, at the same time, to divert the suspicions of the police from himself. The fact that he had not duly informed the police of the proposed meeting of the terrorists might very well direct police suspicion against him. He hastened therefore to take his share in the exposure of the Nijni meeting and informed the police of an "intended attempt" against the Governor of Nijni, but he did this in such a way as not to compromise any of the terrorists. Jakimova alone was sacrificed, for it had become clear to Aseff that she had already been betrayed by someone else and that she was, therefore, dangerous. Aseff played this game with great finesse and forethought. He had good reason to suppose that the "wolves" would be satisfied and the "sheep" preserved, and that his standing would improve in both camps. It was not his fault if things turned out differently and he found himself attacked on both sides.

In the past few months a real revolution had taken place in the personnel of the Police Department. Lopuhin, who had been its director for the previous three years, resigned. He was forced to do this, as Trepoff, the Governor General of St. Petersburg, had, after the assassination of the Grand Duke Sergei, called him a murderer to his face. Lopuhin, in an attempt to rehabilitate himself, went to Moscow to conduct a personal investigation. He hoped to unearth some carelessness on the part of the Moscow Ochrana which, it seemed, had wind of the attempt, and which had not only failed to follow up its information but had even concealed it from the department. But this was a mistake: for the information in possession of the Moscow Ochrana concerned only the local group of the Social Revolutionaries, which had been preparing an attempt, but had given way to Savinkoff, and was not likely to lead it on the track of the Savinkoff-Kalyaeff group. In any case, Lopuhin's visit did not help him. The Czar shortly afterwards expressed his dissatisfaction with the work of the Police Department, and there was nothing left for Lopuhin to do but resign. He retired at the beginning of March and, possibly most galling of all to him, was succeeded by his greatest enemy Ratchkovsky.

Little is known of the beginning of Ratchkovsky's police career. A man of little education, he was already acting as a minor clerk in various government offices in Kiev, Odessa, and Warsaw at the end of the 'sixties. There is some evidence that he had already had some small connection with the police. Officially he did not enter on a police career until 1879, when he became a secret agent of the famous Third Department. He was very soon discovered by the revolutionaries; and he then openly entered the police service, becoming one of the pioneers of the *agent provocateur* system. Coming to the front rapidly, he became in 1884 the chief of the Russian police abroad. Here he was very active and introduced a whole series of his agents into the ranks of the *émigrés*. Simple investigation did not satisfy him, and he attempted to exercise an influence on politics in general. By virtue of his position, he was able to enter into close relations with the French police, and, through them, with the leading representatives of the press and those of the French politicians who were advocating a Russian alliance. By gambling on the Stock Exchange he amassed a considerable fortune, and this made it possible for him to live on a large scale. This, of course, enabled him to strengthen his relations.

He was on friendly terms with Fleurence, Constant, Delcassé, and even President Loubet himself. At the same time he established relations with many Russian notabilities, whom he helped in their deals on the Paris Stock Exchange, and from whom in return he obtained a deal of useful information; he also took advantage of these connections to make his influence felt in Russian politics. He became particularly friendly with General Hesse, the commander of the Palace Guard, who was on excellent terms with the Czar, and through him was pulled into the vortex of Court intrigues. Ratchkovsky undoubtedly played a notable part in laying the foundations for the Franco-Russian alliance. He made a successful, but far from irreproachable, career for himself. His financial operations often exceeded the bounds of strict legality.

In his police work he immediately adopted the latest "French" system of provocation, which did not stop at bomb-throwing or the setting of infernal machines, when it was thought useful to intimidate the man in the street and to create a "public opinion." With his money, and at the instigation of his agents, there were prepared those "Russian bombs" which were discovered in Paris in 1890. His agent Jagolkovsky planned a number of anarchist attempts in Belgium, among them being the blowing up of Liége Cathedral. There is no doubt that these agents acted in all cases under Ratchkovsky's orders and with his help escaped punishment.

This, however, was only a part of the evil. The Russian government turned a blind eye to all this and, for particularly successful cases of provocation, even the Czars themselves, both Alexander III and Nicholas II, graciously thanked Ratchkovsky. Less pardonable, however, was the fact that Ratchkovsky in his zeal often touched upon questions affecting the private life of the imperial family. Thus, in the middle of the 'eighties, he honored with his attention the private life of the Princess Iurievskaya, the widow of Alexander II, who had settled in France; and he sent in the most scurrilous reports about her and her children. But this enraged Alexander III, who reprimanded Ratchkovsky, and he did not dare to meddle in such affairs in the Czar's lifetime. Under Nicholas II, to whom he was personally presented, and who was well disposed towards him, Ratchkovsky once more ventured to interfere in Court intrigues, and sent in a very unfavorable report on the notorious adventurer and "crystal gazer," Philippe, who had been invited to the Russian Court in order to foretell the future of the dynasty and the birth of the long-desired heir to the throne. That ruined him for the moment. Plehve, who disliked him, profited by this opportunity to have him removed. Lopuhin collected all the information he could about Ratchkovsky's exploits; and Plehve then persuaded the Czar to dismiss him. Lopuhin drew up the notice of dismissal in the most offensive way possible and was careful that the text of this should become widely known in official circles. Ratchkovsky never forgave him, and now the moment had come to take his revenge.

As soon as Trepoff was appointed Governor General of St. Petersburg with dictatorial powers, he began to look for somebody whom he could put at the head of the police. His choice fell on Ratchkovsky, and, in spite of the opposition of the Police Department and the Minister of the Interior, Ratchkovsky was appointed on February 18, 1905, the day after the assassination of the Grand Duke Sergei, to the post of special commissioner to the Ministry of the Interior, with the special task of controlling the activity of the St. Petersburg Ochrana. He took into his hands the control of the secret agents and was now personally in touch with Tataroff, supervising all the arrests made on the latter's information. In July, Trepoff was promoted to be assistant to the Minister of the Interior. He obtained promotion for Ratchkovsky too, and a secret order of August 9th appointed him vice-director of the Police Department, with the special control of the whole of the department's political section. Ratchkovsky's star was now in the ascendant; he began, first of all, by settling accounts with those of the department's officials who

had been appointed by Zubatoff and Lopuhin. Ratayeff was one of the first of his victims. Ratchkovsky recalled him and gave him clearly to understand that his
services were no longer required.

This was, of course, a severe blow to Aseff. Ratayeff
could only submit. He summoned Aseff to St. Petersburg and, on August 21st, put him under Ratchkovsky's
supervision. This was their first meeting.[1] Aseff's position was now made more difficult, as he had to deal with
a chief of greater experience and better judgment. The
situation was further complicated by the fact that
Ratchkovsky had many more means of checking Aseff's
reports. Furthermore, Aseff was now kept under observation by Tataroff, who had learned a great deal more
of the party's affairs. Aseff realized that he *must* be
more active in supplying information, and that he must
provide a great deal of it to avoid letting the police discover his treachery. That was the policy he adopted.

August 21, 1905, was an important day in Aseff's
life. On that day he promised to betray Savinkoff,
Breshkovskaya, and many other terrorists; he also had
his salary increased to six hundred roubles and was
promised much more generous expenses. On the following day Aseff received his salary for several months in

---

[1]It has been widely asserted that a close connection existed between
Ratchkovsky and Aseff ever since the latter's early police days. On this hy-
pothesis are built the assumptions of the part played by Ratchkovsky in the
assassination of Plehve and other terrorist acts of the Battle Organization.
But there is no ground for such assertions either in the evidence of well-
informed people or in documents. Aseff in his conversations with Burtzeff,
and Ratchkovsky in his with Ratayeff, both categorically deny the existence
of any such relationship. Lopuhin, who is the only person to state this as a
fact, has often been given to lapses of memory. Documents, on the contrary,
tend to show that during this period Ratchkovsky had no idea of the real part
played by Aseff, and, in his reports of spring 1902, he spoke of him as an
active Social Revolutionary.

advance and one thousand three hundred róubles for expenses and in the evening left for Saratoff to catch "Grandmother" Breshkovskaya. He was accompanied by Mednikoff, the chief of the Investigation Department. Another detachment of detectives set out to arrest Savinkoff, who was resting on the estate of a friend whose address had been given to him by Aseff. Neither of these arrests was made, as both Breshkovskaya and Savinkoff succeeded in escaping. Aseff's betrayals were on the whole insignificant: they amounted to a dynamite factory in Saratoff and one in Moscow, and a number of minor arrests. . . . Not one of the party chiefs was caught, and the whole staff of the Battle Organization was preserved intact. Aseff had contented himself with denouncing Savinkoff. He would, of course, have betrayed the others if Ratchkovsky had brought pressure to bear on him. . . .

Though it saved him from this trial, fate had another and more bitter one in store for him. If a member of the Central Committee had disclosed to Ratchkovsky Aseff's real part in the revolutionary movement, so now, in his turn, one of the most trusted officials of the Department, L. P. Menstchikoff, informed the Central Committee of Aseff's police activities. Aseff was now between two fires.

Menstchikoff was an old and experienced official of the Political Police. In 1887 he had been arrested in Moscow as a member of a small revolutionary group, and he soon became convinced that he was surrounded on all sides by treachery and provocation. According to his account, he then had the idea of "turning the tables" on the police by entering its service with a view to exposing its secrets to the revolutionaries. This intention led Menstchikoff very far. He entered the Moscow

Ochrana and soon drew attention to himself by the precision and clarity of his reports. Morose, silent, and
always coldly polite, he held himself a little aloof from
his associates, but he was valued by his chiefs and came
to hold a responsible position. He had held this for some
two years when Ratchkovsky's "combing out" threatened the security of his position. He had by that time
collected a considerable amount of material dealing
with various police secrets, and he decided to launch
on his exposure of the secret police agents.

On September 8, 1905, a mysterious veiled lady called
upon Rostkovsky, one of the members of the St. Petersburg Social Revolutionary Committee, handed him a
sealed envelope, and quickly disappeared. The letter
contained a warning that the Social Revolutionary party
was being betrayed by two spies, "a certain T——, an
ex-convict," and "the engineer Aseff, a Jew, who had
recently arrived from abroad." The letter further gave
exact details of the betrayals made by these persons.

This letter came to Aseff's knowledge that very day.
He called by chance on Rostkovsky, and the latter, who
was very much upset, showed him the letter. Aseff
turned pale, but did not lose his self-control, and said,
"T——, that can only be Tataroff, and the engineer
Aseff, that must be myself. My name is Aseff." At this
he threw down his cigarette and went out, leaving
Rostkovsky in a still more perturbed state than before.

Events, however, took a very different turn from that
hoped for by the author of the letter. That evening
Aseff saw Ratchkovsky and gave him a full account of
what had taken place. Ratchkovsky was delighted with
Aseff's self-possession, but Aseff was far from delighted
at the department's inability to guard its secrets. Aseff
next went to Moscow, where he spoke of the letter to

Potapoff, a member of the Central Committee, and then he went on to Geneva.

The letter made a tremendous impression both in Moscow and abroad. The revolutionaries could not help feeling that they were hemmed in on every side by the police, and that even their very thoughts were known to the department, which seemed to be playing an incomprehensible game with them. It was clear to all the members of the Central Committee that there was treachery in the very heart of the party, but they all, without exception, refused to credit the accusation against Aseff.

The revolutionaries would not even admit the possibility of treachery on the part of the organizer of Plehve's assassination. No investigation was therefore made into the charge. Nor did the knowledge of the accusation get beyond a very narrow circle of party leaders. Aseff, as before, was kept informed of the party's secret projects, and of the progress of the Tataroff affair, which took on a very different complexion from that of his own. The accusations against the latter looked much less improbable than those against Aseff. Gotz, who had warmly defended Aseff, insisted on a thorough investigation of his case. Tataroff, who had gone abroad, had already roused the suspicion of his comrades. The preliminary inquiry definitely established that he had been deceiving them. The Central Committee then officially set up a commission consisting of Bach, Savinkoff, Tiutcheff, and Tchernoff, to make a full investigation.

Tataroff was taken completely by surprise: he had no inkling of the suspicions directed against him, for Ratchkovsky betrayed him by not telling him of Menstchikoff's letter. Tataroff's answers on a number of points were palpably false. He went back on his evidence and contradicted himself, thus confirming the worst suspicions against him. It was established that he *could* have been responsible for these betrayals, but there was no proof that he was.

The commission unanimously arrived at the conclusion that Tataroff was in some way connected with the police; but the nature of this connection remained obscure. The idea of killing him was therefore given up; instead it was decided to suspend him from further party work and to pursue the investigation. He was allowed to return to Russia, but on the condition of keeping the Central Committee informed of all his movements.

At the time of this sentence Aseff was absent from Geneva, recuperating in the mountains. By the time he returned, Tataroff had gone. Aseff was indignant. He considered that the prestige of the party had suffered through Tataroff's not being executed. "Are there ever any more definite proofs in affairs like this?" he said. All witnesses agree that, had Aseff been in Geneva at the time of the sentence, Tataroff would not have remained alive.

As it was, he had not long left to live. In October, the doors of the prisons opened and most of the revolutionaries arrested on March 29th–30th regained their freedom. Their accounts left no doubts as to Tataroff's treachery; he had even been so imprudent as to go to the Ochrana in order to identify some of those arrested. A friend of his, Freedenson, visited him in Kiev to make one more attempt to get a satisfactory explanation from him. Tataroff persisted in his denials; and he furthermore asserted that he had been told on good authority by a relation of his in the St. Petersburg police

that the real traitor was Aseff. But he brought forward
no facts to support his accusation. His declaration was
therefore interpreted as an attempt to save himself by
calumniating one whom the police had long been trying
to destroy. The terrorists were particularly indignant
at this, and they resolved to kill Tataroff.

They tried to keep Aseff in ignorance of their plan.
"We thought it necessary," recalls Savinkoff, "to spare
Aseff all the worries involved in the killing of this *agent
provocateur*." But Aseff would have nothing to do with
such "sentimentalities." He showed great interest in the
development of the affair, studied the details, and even
made his appearance uninvited at the meeting which
was working out the technical side of the assassination
and gave his own views.

Under other circumstances, Aseff would probably
have been tactful enough not to intrude upon a meeting
of this nature, but at that moment he could not act
otherwise. Savinkoff had no suspicion of the *multiple*
embarrassments which Tataroff had caused Aseff.
From Aseff's point of view, Tataroff had to be killed
even at the risk of something more than lack of tact.

A whole detachment of the Battle Organization, with
Savinkoff at its head, set out for Warsaw, where
Tataroff was living at the time. All the plans were
difficult of execution, as Tataroff was obviously afraid
for his life and scarcely ever left his father's house. The
terrorists were therefore obliged to make a direct attack.
On April 4, 1906, Nazaroff, a worker member of the organization, called at the house of Tataroff's father and
asked to see the son. The father and mother did not wish
to let him in, as they knew of their son's apprehensions.
But at the noise Tataroff himself came into the hall.
Nazaroff pulled out his revolver and began to shoot.

The father had time to knock his hand up, and the bullets went over his head. All three then grappled with Nazaroff. But the latter pulled out a dagger and, slightly wounding the mother in the struggle, struck the son in the left side. Tataroff took a few steps and fell dead. Nazaroff succeeded in making his escape.

When the police archives were opened after the Revolution, documents were found showing what blood money had been paid to various traitors. In the course of his police work, beginning in March, 1905, Tataroff had received sixteen thousand, one hundred roubles. This was a great deal, if we take into account that Tataroff's "work" did not last more than about eight months. But it was not excessive if we consider that he paid for his treachery with his life. . . .

CHAPTER IX

The Days of Revolu-
tionary Battles

THE FIRST STAGE of the Tataroff affair, the collecting of evidence and the inquiries, came to an end in October, 1905. The excitement and alarm caused by this affair were intensified by the news of events then taking place in Russia. Finally news was received of the Czar's famous manifesto of October 17th.

This news caused a great stir among the revolutionary *émigrés*. All parties and groups were now busily discussing the meaning of this manifesto. The executive of the Social Revolutionary party abroad met in Gotz's house on hearing of the manifesto. The latter was now ill and had to be wheeled about in an armchair. The terror was the most debated subject. What was to be done now about terrorist methods? What was to be done with the party's "beloved child," the Battle Organization? The old conflict between the supporters of terror and those of a mass movement was now revived in a new form, giving rise to new groupings within the party executive. Gotz made a most resolute stand against terror. He found the terror no longer admissible under the new circumstances. "The terror is finished," he declared firmly, "and the leaders of the Battle Organization must realize it."

This point of view met with opposition. Savinkoff's defense of the terror was particularly impassioned. He considered that the party must profit by the government's weakness and intensify the terror. But he was almost its only defender. The majority agreed that to use terror under the new conditions would alienate the party from the masses. The party should, rather, concentrate all its energies on influencing the masses, on extending its work of political agitation and on founding open organizations of workers and peasants. The terror should be resorted to only in case the reactionaries attempted to take away these concessions from the people. Therefore the majority agreed with Tchernoff's view that terrorist activity should cease for the moment, but that the Battle Organization should be preserved in case it might be needed in the future.

Aseff remained somewhat aloof in these discussions. In principle he inclined to the idea of putting an end to the terror, but as leader of the Battle Organization he was obliged to give a certain amount of support to Savinkoff. In the course of these debates, however, he made a clear statement of his position. He thought the application of revolutionary methods of fighting only possible in so far as it was a question of fighting absolutism. According to him, revolutionary interference in the progress of the social struggle, and partly in the struggle

of the peasants for the land, defeated its own ends, and
he openly declared that he would leave the party if that
course were adopted. He proclaimed himself to be a
"fellow traveler" of the party until a real constitution
had been attained. As soon as this was achieved, he
would become a "logical legalist and evolutionist"
and an opponent of all violent measures.

Tchernoff relates that Aseff's declarations surprised
many of those present. But there was really nothing
new in the position he adopted. These views had always
made him oppose the advocates of agrarian terror and
mass revolts, and had made him attempt to reconcile the
party with the moderate Liberal groups . . .

No decision was reached at the meeting in Gotz's
house, as the right to make such a decision rested only
with a meeting of all the members of the Central
Committee which was to take place in Russia. All the
émigrés, with the exception of the sick Gotz, decided to
go immediately to Russia and take an active part in
events there. This meeting, however, had a great significance in the history of the Social Revolutionary party;
it defined the positions of those who were going to
Russia.

After the meeting, Tchernoff, Savinkoff, and Aseff
went into a café: they had forgotten about food during
their discussion, and now they felt hungry. They
finished their discussion over supper. Savinkoff vigorously attacked the views of the majority. There was a
lot of passion in his speech, but little practical politics.
He had always connected the attainment of freedom in
Russia with some heroic act of the Battle Organization,
and he now declared that, if no collective attempt such
as the blowing up of the Winter Palace were organized,
he would himself "let off his last bullet" at the first
gendarme he met in the street.

Aseff remained silent during this conversation, for he was preoccupied with his own thoughts. But as soon as Savinkoff had gone, he unfolded a plan for the blowing up of the Ochrana as the "one act which would have any significance" and which would be the "logical conclusion" of the activities of the Battle Organization. "The Ochrana," he said, "is the living symbol of all that is most repressive, cruel, mean, and revolting in Autocracy. . . ." This plan is, indeed, the true reflection of Aseff's temper at the time.

He had, it seemed, come out of his hardest trial, the difficult situation in which Menstchikoff's letter had placed him, with honor. He could have no doubt now of the confidence in which he was held by the revolutionaries. Nevertheless, his mind was not at peace. For the first time in his life, perhaps, he had a vague premonition of the reality of his exposure, and he could feel the cold barrel of a revolver pressed against his head. The danger threatened him both from the revolutionaries and the police. The game could only be played as long as no one guessed it. Once suspicion was aroused, he would either have to abandon the game altogether or give definite allegiance to one side or the other.

Aseff at that period would have been inclined to go over entirely to the revolutionary camp. In the first place, this seemed to be more profitable, as the Revolution looked like getting the upper hand. Furthermore, this also seemed the safer course: there was more chance of his being treated with more consideration by the revolutionaries than by the nephew of one of his victims, the Czar. These were probably the reasons why he had given no news of himself to the Police Department for several months after Menstchikoff's letter. He called, however, on his old friend Ratayeff, who was then living in Paris, and told him that his police work was now at an end since he had been "exposed" to the revolutionaries. This was in the late autumn of 1905, and, as Aseff knew by then that the revolutionaries no longer entertained suspicions against him, we can only conclude that he was abandoning police work because he wished to do so.

In his present mood Aseff could desire nothing better than the destruction of the secret archives of the political police. Thus his past could no longer be a threat to him and he could become a free man.

Aseff set out for Russia only after the other *émigrés* had gone, for, as usual, he was in no hurry to take risks. He went only when he had received news of the others' safe arrival. But he arrived in time for the sessions of the Central Committee. These took place in Moscow, and some thirty members were present. They were made up of those who had been admitted to the executive on the foundation of the party and, also, of all those who had been amnestied after long months or years of imprisonment and exile. The *émigrés* played the leading rôle in these sessions; they were more united as a group and had a definite point of view. Their opinions won the day, and the conclusions at which the majority had arrived in Gotz's house now became the policy of the party.

Aseff spoke very little during these sessions and silently supported the resolutions of the majority. In this way, he also supported the resolution to end the terror. He also defended this point of view in private conversations. One of the few occasions on which he held the floor was during the discussion on the fate of the Battle Organization. Tchernoff proposed that the Battle Organization should not be dissolved but "kept under arms." This point of view threatened to gain the approval of the majority. Aseff stood up then and said with the authority of a specialist versed in the affairs of the Battle Organization: "It is impossible to keep it under arms. That is a mere phrase. I take full responsibility on myself. The Battle Organization is dissolved."

The authoritative tone did its work, and the Central Committee sanctioned its dissolution.

Aseff's impressions on his arrival in Russia did not inspire him with confidence in the victory of the Revolution. He was but little interested in the innumerable gatherings and meetings then being held in St. Petersburg. But he listened attentively to what people said in general, and he very soon came to the conclusion that: "We are far from victory yet. There will still be a reaction." The headquarters of the Central Committee in those days were attached to the editorial offices of *Sin Otetchestva*, a St. Petersburg daily which had become the principal organ of the party. All the leaders of the party came here to discuss questions of party policy, and here were written all the articles which directed propaganda throughout Russia.

In the discussions frequently held there were voiced all those differences of opinion which characterized the ideological development of the party in years to come. Here, too, grew up the moderate wing, which was adopting a purely evolutionist point of view, and which was in a few months' time to form a distinct party—the National Socialists. On the other hand, an extreme left wing, later to become known as the Social Revolutionary Maximalist party, advocated the running of the revolution preparing in Russia on Socialist lines; it was undoubtedly here, in these editorial offices, that the general opinion and policy of the party were worked out.

All these questions and theoretical differentiations were but of little interest to the terrorists, who had a small room opening directly onto the vestibule set apart for their use. They still believed that their only "business" was to throw bombs and that all the rest was "mere chatter." And now that they had been forbidden to undertake any real terrorist attempts, they were almost glad at the impending defeat of the Revolution. Savinkoff played the part of first fiddle in all these discussions. Aseff said little and was content to act the part of stage manager.

Aseff had his own special worries. One evening, late in November or early in December, an attempt was made on his life by two hooligan members of the reactionary "Black Band" who fell upon him in a dark alley. Robbery was obviously not the motive. They stabbed him and then disappeared. Fortunately Aseff's fur coat was very thick and heavy; the knife only cut it, and Aseff was not even wounded. But he was perturbed beyond all reason. "His face was covered with purple blotches, and his lips quivered nervously," a witness tells us. It was strange that such an "inflexible terrorist" should have been so disturbed, for attacks by the "Black Band" were a common occurrence at that time. No one suspected, of course, the conclusion which Aseff could draw from this attempt.

It was general knowledge that the "Black Bands" in St. Petersburg were controlled by the Political Police with Ratchkovsky at its head. It was the police who inspired the attacks on the revolutionaries, and Aseff could not but ask himself if he had to thank Ratchkovsky for the attempt against himself. Had he escaped being killed by the revolutionaries only to fall now a victim to the police? The prospect was not at all comforting. And since he was convinced that the reaction would take the upper hand in the near future, Aseff asked himself whether he had not better "make peace" with Ratchkovsky.

It is not known exactly when Aseff began to feel his

way in this direction. We only know that, after a few
months of interruption, Aseff once more began to write
letters to Ratchkovsky. The first of these letters may
be attributed to the period of the December rising; at
any rate, all the Social Revolutionary projects of the
time, such as the blowing up of a railway bridge to prevent the arrival of troops which had been sent to crush
the Moscow rising, the blowing up of the Ochrana, the
arrest of the president of the Cabinet of Ministers,
Count Witte, and so on, all projects of which Aseff was
informed, could not be executed because, as Savinkoff
says, "the places selected were guarded so strongly as
to suggest that the police had been forewarned." As
there were no other traitors in the narrow circle of those
who had knowledge of these plans, it is very probable
that Aseff tried to get into the good graces of Ratchkovsky by these betrayals.[1] If this were true Aseff
gained little from it, for Ratchkovsky used his information, but did not reply to the letters. . . . The reasons for
Ratchkovsky's conduct became clear only much later.

The December risings in Moscow, in Kharkov, in the
Don basin, in the Caucasus, in the Baltic and in Siberia,
all ended in the defeat of the revolutionaries. The
government crushed all attempts at opposition, and the
revolutionary parties were once more driven under-
ground. Therefore in January, 1906, the Central Committee decided to renew the terror.

The chief attempts were now to be directed against
Durnoff, the Minister of the Interior, who was regarded
as the inspirer of the reactionary policy, and the Mos-

[1]Gerassimoff, who was directly responsible for all the arrests made in
St. Petersburg, categorically denies that he had received any information
from Ratchkovsky leading to the arrest of the Social Revolutionaries; and he
therefore considers as improbable the suggestion that Aseff had supplied
Ratchkovsky with any important information at the time.

cow Governor General Dubassoff, who had put down the
rising of the Moscow workers with an iron hand. Other
less important attempts were to be made against those
government officials who had particularly distinguished
themselves in the suppression of the December revolts.
The campaign of the Battle Organization was to serve
as an answer to the cruelty of the government, which
had put such a brutal end to the days of freedom.

The direction of the work of the Battle Organization
was entrusted as before to Aseff. His nearest assistants
were Savinkoff and Moisenko. Finland, which was
granted full internal autonomy after October, 1905,
served as the base of action; for many of its active
politicians sympathized with or actively helped the
Battle Organization. There was no lack of volunteers,
and all its old members, many of whom had just regained their freedom from prison, responded to its call.
The membership rose to almost thirty; there was also
plenty of material, both money and explosives. At first
sight everything pointed to success. But the campaign
was planned "officially": according to old methods, cabmen and street hawkers were to keep observation on the
victims, and then the bomb throwers were to act. It
was the repetition of the formula which had been successful in the case of Plehve. . . . Zubatoff would never
have called the present members of the Battle Organization "artists in terror," for they worked without
invention or inspiration.

Under these circumstances the campaign might very
well have proved unsuccessful even if there had been
no question of treachery. But there was—and, in the
conditions created by a victorious reaction, it assumed
an intricate form such as no novelist, even though
gifted with the richest fantasy, could imagine.

CHAPTER X

Gapon's Treachery

THE NEWS of the tragic events of "Bloody Sunday" in St. Petersburg, on January 22, 1905, portrayed in mysterious and heroic tones the priest Gapon, who, with a cross in his hand, had led the masses to the Czar's palace in search of justice and freedom. The readers abroad were for several days afterwards anxious as to his fate and wondered whether the bullets had spared him or if he had escaped arrest. The Berlin *Vorwarts* was the first to announce his safe arrival in Geneva. Everybody hurried to welcome him. Only old Adler, who was a good judge of men, remarked skeptically that it would be better for the Revolution if it could count Gapon on the list of its perished heroes. His opinion was soon shared by everybody.

Fame and money ruined Gapon. All the papers were full of him, his photographs were in all the shops, and he was paid a fortune for his autobiography. His vanity knew no bounds, and everywhere he wished to be the central figure. But he did not succeed in making any headway in any of the revolutionary groups. He began by proclaiming his adhesion to the Social Democratic party, but he abandoned it as soon as he saw that he would be allowed to play only a secondary part in it. He stayed a little longer with the Social Revolutionaries, but they, too, were not prepared to proclaim him their "leader." For this, indeed, he had no qualifications.

Then he broke with the Social Revolutionaries and made an attempt to form an independent party of his own. There he was indeed a "leader," but he was also its sole member; it did no revolutionary work and had no real support. All it had was plenty of money, for many Russians and foreigners subscribed to his name. In his private life Gapon sank lower and lower: he became the habitué of the smartest cabarets in Paris and other towns, gambled at Monte Carlo, spent money on women, and, in the drunken fumes of his debauchery, lost all contact with revolutionary ideals.

His conduct inspired general mistrust, and when, in November, he went to St. Petersburg and attempted to found an organization of his own, he was unable to get any followers. There were not wanting, however, people ready to exploit his popularity in the interests of various shady activities. He entered into particularly close relations with a certain Manasevitch-Manoiloff, a police agent and popular journalist, who was at that time in the secret service of Count Witte. He realized very soon that Gapon was ready for anything and began to put him in touch with the police chiefs. Gapon, first of all, met Lopuhin, who, though now in retirement, was making great efforts to gain readmittance into the Police Department. Later he met Ratchkovsky.

Ratchkovsky could get round abler men than Gapon, and he had, above all, sufficient means to buy the latter. First of all came discussions on high politics; Ratchkovsky argued that the government regretted the events of Bloody Sunday, that it had all been a "sad misunderstanding," and that it now valued Gapon and was in need of his services to direct the labor movement in Russia along peaceful lines, and thus to remove it from the influence of the Social Democrats and the Social Revolutionaries, who had treated Gapon so contemptuously. When it became clear that Gapon was swallowing the bait, the conversation took a more concrete turn, and Ratchkovsky complained that the terrorists were impeding the normal development of the country, and that the government, if it succeeded in ridding the country of the danger of the terror, could more easily pursue the policy of reform.

These meetings usually took place in the private rooms of the best St. Petersburg restaurants. Ratchkovsky did not grudge money for entertainment. Good wine loosened Gapon's tongue, and Ratchkovsky, of course, profited by this to make direct proposals. "I am old now," he complained, "and there is nobody to take my place. Russia (that is, the Russian Political Police) has need of men like you. Why shouldn't you succeed me? We should only be too glad. But you must help us first of all. You must tell us what the revolutionary organizations are doing." Gapon yielded to these flattering suggestions and gradually revealed all he knew of the revolutionary activities, and particularly what he knew of the terrorist activity of the Battle Organization.

Nor did he refuse further help to Ratchkovsky; he assured him that he could count on the assistance of his good friend the engineer Rutenberg, who was close to the Battle Organization and who would keep him informed of the terrorists' new plans. Ratchkovsky was now very pleased with himself; it seemed to him that he had created a reliable central source of information as to the activities of the Battle Organization. He realized that Gapon would be expensive, but the game was worth the candle.

As this was an important decision, Ratchkovsky told Durnovo, the Minister of the Interior, of his association with Gapon. The former took Colonel Gerassimoff, the chief of the St. Petersburg Ochana, into his confidence. Ratchkovsky made a detailed and very optimistic report on these negotiations. Gerassimoff, according to his own account, was far from sharing this optimism. He was especially doubtful of the possibility of winning over Rutenberg, for his impression of him was that of a convinced revolutionary, and, as it was known from police reports that Rutenberg led a very temperate life, Gerassimoff doubted whether he could be tempted by money. In view of these doubts, Durnovo suggested that Ratchkovsky should arrange an interview between Gapon and Gerassimoff, and, much against his will, Ratchkovsky was forced to accede to this.

The interview took place in the Café de Paris, but its only result was to strengthen Gerassimoff in his doubts, for Gapon gave the impression of a shallow and boastful man. He was ready enough to betray all he knew, but his answers showed that he had no real connection with the terrorists, and that his one hope lay in Rutenberg. As a result, Gerassimoff reported adversely to Durnovo, but, in view of Ratchkovsky's insistence, the Minister consented to the negotiations being pursued.

Rutenberg was at that time "wanted" and was in hiding in Moscow. Gapon, who had managed to get hold of his address from a mutual friend, called on him on February 19, 1906. Rutenberg was, indeed, personally attached to Gapon, for he saw him in the light of the January movement of 1905, when he had helped him to draw up the famous petition to the Czar, had lain beside him in the snow under the hail of the soldiers' bullets, and had later helped him to escape. But now, on Gapon's first words, Rutenberg realized that he had to deal with a different man. Gapon tried cunning. He attempted to draw Rutenberg into the police net by stories of grandiose revolutionary undertakings such as terrorist attacks against Ministers and the "repetition—only on a larger scale—of the 9th of January," and so on.

But he played his part badly: his stories were full of contradictions; he mentioned his meetings with Ratchkovsky, whom, it would seem, he was going to use for his revolutionary aims; and his eyes shifted uneasily, betraying his uneasy conscience. Rutenberg very soon convinced himself that Gapon had entered into relations with the police and was trying to inveigle him into treachery. As this game might have the most disastrous consequences, Rutenberg decided to find out as much as he could about it and so pretended to fall in with the scheme. This ruse succeeded, and Gapon told him most of his plans: Rutenberg was to help him to betray the attempts projected by the terrorists, for which Ratchkovsky would pay considerable sums amounting to many tens of thousands of roubles.

Rutenberg, while pretending to agree, informed the party chiefs and the Battle Organization of this. Gapon, very content with himself, made a further appointment with Rutenberg in St. Petersburg and called on Ratchkovsky to report on his success. The latter knew from his agents that Gapon had met Rutenberg several times, and accordingly treated Gapon with greater confidence than ever. This had a favorable effect, too, on Durnovo. The negotiations now took on a much more concrete character: the discussion turned on the amount that Gapon and Rutenberg were to be paid for betraying the terrorist attempt. Gapon asked no less than one hundred thousand roubles. Ratchkovsky was aghast at such an appetite, and assured Gapon that the police never paid such exorbitant prices. Durnovo made a counter proposition of twenty-five thousand roubles. Gapon, however, insisted, and the question was referred to higher authority. Durnovo consulted Count Witte, the president of the Cabinet. Witte states in his memoirs that he had advised caution in dealing with Gapon; but Gerassimoff holds him chiefly responsible for the Gapon incident. In any case, as far as money is concerned, Witte himself admits that he advised the police not to bargain too much.

In the meantime, Rutenberg went to Helsingfors, where he found Aseff, whom he told about Gapon. Aseff's indignation knew no bounds. "He thought," Rutenberg recalls, "that Gapon should be killed like a snake. I was to arrange an interview with him, take him out to dinner, and after dinner, while driving back through a wood in a sledge belonging to the Battle Organization, stab him and throw his body out." Aseff was always ruthless where traitors were concerned. . . .

The question of Gapon, however, could not be decided so simply. He had already lost all prestige in the eyes of active revolutionaries, but the masses still had faith in him. For them he was still the hero of Bloody Sunday, and there was reason to suppose that they would not believe in his treachery, but would impute the accusation to an intrigue on the part of his political opponents. It was therefore decided, in order to make Gapon's connection with the police clear, to kill both him and Ratchkovsky.

This task was entrusted to Rutenberg, who was to continue to pretend to play the part of a traitor and was to persuade Gapon to arrange an interview with Ratchkovsky. The plan was thought out in all its details, and Rutenberg was to be given the assistance of another member of the Battle Organization, who was to act the part of a cabman who was keeping observation on Durnovo. Rutenberg's relations with him were to convince the police that they really had to do with a projected attempt. Rutenberg disliked his rôle, but agreed to undertake it in view of the important consequences it might have on the revolutionary movement.

About March 10th, Rutenberg returned to St. Petersburg and renewed his relations with Gapon. The latter was impatient at the delay but was content at Rutenberg's final agreement. They bargained a great deal about money; Gapon was very anxious for Rutenberg to meet Ratchkovsky as soon as possible, and the latter was also eager for the meeting to take place, for on its results depended any further offers he would make.

After much hesitation and delay—for he found it difficult to overcome his scruples—Rutenberg agreed to this. This interview was appointed for March 17th, in a restaurant. Ratchkovsky was very content, but at the very last moment Gerassimoff telephoned to him and advised him not to go to the meeting, in view of Rutenberg's suspicious behavior. Ratchkovsky was some time in making up his mind not to go, as he felt sure that Gerassimoff was mistaken. In any case, Gerassimoff took precautionary measures, and Ochrana agents were stationed in the room next to that in which the meeting was to take place. In the end, Ratchkovsky did not go, and Rutenberg waited for him in vain. Soon after, a change came about in Ratchkovsky's attitude towards Gapon and Rutenberg; he took less interest in them and became very prudent and cautious.

The reasons for this change have only recently become clear. Aseff felt very uneasy in the period which followed the crushing of the December rising. The reaction was obviously triumphant. And Aseff had ceased to believe in the victory of the Revolution for some time to come. His control of the Battle Organization's treasury continued to remain a much more paying proposition than his work for the department, but it was profitable only so long as he remained on good terms with the latter. A conflict with the department would not only reduce Aseff's material profit to nothing, but would also bring him face to face with dangers which he could not underestimate. Ratchkovsky's attitude now particularly disturbed him, for his letters had remained unanswered. He knew that Tataroff had learned of his activities, and there could be no doubt that he had told Ratchkovsky all he knew. This was a direct threat, and Aseff was therefore all the more anxious to allay the wrath of the gods of the police Olympus. That actually was the situation.

We have no exact facts to account for Ratchkovsky's behavior, but we can only assume that Ratchkovsky distrusted Aseff and did not wish to have anything to do with him. Ratchkovsky later told the gendarme colonel, P. P. Zavarzin, that he had caught Aseff playing a double game, and that he had therefore broken all relations with him. Zavarzin's account does not inspire confidence in all its details, but his story answers in the main to what we know of the relations between Ratchkovsky and Aseff, and is therefore worthy of credence. Aseff's fury may well be imagined when he learned from Rutenberg that Gapon had told Ratchkovsky of the part he was really playing among the revolutionaries. Gapon's death, therefore, became a necessity.

More complex was the problem of how to deal with Ratchkovsky. On the one hand, Aseff might have him put out of the way and thus remove the one department chief who regarded him with suspicion. On the other hand, he might win his good-will by informing him of Rutenberg's plans. We can only guess at what Aseff really thought during this period, but his conduct gives us ground for supposing that he first favored the double assassination of Gapon and Ratchkovsky, and only later, on seeing that Ratchkovsky was on his guard, did he attempt to profit by the situation in the only way he could, by betraying Rutenberg's plan. This we learn from Gerassimoff, who declared before the Commission of Inquiry, in 1917, that Aseff had, during his later interviews with Ratchkovsky, reminded him of his letters of warning against Rutenberg.[1] These warnings apply, of course, to a later period, for, as we know,

[1] Gerassimoff's declaration is as follows: "I remember that Aseff spoke to Ratchkovsky of a letter in which he had warned the latter that his life was in danger from Rutenberg."

Ratchkovsky was at first eager to meet Rutenberg.

There can be no doubt that Aseff had at a certain moment set himself the double problem of having Gapon assassinated on the one hand, and, on the other, of saving Ratchkovsky. Aseff in general liked to show himself in the rôle of savior of the lives of his police chiefs. Experience taught him that the chiefs whose lives he had "saved" were inclined to be more indulgent to him. But the situation was now complicated by the fact that the Central Committee had resolved to kill Gapon and Ratchkovsky together. Aseff found a way out of this. Assuming the whole responsibility for the undertaking, he instructed Rutenberg to kill Gapon in any case, even if he failed to entrap Ratchkovsky. Aseff succeeded in fully realizing his plan.

The dénouement was close at hand. Rutenberg felt that the police net was being drawn more tightly round him and that he would not be able to surprise Gapon and Ratchkovsky together. As his nerve failed him for the double attempt, he at last made up his mind to take the easiest course and to kill Gapon alone.

It was decided that Gapon's assassination should be preceded by a trial held on him by a group of his worker friends, who had taken part in the events of January, 1905. An isolated villa was taken not far from St. Petersburg. Gapon was enticed there under the pretext of discussing the final terms for the betrayal of the Battle Organization. Gapon, who had no suspicion of the trap set for him, and who was angry with Rutenberg for his procrastination, now spoke with the utmost frankness and crudeness. "What are you dilly-dallying about?" he said persuasively to Rutenberg. "Twenty-five thousand is good money!"

When Rutenberg pointed to his scruples, and his fears

that the terrorists would be hung if arrested, Gapon harshly replied:

"Well, what of it? It's a pity, of course, but we can't help that! You can't cut a tree down without the splinters flying."

And he comforted Rutenberg with the thought that his treachery would never be made public.

"Ratchkovsky is such a clever man, he will arrange everything perfectly."

Through a thin partition this conversation was overheard by the workers invited to act as judges. They had formerly almost deified Gapon as the leader of the January movement. Now they could contain themselves with difficulty, and, when Rutenberg finally decided to put an end to the game and opened the door for them, they literally burst into the room and with cries, almost with groans, threw themselves on Gapon. The latter recognized them, for among them were several of his close friends. He fell on his knees and, clutching their hands, begged for mercy.

"Brothers . . ." he implored, "forgive me, forgive me, for the sake of the past. . . ."

"Ratchkovsky is your brother, not we!" came the answer.

"You sold our blood to the police, there's no forgiveness for that!" others added.

Rutenberg had not the strength to remain to see justice done. He went out of the room, sobbing almost hysterically: "He was once my friend. . . . My God! . . . How terrible! . . ."

By that time a noose had been thrown round Gapon's neck, and the rope was attached to an iron hook which had been put in over the clothes rail. In a few seconds all was over. This took place on April 10, 1906, about seven o'clock in the evening. . . . They all left the villa silently, locking it behind them.

In Finland, where Rutenberg went immediately afterwards, an unexpected piece of news awaited him. Aseff now, apparently, denied that he had given permission for the assassination of Gapon alone, or that he had been warned of its imminence. He declared categorically that he had never countenanced any departure from the decision of the Central Committee, and that he would take it as a personal affront if anybody thought even for a moment of taking Rutenberg's word against his. Rutenberg, as a result, found himself accused not only of violating the party discipline, but also of slandering one of the most "respected" members of the Central Committee. The party denied all responsibility for Gapon's assassination, which was declared to be a personal affair of Rutenberg's. The reactionary papers soon began to hint that Rutenberg had been in relation with the Political Police and that he had killed Gapon either as a rival, or out of fear of exposure. . . . Rutenberg, completely overcome by this, withdrew from the revolutionary movement.

CHAPTER XI

Aseff'sReconciliation with the Police Department

LOOKING BACK now at the past, it is difficult to understand how the chiefs of the Central Committee and of the Battle Organization, men it would seem of sufficient experience, could have been capable of such gross elementary errors in the Rutenberg and Gapon affair. The success of terrorist undertakings always depends on the unexpectedness of the attack. Yet, while playing their own game with Rutenberg's help against Ratchkovsky, the chiefs of the Battle Organization not only let the police know that they were preparing an attempt against Durnovo, but also that the observation of the intended victims was usually conducted by terror-

ists disguised as cab drivers. The pretended attempt
against Durnovo, staged specially for Ratchkovsky's
benefit, was an exact copy of the genuine attempt which
was being prepared at the same time.

Neither Rutenberg nor his immediate assistants had
any contact with the terrorists who were preparing the
real attempt, and the police, while observing Rutenberg,
had therefore no means of getting on their track. The
assumption of the terrorists was correct as far as this
went, but they overlooked that the police had now
another clue which they could follow up: they could keep
a careful look-out for terrorists disguised as cab drivers.

The police had already taken measures for keeping
observation on cab drivers immediately after the March
arrests, when it was learned that the terrorists had often
adopted that disguise. Following the news of the intended attempt on Durnovo, a closer watch was kept
on the cabmen's quarters. The owners of these quarters
were now required to inform the police about any cabmen whose behavior was at all strange or out of keeping
with the general run of cab drivers. All such reports
were carefully examined. One of these did in fact concern one of the terrorists who was keeping observation
on Durnovo, and the detective who was detailed to
watch him discovered that he usually took up his stand
near Durnovo's house, and that he remained there for
hours on end, refusing chance fares. It was gradually
found that he was in touch with two other cabmen and
another man, who met all of them regularly and was
obviously directing their work.

The police had no doubt as to the meaning of these
maneuvers, and it only remained to effect the arrests.
But a difficulty now arose. Titushkin, the detective in
charge of this investigation, in his reports called the

fourth terrorist "our Philipovsky." "This could not help attracting my attention," says Gerassimoff, then chief of the St. Petersburg Ochrana. Titushkin, who was asked to explain this, stated that he had known the person in question for some time, as he had been pointed out to him five or six years before in the Philippoff café by Mednikoff, then chief of the Investigation Department, as one of the most important secret agents, who had to be carefully shielded in case of arrest.

This made the arrest impossible without endangering the secret agent. Gerassimoff applied to the department for "Philipovsky's" identity and the nature of his relations with the police. This he did all the more willingly as he had been vigorously opposing the department's system of an independent secret service, insisting that it should pass under his control. The department denied all knowledge of "Philipovsky." "I asked them," says Gerassimoff, "to make absolutely sure, for he might have been some agent whom the department usually knew under some other name, or some agent of our secret service abroad. But Ratchkovsky assured me that there neither was nor could be any agent of ours near the Battle Organization."

Titushkin's evidence was, however, too precise to be disregarded. It was, therefore, decided to tackle "Philipovsky" himself, and detectives were instructed to arrest him without attracting any attention.

This order was carried out to the letter. About April 15th, "Philipovsky" was waylaid in a deserted street near the Letnyi Sad as he was walking back at dusk after an interview with one of his cab drivers. The detectives caught him by the arms and asked him to accompany them. "Philipovsky" tried to protest, but he was advised to come quietly in his own interests, and he was taken in a closed cab to the Ochrana. Here "Philipovsky" renewed his protests, produced papers in the name of Engineer Tcherkass, and demanded his immediate liberation, threatening to bring the matter to the notice of the newspapers. These threats had little effect on Gerassimoff, and the arrested man was told that they knew that he was serving, or had in the past served the department and that he had better be "frank." "Philipovsky" adopted a milder tone but declined to give any further information.

"If you don't want to speak," Gerassimoff replied, "you needn't. We are in no hurry. You will have leisure to think it over here, and when you have made up your mind, tell the warder."

And "Philipovsky" found himself in one of the Ochrana cells. He took some two days to arrive at a decision. He was evidently thinking over the new situation. Finally he announced that he was ready to speak. Gerassimoff did not keep him waiting. "Philipovsky" now spoke in a very different tone.

"I am willing to be frank," he at once declared. "But I should like my former chief, Piotr Ivanovitch, to be present."

Piotr Ivanovitch was none other than Ratchkovsky. Gerassimoff had no objection, especially as he thought the conversation would be embarrassing to Ratchkovsky. Gerassimoff immediately rang him up.

"'We have caught "Philipovsky" about whom we asked you, Piotr Ivanovitch [said Gerassimoff]. And just imagine, he says that he knows you very well and that he served under you. I have got him here now, and he wishes you to be present when he speaks.'

"Ratchkovsky [Gerassimoff continues] tried to hedge. 'How can it be "Philipovsky"? It may be Aseff.'

"That was the first time [Gerassimoff adds] that I had heard that name."

Ratchkovsky came at once to the Ochrana, and a stormy discussion followed in Gerassimoff's private room. Ratchkovsky turned to Aseff with his usual "sweet smile."

"Ah, my dear Aseff, we haven't seen each other for a long time."

But Aseff, after two days of solitary confinement and scanty prison fare, was in no humor for pleasantries. He realized, too, that this was the moment for attack. He at once turned a stream of vulgar abuse upon Ratchkovsky. "I have rarely in my life heard such choice abuse," Gerassimoff says. "But Ratchkovsky did not turn a hair. He merely smiled and repeated, 'Don't excite yourself, my dear Aseff; keep calm!'"

When the conversation became more normal, it was established that Aseff had not seen Ratchkovsky for over six months, in fact, ever since the day of the letter compromising Aseff and Tataroff. Aseff had shown no signs of life, to begin with, as he was afraid of compromising himself still further in the eyes of the revolutionaries, but in the last few months he had made several attempts to renew his relations with the department and had sent to Ratchkovsky several letters containing information of various kinds. But Ratchkovsky had ignored his request for an interview and had abandoned him to the "mercy of fate." It was for this that Aseff now rated him.

Aseff's attack was quite well executed. According to Gerassimoff, Ratchkovsky made not the slightest allusion to his suspicions of Aseff. He was evidently afraid to touch upon this question, knowing well that if investigation was made into the obscurer sides of the department's activities, much that was embarrassing to him personally would inevitably come to light. Ratchkovsky undoubtedly felt himself now under an obligation to Aseff, for the latter, by warning him of the Rutenberg plot, had "saved" his life. Aseff made the most of this point, and Gapon's death only went to prove the real danger of this plot. All these facts compelled Ratchkovsky to postpone the raising of those arguments which had influenced him to break off relations with Aseff. Since he did not advance those accusations, he could scarcely defend his position. The defense he put forward was confused and improbable and did not impress his hearers. "I myself felt a twinge of conscience about Ratchkovsky's treatment of Aseff," writes Gerassimoff in his unpublished Memoirs, "and was astonished that such incompetent people were at the head of the Political Department. Aseff read Ratchkovsky a necessary and well-deserved lecture."

In the end, however, Aseff and Ratchkovsky made peace. The latter, according to Gerassimoff, admitted that he had behaved badly and asked Aseff to renew his police work. Aseff, to preserve a show of decency, at first demurred but finally consented. And in reality that was the one thing he wanted.

It was, however, impossible to avoid altogether broaching the question as to why Aseff was involved in the preparation of an attempt against Durnovo. Aseff's explanations were typical. As Gerassimoff says in his Memoirs, Aseff declared that, since he had been deserted by Ratchkovsky he "considered himself no longer in the service of the department" and therefore thought it right to "go on with his professional party work," thus becoming a member of the Central Committee and taking part in the work of the Battle Organ-

ization. This explanation satisfied both Ratchkovsky
and Gerassimoff: they evidently thought it natural
that their secret agents, when left without police work,
should occupy themselves with the organization of
attempts against ministers. Perceiving their attitude
towards him, Aseff grew more brazen and demanded
the payment of what he had lost through his temporary
break with the department. And he gained his end: it
was decided that he should be given five thousand
roubles; that is to say, not only his salary for those
months, but also a certain sum for expenses. . . .

In return for this he gave a certain amount of information about the activity and plans of the Battle
Organization. This information was by no means complete. Of the two chief attempts planned by the Battle
Organization, Aseff did not mention that against Dubassoff. The second attempt, that against Durnovo, was
being prepared by two groups of terrorists. On the one
hand there was the group of "cab drivers"—A. R.
Gotz, Pavloff, and Tretyakoff—who were in contact
with Aseff, and on the other a mixed group of "cabmen"
and "hawkers"—Kudriavtzeff, Piotr Ivanoff, Gorinson,
Piskareff, and Smirnoff—whose work was being directed
by Savinkoff. The police had already full knowledge of
the first group, and Aseff could only confirm the
Ochrana's evidence, but this he did not even suggest
doing. As to the second group, of whose existence the
Ochrana had no suspicion, Aseff made no mention of it.
In this way he gave the police at the moment absolutely
no fresh information about the two principal attempts
undertaken by the Battle Organization.

What news he gave was contained in his accounts of
the Battle Organization's comparatively unimportant
projects, the proposed assassinations of General Min

and Colonel Riman, two officers of the Semeonovsky Regiment who had particularly distinguished themselves by their cruelty in crushing the Moscow rising. The general direction of these attempts had been entrusted to Zenzinoff, who, with Aseff's assistance, worked out a simple plan. Two terrorists, the former students Samoyloff and Iakovleff, were to call on the officers disguised in military uniform. Aseff betrayed this plot, without, however, mentioning any names; but his account made it possible for the police to take precautionary measures. Such were the results of Aseff's interview with his police chiefs, the first for many months. It is clear from it that Aseff had no intention at the moment of giving up his double game.

Aseff took great pleasure in going into the details of the Gapon-Rutenberg affair and did not conceal his gibes at Ratchkovsky. "Well," he said, "did you succeed in buying Rutenberg? That's a fine secret service you established in the Battle Organization—there's no denying that!" It was from him that Ratchkovsky and Gerassimoff first heard for certain that Gapon was dead. Ratchkovsky suspected that all was not well, but it was only now that he learned that Gapon's corpse had been hanging for some days in a deserted villa on the Finnish frontier. Aseff did not give the exact address of the villa, and he may really have forgotten it. Search had to be undertaken through the local police along both sides of the Russo-Finnish frontier, and the body was found only a month later. . . .

It was decided not to arrest the terrorists working with Aseff; the latter had argued that this would finally compromise him in the eyes of the revolutionaries, and that he would be forced to give up his police service. The terrorists were therefore only to be "frightened" by the spreading of a rumor that the police were on their tracks. Aseff himself was, of course, liberated.

Gerassimoff brought all these conversations to the knowledge of the Minister of the Interior, Durnovo. According to Gerassimoff, he himself had expressed his doubt in Aseff's further success as a secret agent, because there was suspicion against him among the revolutionaries and because, now that he was known to so many detectives, there was no certainty of his not being betrayed again. Betrayal would, of course, mean Aseff's death. Gerassimoff was, therefore, inclined to refuse Aseff's services. Durnovo, who was a cynic, looked at the matter in a different light. The terrorists were a source of too much annoyance to him: he had lately lived like a caged animal; police reports too often prevented him from keeping the most private and intimate appointments. He was therefore glad of anything that brought relief to his mode of existence.

"It's his risk, not ours," is approximately what Durnovo said. "If he is willing, why should we worry about it? At the moment we need all the assistance we can get. Let him work; we shall see later."

Durnovo signed the order for five thousand roubles without demur. The deal with Aseff was thus concluded. Ratchkovsky was to supervise his work, but Gerassimoff was to assist at the interviews.

Aseff's absence due to his arrest lasted several days, but the revolutionaries were not perturbed. Aseff explained that he had gone into hiding from the police, who were on his track. This was all the more feasible since by now the rumor had spread that the police were watching the terrorists. The cab drivers were the first to notice that they were being watched, for Gerassimoff had instructed his detectives to make their presence obvious. Rumors of the impending arrest, spread by the police, also reached the executive of the Battle Organization. The wife of one of the members of the Central Committee, while visiting a leading member of the Cadet party, had heard at table a conversation about three "cabmen" who were keeping watch on Durnovo and who were to be arrested in the near future.

Another member of the Central Committee, Argunoff, was told much the same by a sympathizer. This information was immediately passed on to Aseff, who hastened to inform Savinkoff of it. After careful consideration they came to the conclusion that the only thing to do was to disband the "cabmen" at once. Aseff worked out the plan of this disbandment. No one was arrested at the moment, but all the cabmen were arrested one by one, several months later, and were sentenced to penal servitude on the evidence supplied by the detectives. This disbandment coincided with an acute general crisis within the Battle Organization. The latter's program had been confirmed by the Central Committee on condition that it should be carried out before the day on which the Duma would open. It was thought that the political situation following the opening of the Duma would be such as to necessitate the abandonment of terrorist methods. The day of this opening, May 10, 1906, was close at hand. Everywhere the elections were going in favor of the progressive parties. There could be no doubt that the majority of the new members would join the ranks of the opposition, and it was not only the moderate Liberals who comforted themselves with the hope of seeing the capitulation of the old régime before the "will of the national representatives," who were appearing for the first time in the arena of Russian political life.

It was becoming more and more obvious that the activities of the Battle Organization were drawing to an end. And yet no part of its program had been realized. Failure had dogged all its attempts. The arrest of the cabmen was almost followed by that of the second detachment, which was preparing an attempt against Dubassoff. Though Aseff had given the department no information regarding it, the Moscow police had come upon its track unaided, and Savinkoff and his friends escaped arrest only with the greatest difficulty.

This blow was followed by the utter failure of the attempts against Min and Riman. On Aseff's information, Gerassimoff had the houses of these officers specially guarded, and nobody except those personally acquainted with them was allowed to see them. Strangers were admitted only after previous inquiries had been made. As a result of this, the two terrorists, although they came in officers' uniforms and gave high-sounding names (one called himself Prince Vadbolsky and the other Prince Drutzky-Sokolensky), were refused admittance, on the pretext that the officers were out. Their uniforms and princely titles helped them only in that they were not detained on the spot. But when Iakovleff (Prince Drutzky-Sokolensky) called on Riman again a few hours later, he was detained, for by that time the police had established that he was an impostor.

The ambitious plans of the Battle Organization threatened to come to nothing, and its members tended to interpret this fact as a stain on their honor. The young men wished to *rehabilitate the honor of the Battle Organization* at any cost, and were prepared to undertake the most desperate enterprises. Gotz had a plan for an open attack on Durnovo's house. The terrorists, wearing "coats" of dynamite, were to make their way

into the house by force, and there to blow themselves
up and bury Durnovo and all those present in the ruins.
For various reasons this plan was abandoned. It was
resolved, however, to reorganize and to assassinate
Durnovo and Dubassoff before the Duma opened.
Savinkoff was to direct the attempt against the former,
while Aseff took charge of that against the latter.

Savinkoff's efforts proved fruitless. Though the police
never got on the track of his group, the measures for
Durnovo's protection were so thorough that the terrorists never even succeeded in catching sight of him.

Aseff was more successful. He picked on May 6th, the
Empress's birthday, for the attempt. On that day,
Dubassoff, as the Governor General of Moscow, would
be present at the service in the Kremlin. The attempt
was to be made on his way back. Aseff proceeded very
carefully: he sent the other members on in advance,
and he himself remained in Finland up till the last
moment. He did really seem to want to succeed in the
attempt. A week before the attempt was due, the techni-
cians perished in an accidental explosion in Moscow
and almost the whole supply of dynamite was lost.
Had he liked, Aseff might have given up the attempt,
and nobody could have blamed him for its failure. But
instead, he took extra measures, and the breach in the
organization was filled.

Aseff himself went to Moscow only on the eve of the
appointed day. He came there with the permission of
both Ratchkovsky and Gerassimoff, to whom he gave
his personal affairs as the reason for his journey. He
did not say a word of the intended attempt.

The attempt duly took place. Dubassoff was driving
in an open carriage accompanied by his adjutant,
Count Konovnitzin. Close to the Governor General's

house, at the corner of Tchernishevsky Street and the
Tverskoy Square, one of the terrorists, Vnorovsky,
broke through the line of sentries and threw a bomb
which exploded underneath the carriage. The explosion
killed the adjutant and Vnorovsky himself. Dubassoff
was thrown·out of the carriage, and received several
wounds and injuries which did not endanger his life,
but which necessitated a prolonged treatment. He went
on leave, but he never resumed his active work. At the
moment of the explosion Aseff was in the vicinity in
the Philippoff Café, which immediately after the attempt was surrounded by the police, who wished to
make sure that none of the terrorists was there. Aseff
was not detained, for an old detective, who was supervising the search, recognized him as a secret agent and
ordered his release.

This attempt, although it was not fully successful,
was the only positive achievement of the Battle Organization during this period, and it served to strengthen
Aseff's reputation. The doubts sowed by Menstchikoff's letter had persisted in the minds of many people
in spite of Aseff's complete rehabilitation. All were
united in believing that Aseff had been a sincere revolutionary at the time of Plehve's ·assassination, but some
had begun to admit the possibility that he may have
entered into relations with the police after that date.

A good judge of people, Aseff felt the growth of this
mood. It was the desire to counteract it that made him
run the risk of having Dubassoff assassinated. He was
not mistaken; the attempt rehabilitated him in the
eyes of even the most suspicious of the revolutionaries.
For this he had risked putting himself in a very difficult
position with Ratchkovsky and Gerassimoff.

There was a police tradition in Russia. Each Ochrana

"worth its salt" had its agent in the local terrorist
organization. Neither pains nor money was spared to
this end. Not to have such an agent was accounted a
sign of "bad tone." The Moscow Ochrana could not be
reproached for its unwillingness to keep up this tradition. It had its own trusted agent, Zinaida Zhutchenko,
who was in touch with the local terrorists and who was
informed of all the attempts organized locally. Although
she was not a member of the central Battle Organization, she nevertheless always succeeded in getting some
information as to its activities. It was she who had a few
weeks before put the police on the track of Savinkoff's
group. Aseff was more prudent and kept clear of the
local organization. But one of its leaders, Sladkopevtz-
zeff, met him accidentally in the street and afterwards
told his comrades that he thought the attempt on
Dubassoff had been organized by Aseff himself. Zhutchenko hastened to report this statement to the
Ochrana, which immediately telegraphed this news to
St. Petersburg. The department was therefore already
informed of this before Aseff's first interview with
Ratchkovsky and Gerassimoff after the attempt.

The interview was stormy. Later, Aseff told Burtzeff
that Ratchkovsky had shouted, pointing at him:

"That affair in Moscow was your doing!"

To this Aseff had challengingly replied:

"If it was my doing, why don't you arrest me?"

Aseff's calculation was that the police would be
afraid of a grave scandal. He not only denied any participation in the Dubassoff affair, but he asserted that
its real organizer was none other than Zhutchenko.
It is difficult to know whether Aseff and Zhutchenko had
any idea of the real part the other was playing, but
their assertions placed the police in a quandary. If this

affair became public—which would be inevitable in case of Aseff's arrest—the police would not only have lost its two most important agents in the Social Revolutionary party, but would have had to face a storm of indignation called up by the discovery that its agents were acting as *agents provocateurs* in the most important revolutionary organization. In view of the fact that the Duma was to open in a few days' time, these revelations might have produced important political repercussions, and the government's position, already shaky, might have become untenable. In these circumstances, Ratchkovsky and Gerassimoff could do nothing but hush up this unpleasant affair in the interests of the groups they represented. Aseff's calculation was fully justified.

The official version adopted was that to which Gerassimoff still holds in his memoirs. "It is possible to admit," he writes, "that Zhutchenko may have helped in the organization of this attempt, but this does not exclude the supposition that Aseff, who for many months had been out of the service of the Police Department, may have been forced to organize the attempt at the instigation of the party, and could not succeed in frustrating it. One fact is perfectly clear, that both Aseff and Zhutchenko knew of the intended attempt, but gave no information about it for their own safety's sake, as they were already regarded with suspicion by the party."

This version in no way corresponds with the facts. Zhutchenko was definitely not involved in the attempt: she learned of it at second hand and gave all the information she knew "honestly" to the police. As to the part played by Aseff, that has already been made clear. It may be doubted whether Gerassimoff and Ratchkovsky seriously accepted his version, for they had enough evidence in their hands, and enough experience in similar affairs, not to accept such a contradictory explanation.

Events tend to show that they were not content to let matters rest there, that, after this interview, Aseff stopped playing his double game and that, for some time, at least, he acted as the obedient and diligent servant of his police chiefs. If he did this, it was no doubt because he became convinced that the continuation of his double game was fraught with the gravest danger to himself.

He had, of course, to pay a "price" for his participation in the Dubassoff affair; this was no less than Savinkoff's head. The police had an exaggerated idea of the part played by the latter, believing him to be one of the chief organizers of the Battle Organization. Aseff, in his first conversations with Gerassimoff, gave every support to this theory. Gerassimoff now insisted on his betrayal. Aseff agreed to this, and it was through no fault of his that Savinkoff escaped from the noose prepared for him.

On May 19th, the Duma—the first representative institution in the history of Russia—was opened in the midst of the general jubilation of the capital. The opposition parties had an overwhelming majority. The Central Committee decided to suspend the terror while the Duma was in session. The formal resolution, however, was postponed for ratification by the Party Soviet. Aseff was kept informed of these resolutions of the Central Committee. This did not prevent him, however, from sending Savinkoff, a few days before the session of the Soviet, to Sebastopol in order to organize the assassination of Admiral Tchuchnin, who, in 1905, had ruthlessly put down the unrest in the Black Sea Fleet.

From St. Petersburg onwards, Savinkoff and his comrades were watched by Ochrana detectives. They were to be arrested in the south, and in this way the suspicion was to be diverted from Aseff. There, incriminating evidence was to be found which would make it impossible for him to escape the death penalty.

An accident helped the realization of these police plans. Two days after Savinkoff's arrival in Sebastopol, the local Social Revolutionaries organized an attempt against the commandant of the town, General Nepliueff. Though Savinkoff and his friends were in no way involved in this affair, a fact of which the police were perfectly well aware, they were nevertheless arrested and brought before a court-martial. The death penalty was assured. But another "accident" saved Savinkoff: his comrades of the Battle Organization hastily arrived from St. Petersburg and organized a daring and successful rescue. Disguised in a soldier's uniform, Savinkoff was taken out of the prison, and he later succeeded in crossing the frontier. With the chief accused missing, the trial lost much of its significance, and the death penalty was not passed on the other accused. After a short rest abroad, Savinkoff had by the autumn once more joined the ranks of the Battle Organization. In the meantime, many changes had taken place within the Battle Organization. Savinkoff arrived back just in time to help Aseff—his betrayer—to put into execution a plan for its dissolution.

CHAPTER XII

Gerassimoff and Stolypin, Aseff's New Chiefs

THE SOCIAL REVOLUTIONARY PARTY SO-
viet met in Moscow a few days after the opening of
the Duma and passed a resolution to bring the terror
to an end. As it had little faith in the government's
readiness to work in harmony with the Duma, the
Soviet empowered the Central Committee to renew the
terror whenever they might consider it necessary in
the interests of the Revolution.

Aseff took part in these Soviet sessions. He adopted
a dual position on the question of putting an end to
the terror. Before the terrorists, he attacked this resolution, thus continuing his policy of fostering differences

between the Battle Organization and the Central
Committee. But before the chiefs of the latter he not
only supported the resolution, but he even went further
and said that, in his opinion, the rôle of the revolutionary parties in general was at an end and that the political development of the country would now take place
under the guidance of the Liberals. Aseff, in any case,
obeyed the resolution and temporarily dissolved the
Battle Organization. This was, for him personally, the
best solution at the time. The cessation of the terror
gave him time to review the new situation, with which
he had now to cope in his police work. And, indeed, the
situation had entirely changed: the methods which
Aseff had used for a number of years in his double game
were now no longer applicable.

The changes which had taken place in the government naturally affected the leading personalities in the
Political Police. The Ministry of the Interior, which
finally controlled the Political Police, fell to P. A.
Stolypin, a newcomer to official life in St. Petersburg,
who at first felt himself very insecure and took care to
surround himself with people whom he could trust.
One of his first measures was to change the directing
body of the Police Department. Ratchkovsky was at
once deprived of practically all his power, and soon
afterwards, in June, 1906, formally dismissed. His dismissal was not due to the part he had played in organizing pogroms. Lopuhin, an intimate friend of Stolypin's,
had not delayed in informing him of Ratchkovsky's
"exploits" in this direction.

But this did not prevent Stolypin from defending the
latter in the Duma, when the question of his activities
had been raised there. For he knew very well that
Ratchkovsky was supported not only by influential

people at Court, but by the Czar himself, who had given
newly appointed governors to understand that he would
be glad if the number of Jews in their provinces could
be somewhat diminished as a result of pogroms. Stolypin
was aware of this, and therefore hoped to inspire the
confidence of the Czar by his defense of Ratchkovsky.
But the latter's Court connections made the new Minister regard him as unsuitable for the post of chief of the
Political Police: with such connections Ratchkovsky
would always be inclined to conduct his personal policy,
which would not always be in agreement with the wishes
of the Minister. He had in view for this post somebody
who would be devoted and answerable to him alone.
Ratchkovsky's position, too, was particularly preju-
diced by his close connection with Trepoff, who was
at that time trying to persuade the Czar to form a
Duma Ministry without Stolypin. Thus, by the irony of
fate, Ratchkovsky, the organizer of the pogroms,
suffered his final official defeat as a potential supporter
of the Liberal policy.

Ratchkovsky's place in the department was taken by
newcomers, such as Trussevitch and others, who were
little acquainted with police work and who therefore
had no independence of policy. In fact, it was Gerassimoff, the chief of the St. Petersburg Ochrana, who became the central figure in the Political Police world.
And indeed he proved to be one of the most influential
chiefs of the Political Police in the decade preceding the
Revolution.

Born in 1861 of plebeian origin, Gerassimoff entered
the gendarmerie in the hope of making a career for
himself: and now he was still full of initiative, energy,
and plans, in the realization of which he was ready to
sacrifice any number of people. He had found it both

difficult to enter and to gain promotion in the gendarmerie, for gendarme officers were usually recruited only
from the upper classes, and all sorts of obstacles were
put in his way. His peasant's tenacity and his talents
for police work, which soon revealed themselves, helped
him to overcome them. By 1900, his position had improved, for, in view of the growth of the revolutionary
movement, the authorities became less particular in
inquiring into the "social origin" of its gendarme officers. In February, 1905, when the police had become
disorganized throughout the Empire, and in St. Petersburg in particular, Gerassimoff was appointed head of
the St. Petersburg Ochrana. This was one of the most
responsible posts in the Russian Political Police, but
Gerassimoff soon succeeded in making it still more
important.

He came specially to the front in October–December,
1905, when the confusion among the police chiefs was
at its height. The police were afraid of taking any
measures against the open manifestations of the revolutionary movement. The revolutionary agitation was
now being conducted openly, steadily gaining new adherents and shaking the very foundations of the *ancien
régime*. Gerassimoff advocated a policy of repression.
The authorities, according to him, had only one alternative, "either the revolutionaries will use us to adorn
the St. Petersburg lamp-posts, or we must send them
to jail and the gibbet." He demanded, therefore, the
immediate arrest of the St. Petersburg Soviet of Workers' Deputies. The department chiefs, including Ratchkovsky, were opposed to these arrests for fear of provoking an outburst, which the government might not
be strong enough to crush. Gerassimoff had a hard
fight. On his insistence, a special interdepartmental

council was summoned to discuss the matter. Its chairman was Stcheglovitoff, who afterwards became Minister of Justice in the worst years of reaction, and who was shot in Moscow in September, 1918, on the sentence of the Extraordinary Commission. This council almost unanimously agreed with the Police Department. Gerassimoff was supported only by Kamishansky, who later became famous as a prosecutor in political trials.

This setback did not deter the Ochrana chief, who now urged his point of view before the Minister of the Interior, Durnovo. Here he met with no better success. According to Gerassimoff, it was Akimoff, the Minister of Justice, who came forward to his support at the last moment. On hearing of Durnovo's refusal, Akimoff declared: "We cannot afford to waste time; it's a matter of life and death." As Durnovo was still wavering, Akimoff said that he would take full responsibility on himself as Chief Public Prosecutor of the Empire, and he thereupon wrote out an authorization for Gerassimoff to effect all searches and arrests he might think necessary. Thus, in December, 1905, the fate of the St. Petersburg Soviet of Workers' Deputies was decided.

From the government point of view, the arrests took place quite smoothly: there was no explosion in St. Petersburg, and the risings in Moscow and the provinces were suppressed with little difficulty. From local reports, it soon became clear that delay in repressive measures would merely prejudice the government's chances of victory over the Revolution. After this, Durnovo had the highest respect for Gerassimoff's police talents, and he advanced him in every way.

Gerassimoff had now no grounds for disappointment over his career, but his appetite was only whetted. He was not satisfied with his position, especially as he was

still under the orders of the department, for whose
chiefs he had always the greatest contempt. He was
freed, however, from this dependence on the department
by Stolypin, who was quick to understand the importance of having the chief of the Political Police entirely
on his side. In consequence, Gerassimoff received such
privileges and influence as no other chief of the Ochrana
possessed either before or after. The department was
completely overshadowed. There was no longer any
question of its controlling Gerassimoff: he did all he
wished and dictated his will to the department. All its
secret agents now came under his supervision, and it
was to inform him of any steps it proposed to take.
The chiefs of the local Ochranas now referred all questions directly to him, and it was decided between them
what matters should be brought to the notice of the
department.

The St. Petersburg Ochrana became for a time the
actual center of all the political investigation within
the Empire, and Stolypin alone controlled its chief.
Gerassimoff made frequent and regular reports to the
Minister on all matters of any importance. Stolypin
was particularly interested in the activities of the revolutionary parties, and it was the business of the Ochrana
to provide him with inside information as to this. He
had to be kept informed, too, of the activities of the
left wing of the Duma. He entered thus into the details
of the work of the Political Police and from time to
time gave direct orders as to who should or should
not be arrested. Stolypin, in fact, was the real political
chief of this department throughout this period, that is,
from the summer of 1906 until Gerassimoff's retirement
in 1909, and, through it, of the Political Police throughout the Empire.

One of Gerassimoff's principal tasks was to organize
an efficient secret agency within the revolutionary
parties. According to Gerassimoff, the official point of
view of the department on this question impeded the
efficient working out of this system. The official ideal
held that the secret agent should in no case be an active
member of a revolutionary organization, but should
receive all his information from such members as re-
posed confidence in him. It was considered undesirable,
though admissible, that an agent should belong to the
less important organizations in which he might play a
subordinate part, but, even so, he was not supposed to
direct the activity of others. It was considered absolutely inadmissible for agents to be members of the
central executive organizations.

Such was the official conception, but it was rarely
followed in practice. The police chiefs, in a number of
cases, gave their agents direct instructions to enter into
the revolutionary executives, and we have seen that
Aseff became a member of the Battle Organization on
the instructions of his department chiefs and of Plehve
himself. In taking this course, the police chiefs realized
that, although inevitable, it was nevertheless a violation
of their principles. As a result, there was in practice a
tacit understanding between the agent and the police:
the agent became a member of such an organization,
but did not officially inform his chief of the fact, and
the chief pretended to believe that he was still merely a
"sympathizer."

Gerassimoff considered such a procedure both errone-
ous and dangerous from the police point of view. It was
obviously more difficult to control an agent whose
position within the revolutionary organization was not

officially known, and the chances of abuse were much greater. Gerassimoff, therefore, decided to legalize this "secret disease." He not only allowed his agents to become members of the revolutionary executives, but he encouraged them to do so, putting them at the same time under stricter supervision and making each of them responsible to the police for the entire activity of the organization in question.

While adopting this policy, Gerassimoff considerably changed the tactics of the police towards those revolutionary executives in which he had agents. The police problem had always been to get at the very heart of a given organization, to learn the identity of its leaders, and then to crush it at one blow. Such was Zubatoff's system. Gerassimoff, on the contrary, introduced a system by which all those revolutionary executives, where he had agents, were carefully shielded from arrest. One of the chief reasons for this policy was that had it become practically impossible to stamp out all the revolutionary organizations and to arrest all the revolutionaries now that the revolutionary movement had assumed a mass character. There would always be volunteers to take the places of those arrested. Every such arrest, too, would either compromise the police agent involved or put him out of action if arrested. In view of this, Gerassimoff judged such arrests undesirable. The police were now to approach the matter in a different way. The revolutionary executives were to be protected, but supervised in such a way that the police would be able to paralyze any action on their part.

If, for example, the revolutionaries set up a secret printing press, a dynamite factory, or a store of arms and explosives, the police were to arrest only those immediately concerned, but were to leave the executive center untouched. Individual members of the executives, who had become too dangerous, might also be arrested, but such arrests were to be made gradually, taking into account their effect on the position of the agent implicated. Those of the revolutionaries on good terms with the agent should, as far as possible, be left alone, whereas his party opponents should be arrested at the first opportunity. The wholesale arrest of the executive was permitted only at moments, for example, of political crisis, when the organization in question threatened to strike some telling blow against the government.

This policy was by no means entirely new. Its various features were present in the police work of the previous period. But Gerassimoff unified these elements in an orderly system. In its final and logically reasoned state, this system was a police Utopia. With all the necessary information at their disposal, the police were to decide whether to allow or to stop this or that action, depending on its degree of danger, or to arrest this or that revolutionary, depending on whether he was more or less able. Gerassimoff tells us that he put this system into practice before Stolypin's advent to the Ministry of the Interior, but that he had to face the opposition of the older chiefs of the department, who objected to his innovations. They even tried to bring Stolypin over to their point of view, but the latter soon understood the advantages of Gerassimoff's system and gave him *carte blanche*.

Gerassimoff failed, of course, to put his system into practice completely, in spite of his unlimited powers and funds, for even police Utopias are not so easily realized. He was able, however, to arrive at important results, and a strict "control" was established over a whole series of revolutionary executives.[1]

Aseff, who now passed under his exclusive control, proved his most valuable asset. In well-informed police circles, rumors had it that Gerassimoff had, knowing Aseff's past, given him the alternative of either serving the police "loyally" or of going to the gallows. But Gerassimoff himself declares that he never made an ultimatum of this kind; he insists, further, that Aseff's complicity in the assassinations of Plehve and the Grand Duke Sergei was unknown to him, and that Ratchkovsky, if aware of these facts, had said nothing to him of them.

It is difficult to judge whether this version is correct or not. But it is certain, and Gerassimoff himself admits it, that he had definite grounds for suspecting Aseff over the Dubassoff affair, and that he had accordingly exercised great caution in dealing with him at the beginning. But Aseff soon succeeded in dissipating these suspicions and in gaining Gerassimoff's entire confidence. In his unpublished memoirs the latter writes, "In view of Aseff's unsatisfactory explanations of the Dubassoff affair, all his reports were treated with great reserve, but, as a result of the honesty, zeal, and preci-

[1]Gerassimoff asserts that far from all of his most important agents were discovered. The activities of many of them still remain entirely unknown. This may be explained by the fact that Gerassimoff did not inform the department of their existence (it was on the evidence of the department that the names of the majority of the secret agents in St. Petersburg were discovered in 1917, for the archives of the St. Petersburg Ochrana were almost entirely destroyed in the first days of the Revolution), for he alone was in personal contact with them and, after his retirement, they likewise abandoned their police work. Gerassimoff also relates that, on retiring from the Ochrana, he gave his more responsible agents the choice of either continuing their work under his successor or of giving it up entirely, and the majority took the latter course. Of these, according to Gerassimoff, not one has so far been traced.

sion with which he carried out the duties imposed on him, all doubts of him were soon dispelled." The information he supplied was correct as far as it could be ascertained, and his knowledge of what went on inside the party was exceptional. His value quickly became apparent, and confidence grew in him.

Aseff made every possible effort to strengthen this confidence in himself and to allay any suspicions against him. He talked a great deal about his former work and played on Gerassimoff's vanity by speaking contemptuously of "their empty-headed excellencies" of the department, who did nothing but compromise him in the eyes of the revolutionaries. "He complained," writes Gerassimoff, "that his chiefs took little care of him, and he expressed surprise at being able to retain the confidence of the revolutionaries in spite of the rumors of treachery circulated against him." This seemed a satisfactory enough explanation of Aseff's past conduct, and besides, he had carefully hinted that he would work very differently now that he was under Gerassimoff's direct orders.

Aseff's victory was complete. He won Gerassimoff's full confidence, and the latter doubts even to this day the correctness of the evidence that held Aseff responsible for the assassinations of the Plehve and the Grand Duke Sergei. As to his work under Gerassimoff's direct supervision, the latter still maintains that he was sincere in every way. "During this time," Gerassimoff writes, "I assume full responsibility for all provocative acts on Aseff's part, if any such took place, and I assert that I was never deceived by Aseff, and that, therefore, the question of provocative acts is beside the point." This declaration is most overconfident, for, as we shall see, Aseff still continued to conceal a great deal from

Gerassimoff, and was, besides, preparing a blow which
would have been a thunderbolt for him.

In its essence, Aseff's relation with Gerassimoff in
no way differed from that with Ratayeff, whose confidence Aseff had gained in order to make use of it for
his own ends. The only difference lay in that Aseff's
position was now more difficult, and that he had to
pay a greater price for the confidence. Gerassimoff's
readiness to answer for Aseff even today throws a very
interesting light on their former relationship. The fact
that Aseff, who had already been compromised in the
eyes of the police, succeeded in winning the confidence
of Gerassimoff, who was usually chary of taking people
on trust, is perhaps the best evidence that he was an
astute judge of men and that he knew how to play
upon their weaknesses.

Gerassimoff based his relations with Aseff on solicitude for the latter's interests. Aseff apparently told his
chief that the department had promised him, in case of
exposure, a pension or a position as an engineer in some
remote part of the Urals. Gerassimoff frankly replied
that he must not count too much on such promises, as
the department was not in the habit of fulfilling them
honestly. Instead, he advised Aseff to save up money
for the black day, and of his own accord doubled Aseff's
salary, bringing it up to a thousand roubles a month.
"I advised him," Gerassimoff says, "not to spend his
salary, but to put it into a bank, for he had enough
money from the party for his living expenses. He followed this advice and drew up a will—which is still in
my possession—by which this money should go to his
wife on his death." At the same time, every precaution
was taken to prevent Aseff's exposure. His duties as a
secret agent were very carefully defined. He was ex-

empted from giving information, even if he had it, about the less important revolutionary activities such as illegal publishing, agitation in the provinces, and so on. "We had other sources of information as to these," says Gerassimoff.

Aseff's task was to supply information about people and events of major importance, about everything that happened in the Central Committee of the party, in its Soviet, Congresses, and Conferences, as well as about what was going on in the heart of those groups in the Duma which were working closely with the Social Revolutionaries. His special and most important task was, of course, to keep Gerassimoff informed of all that happened in the Battle Organization, for the latter had, on learning that Aseff was actually its chief, made him directly responsible for its activities to the Ochrana. In return, Gerassimoff promised to take no action against any of these revolutionary groups without previously consulting Aseff, and to keep all such information strictly secret, not even bringing it to the knowledge of the Department for fear of its leaking out.

Aseff "worked" very well. His information was extremely rich in facts, very valuable and precise. He was Gerassimoff's chief source of information as to the temper of the opposition, and that of the revolutionary groups in the Duma which, during the first months of Aseff's collaboration with Gerassimoff, occupied the central position in Russian political life. He provided the material for Gerassimoff's daily report to Stolypin, who soon took note of its value and desired to know its origin. Gerassimoff told him all he knew of Aseff. Stolypin became very much interested in Aseff's personality and, from then on, made a point of specially studying his information: when any problem of par-

ticular interest had not been sufficiently elucidated by
Aseff, he used to ask Gerassimoff to put this problem
directly to him. Later, Stolypin even expressed the wish
to meet Aseff personally in order to acquaint himself
more fully with the temper and opinions in revolutionary circles.

For various reasons Gerassimoff could not arrange
such an interview, but he often passed on those of
Stolypin's questions which were not confined to police
matters into which Gerassimoff went closely enough
himself. Stolypin was usually interested in Aseff's opinion as to the possible reaction of revolutionary groups
to this or that projected government measure, and as
to the groupings inside the Duma on this or that question. Aseff knew the source of these questions and,
undoubtedly flattered by Stolypin's attention, took
particular pains over his answers, which were the result
of expert political judgment. Gerassimoff recalls that,
on the dissolution of the first Duma, he had to commu-
nicate to Stolypin Aseff's opinion as to the possibility
of introducing into the government such moderate
Liberals as Shipoff, Gutchkoff, and others.

He likewise remembers Aseff's views of Stolypin's
agrarian reforms. Aseff favored the abolition of the old
village communal system and its replacement by peasant proprietorship as the best means of warding off the
threatened agrarian revolution. His political opinions,
according to Gerassimoff, were generally those of a
"moderate Cadet or, rather, a Left Octobrist." Stolypin
always paid the closest attention to these communica-
tions, and his only surprise was that a man of such
views could have become a member of the executive of
the Social Revolutionary party, which took up a completely different position.

Later, in the days following Aseff's exposure, all were astonished when the first government report referred to him as "an adviser of the government." All were convinced that to have called a police agent "an adviser of the government" was a pure error on the part of the compiler of the report. But, in the light of Gerassimoff's account, this expression has a definite significance. For even if it got into the report by mistake, it did sum up the real part played by Aseff during the last years of his work for the police much more accurately than the stereotyped term "police agent."

CHAPTER XIII

The Campaign of Aseff, Gerassimoff and Stolypin against the Battle Organization

THUS PASSED BY the short months of the existence of the first Duma—a period, too, of brief holiday for the Battle Organization. It soon became clear that no agreement could be arrived at between the Duma and the government, and that their dispute would have to be settled by force. In these circumstances, the party leaders began to reconsider their decision not to employ the terror.

The Sebastopol branch finally forced the hands of the Central Committee. Its leader came specially to St. Petersburg to demand permission to kill Admiral Tchuknin. His death had already been decided on soon after his suppression of the Sebastopol mutiny in November, 1905, but all the attempts on his life so far had failed. The Central Committee had now to resolve whether it would abide by its decision of two months earlier to discontinue the terror. The Sebastopol leader argued that Tchuknin's assassination, far from harming the revolutionary cause, would, on the contrary, encourage the revolutionary temper, particularly among the soldiers and sailors, who detested the admiral. This would be a great asset to the party, which was already trying to stir up mutiny. The Central Committee finally accorded its permission, and Tchuknin was soon afterwards killed by the sailor Akimoff, who made his escape after committing the deed.

The situation in Sebastopol was no exception: preparations for mutiny were everywhere in full swing, and the Central Committee now judged that individual terrorist acts could only help the rising tide of revolution. It was, therefore, decided to renew the activity of the Battle Organization. The first and only task given it was that of killing Stolypin, since there could be no doubt now that he was chiefly to blame for the rift between the government and the Duma on the question of a responsible Ministry.

It was Aseff, needless to say, who assumed leadership of the Battle Organization. He found no difficulty in enrolling the old members, the majority of whom were living in St. Petersburg or Finland, waiting for the moment to resume their work. Nor was there any lack of new volunteers. The necessary detachment was quickly formed, and it soon set to work. Their temper was of the most sanguine. The general atmosphere at the time fired people and made them believe in the success of their undertakings. Only Aseff showed himself very reserved and did not hide that he was far from sharing the general confidence. This was part of his plan, since he was, of course, arranging for the failure of the undertaking.

From the beginning, Aseff kept Gerassimoff informed of all the particulars of the renewed activity of the Battle Organization. He made no mention, however, of the Sebastopol incident, profiting, no doubt, by his right to overlook "trifles." But where St. Petersburg was concerned, the Ochrana knew all the details of the Battle Organization's plan, the names of all its members, and all that happened inside it. Arrests could have been made at any moment, but these did not enter into Gerassimoff's calculations, for Aseff had insisted that the arrest of any terrorist working under him would mean his downfall. The loss of Aseff was no part of Gerassimoff's plan, and the suppression, merely of one terrorist detachment, was far too insignificant a result of the close coöperation now established between the chief of the Ochrana and the head of the Battle Organization. The possibilities of this alliance might be exploited in a more brilliant fashion.

It was difficult, however, to find the most profitable line of action. They followed at first the line of least resistance, making no arrests but nipping every plot in the bud. Aseff could do this very well himself, since he was able to direct the terrorists on false trails. The terrorists were now keeping a lookout for Stolypin whenever he drove to see the Czar or to the Duma. By agreement with Gerassimoff, Aseff so posted the terrorists that for a considerable time they did not once succeed in catching sight of the Minister. Becoming aware of the fruitlessness of their work, they soon began to get nervous.

Aseff, noting the first results of his methods, suggested a further plan, which was both daring and original. This was to systematize the policy of frustration and thus force the terrorists and the Central Committee to the conclusion that terror on a grand scale had become impossible. The Battle Organization was to be made to work like a machine that is running at full pressure yet producing nothing of any consequence; and the terrorists were to be made to feel that they were doing all in their power but that their attempts broke themselves against an impenetrable wall. All this was to convince them and the Central Committee that the terror could not be pursued by the old methods and that the Battle Organization had, for a time at least, to be dissolved. This plan was greatly to Gerassimoff's liking, and he helped to work it out in all its details. The result was a far-reaching plan of campaign, which was to combine Aseff's party experience and authority and all the machinery of the Ochrana.

The plan was submitted for Stolypin's approval. The Minister against whose life Aseff was to pretend to organize an attempt at first hesitated and went carefully into all the details. He was apparently afraid of some hitch in the working of the "machinery" and of losing his life in consequence. But Gerassimoff guaranteed that there would be no "unfortunate accidents," and he got a similar assurance from Aseff. The latter agreed to do so because he was perfectly well aware of the strictness of the Battle Organization discipline, and that none of its members would dare to act on their own initiative. Moreover, the terrorists carried no arms during their preparatory work in order to avoid imperiling themselves needlessly in case of chance arrest. Gerassimoff also guaranteed that every possible measure

of precaution would be taken and that the terrorists
would be kept under the closest observation. Thus,
according to Gerassimoff, no real danger threatened
Stolypin, while the result of the scheme would be to put
the Battle Organization under sure and permanent
control. In the end, Stolypin was even pleased with this
plan and set the seal of his approval upon it.

Thus began the campaign of the Battle Organization
against Stolypin—a campaign, really, of Aseff, Gerassimoff, and Stolypin against the Battle Organization.

If we were to look at the work of the Battle Organization through the eyes of its members, it would seem
to be progressing normally. Secret meeting places were
arranged; some of the terrorists disguised themselves
as cabmen, others as messengers, hawkers, and so
forth. The attempt was being prepared on a grand
scale, and no expenses were spared. The treasury of the
Battle Organization was at that time full: hundreds of
thousands of roubles passed through it, and its treasurers followed the rule, now consecrated by tradition, of
satisfying all the demands of the Battle Organization
without question.

Once the initial steps had been taken, the terrorists
began their watch on Stolypin. They worked with zeal
and self-denial but without any tangible results. It was
rarely that one of them succeeded in catching sight of
the Minister as he drove by, and more often they had
to content themselves with seeing groups of Ochrana
agents, who carefully scrutinized everybody who came
their way. If they happened to get hold of some detail
which, they hoped, might enable them to take more
direct action, there invariably appeared on the horizon
some alarming sign, which not only dashed their hopes
of outwitting the police, but even made them feel

anxious for their own safety. That was the doing of Aseff's secret ally, Gerassimoff.

Aseff relied as far as possible upon his own resources and frustrated the work of the terrorists by misdirecting them. There were obviously limits to this procedure, since he had to create the illusion that the organization was doing everything in its power to achieve positive results. The terrorists, too, seeing that continual failure attended their efforts, began to show initiative and suggested plans of their own. When their independence began to importune, Gerassimoff, with Aseff's consent, resorted to "frightening" them.

To this end, the terrorists were permitted to try to put their plans into execution. Aseff criticized them beforehand but agreed to the attempts being made. The first steps raised hopes; but as soon as the terrorists' nerves became strung to their utmost, Gerassimoff let loose his "branders," as those not very competent detectives were called in Ochrana slang, who could not keep anybody under observation without making the fact immediately obvious. "We had real specialists in this line," Gerassimoff relates. "When following anybody, they almost breathed down the back of his neck. Only a blind man could fail to notice them. No self-respecting detective would accept such a mission and, besides, it would have been most inadvisable to use him in that way, as it would either spoil his work or make him too well known."

The terrorists, of course, noticed the "branders." They would immediately inform Aseff of the fact; the latter would sometimes pretend to doubt them at first and wonder whether they had not become too nervous. But examination of the evidence soon showed that the police were really on their track. Then Aseff would take the decision, which had become a rule, to abandon the plans and think only of the safety of the terrorists. And he would give them detailed instructions as to how to effect their escape. The horses, cabs, apartments, and other weapons of conspiracy, were naturally abandoned to their fate, but the terrorists safely eluded the spies.

Such "frightenings" were practised comparatively rarely, and every time the details were slightly varied. But all this helped to convince the terrorists that the police had learned their methods so well that there was no possibility of getting near Stolypin. And each time that the terrorists came together again somewhere in Finland, after a successful escape, and reviewed the past events, they all came to the conclusion that the police had come upon their tracks absolutely by chance, and that they had not even had the time to find out who they were (that is how they explained the ease with which they made their escape). But the fact that this "chance" repeated itself as often as they got anywhere near the Minister forced them to conclude that the Minister was ringed by an impenetrable wall of police protection. But as Aseff had "foreseen" the weaknesses of the terrorists' plans and had so successfully organized their escape, his authority only tended to increase, while the legend of his "coolness" and "foresight" seemingly received every confirmation.

After every such failure Aseff insinuated with ever greater insistence that the terror could not be pursued any longer by the "old methods." "The police," he said, "have become too well acquainted with our old devices. And there is nothing surprising in this, for we have still the same cabmen, hawkers, and so on, who figured in Plehve's assassination. We rely too much on the old technique to think of anything new. This is hard, but it must be admitted. . . ."

Weeks and months went by in this fashion. . . . The Duma had already been dissolved. Risings had already flared up and had been crushed in Kronstadt, Sveaborg, and Reval. A wave of terror, of widespread and sporadic partisan attempts on governor generals, gendarmes, policemen, and public buildings swept over the country. But there was no mass explosion such as had occurred in 1905. The workers, who had been the backbone of the 1905 movement, now remained silent, tired out by their defeats and worn out by unemployment and the industrial crisis. Under these circumstances the government soon overcame its temporary hesitation and set up courts-martial everywhere to cope rapidly with armed risings. Reaction grew stronger every day, and Stolypin, its chief inspirer, had already become the best hated representative of authority.

The Battle Organization, at this moment, found itself up against a competitor. The "Maximalists," who had broken away from the Social Revolutionary party and had decided to conduct a terrorist campaign of their own, were now planning an attempt on Stolypin. They organized their attempt very differently from the Battle Organization, relying on short, swift blows, without long preparatory work and observation. Thus three of its members, armed with bombs, called at Stolypin's villa at the hour of official reception. The guards suspected that all was not well and refused to let them pass. They threw their bombs in the hall. The explosion destroyed the greater part of the Minister's villa: several dozens of people lost their lives, including the guards, many callers, and, of course, the terrorists themselves. The Minister's small children were also severely injured, but Stolypin himself escaped almost without a scratch. The shock of the explosion was only slightly felt in his study.

The news of this attempt reached Aseff in Finland. It put him into a state bordering on panic. "In August, on the day that Stolypin's villa was blown up," Popova, a member of the Battle Organization working in its Finnish laboratory, writes in her Memoirs, "Ivan Nicholaievitch [Aseff] unexpectedly called upon us. He was very agitated and also seemed depressed and distraught. He sat for a time in silence, nervously turning over the pages of a railway guide. At first he wanted to spend the night with us, but then thought better of it and went off to the station."

The reasons for Aseff's agitation are clear. He was afraid that Stolypin and Gerassimoff would hold the Battle Organization responsible for the attempt; and he knew that, since he had pledged the Minister's safety with his head, he would find it much more difficult to justify himself than after the Dubassoff affair. There was the danger, too, that the Ochrana would, for want of better information, arrest those members of the Battle Organization whom it had under observation and would thus disgrace him in the eyes of the revolutionaries. That was why Aseff hastened to St. Petersburg to explain things personally to Gerassimoff.

Fortunately, at this time he enjoyed Gerassimoff's complete confidence, and the latter took no action that would have compromised him. But, in order to whitewash the Battle Organization in Stolypin's eyes, Aseff was obliged to induce the Central Committee to publish an official manifesto, disclaiming all participation of the party and of the Battle Organization in the affair, and even containing a "moral and political" condemnation of the means employed in this attempt. Such declarations were hardly in keeping with the revolutionary movement; the Central Committee had doubted its necessity, but Aseff's insistence prevailed upon them. It fell to him to draw up the text of this manifesto, which is the only official party document of which Aseff is the direct author. This manifesto was obviously of paramount importance to him. Aseff also settled his score with the "Maximalists," the organizers of the attempt. From that time onwards, he gathered all the information he could about them and brought this to notice of his police chiefs.

The Central Committee's manifesto about the "Maximalist" attempt did not meet with unanimous approval in the party. There were many who believed that terrorists should not be bound by considerations of possible accidental victims in the course of attempts organized by them. Many others thought the manifesto tactless and unnecessary, especially as the "Maximalists" had soon afterwards openly avowed their responsibility. The Central Committee's manifesto produced too strange an impression not to call for a certain amount of protest.

The ensuing discussions helped to raise the whole question of the work of the Battle Organization. "The Central Committee condemns the means employed by the Maximalists. . . . Why doesn't the Battle Organization do something better?" such was the question asked on every side in the party. Many, including even some members of the Central Committee, began to criticize the work of the Battle Organization. Some of the revolutionaries well versed in terrorist work even formed a special group, which set itself the task of controlling the work of the Battle Organization. They acted without Aseff's knowledge, and very soon established the fact that the preliminary work of the terrorists under him was being conducted on false lines.

STOLYPIN'S VILLA AFTER THE "MAXIMALIST" ATTEMPT.

This gave ground for conflict between the Battle Organization and its critics. Aseff was, of course, the principal instigator of these, but he usually preferred to remain in the background and let Savinkoff play the leading part.

Savinkoff had recently rejoined the ranks of the Battle Organization after an absence of four months made necessary by his arrest in Sebastopol. The death penalty hanging over him and his escape made him very popular in the party. The members of the Battle Organization were particularly solicitous for him. He was, after Aseff, the senior member. Entering the Battle Organization some three years previously, in the heroic days of the attempt against Plehve, he had ever since worked uninterruptedly in its ranks in the most dangerous positions. In the eyes of the younger terrorists, he was the incarnation of the history and the traditions of the Battle Organization. A close friend of Sazonoff, Kalyaeff, and Schweitzer, around whose names there had grown up a legend of enthusiastic admiration, he liked to recall the past at the rare social gatherings organized in moments of rest. He spoke with particular elation of the atmosphere of true brotherly love and confidence which had existed in the Battle Organization of those times and which he attempted to cultivate now also. He treated every member with the utmost consideration, and he wished, indeed, to become the "heart of the Battle Organization," as he was later called by one of its members, Zenzinoff.

These were the sympathetic sides of Savinkoff's character, but they were no longer so much in evidence. By nature he was intended to play ideally any secondary part as long as there was a capable leader at his elbow. Undoubtedly possessed of great courage, he had more than once looked death in the face; but his courage, that of a soldier, was of a different kind from that of a leader. Savinkoff was no leader, lacking as he did the courage of initiative, of independent decision and thought, if we think in terms of a far-reaching plan of action.

Savinkoff's misfortune was that, throughout his years of work for the Battle Organization, he relied too much upon Aseff. There can be no doubt that the latter won him by his lack of any of the doubts and scruples which were characteristic of the intellectual terrorists of the time. These latter were usually preoccupied with the problem of "the right to kill." They were convinced that the representatives of authority against whom they fought were injurious to the good of the millions, but many of them were sorely troubled with the question whether a man has the right to take the life of another under any circumstance whatsoever. And what if human life were so precious that no one had the right to take it? In search of an answer to this question, many involved themselves in flights of pure philosophy, and the peaceful Königsberg professor, Kant, would have been amazed could he have risen from his grave and seen that his Law of Nature was often the categorical imperative which compelled many of the Russian terrorists at the beginning of the twentieth century to take bombs into their hands.

Any such doubts were quite foreign to Aseff. He scarcely ever thought of his "right" to do what he did. He followed the road that was most profitable to him, and this question of profit dictated all his scruples and hesitations. Aseff could not, of course, explain the real motives of his conduct to anybody, and his contempt was therefore natural enough when such questions were raised. Why all these complex theories, when it was clear that this or that action was dictated by the in-

terests of the action itself, by the interests of the
terrorist campaign?

Savinkoff had entered the Battle Organization with
very different ideals. He devoted a great deal of thought
to these sore questions which tormented the consciences
of the terrorists; and those who held that these moods
were not the real reflection of his intimate thoughts
did not do him justice. It was not by chance that Gotz
called him "a broken Stradivarius." But his future
development depended, rather, upon the position which
by the will of fate he was to occupy within the Battle
Organization.

Those who believed in Kant's Law of Nature thought
they could kill and then pay for killing with their own
lives. Thus the best of the terrorist intellectuals gave
more thought to the question of how they themselves
would *die* than to how they would *kill* others. The latter,
from their point of view, was an unpleasant necessity,
while the former was a joyous adventure. That Savinkoff would have gone to his death as joyfully is proved
by his behavior at the time of his arrest in Sebastopol.
His misfortune, however, lay in that he was obliged to
direct his activities into other channels.

The terror had need of organizers as well as of men of
action. For a number of reasons Savinkoff became one
of the former. He still risked a great deal in his work,
but he was an adroit and talented conspirator and
always succeeded in escaping from the most difficult
situations. It was to this ability that he owed in no
small measure his position of organizer. All this is true,
but it counts for little where the final *result* is concerned.
And the result was that Savinkoff's closest friends
perished, while he himself remained alive and continued
to send others to their death.

A man in Savinkoff's position, too, was obliged,

whether he wished or not, to concentrate his thoughts
not so much on how to die, as on how to kill, that is,
on how to organize an assassination. This fact created
in him a different outlook from that which had guided
Sazonoff, Kalyaeff, and others—that of a professional
"head-hunter," and the terror tended to become for
him an end in itself.

Zenzinoff recounts in his memoirs how Gotz and he,
at the beginning of 1906, had a discussion with Savinkoff about the motives underlying their personal conduct. Zenzinoff and Gotz, who had both passed through
German universities, were Kantists in their philosophy,
and Kant's Law of Nature was at the foundation of
their terrorist conceptions. "With surprise we heard
Savinkoff say," writes Zenzinoff, "that his only categorical imperative was the will of the Battle Organization. In vain we demonstrated to him that human
consciousness could not accept the will of more or less
chance individuals as a 'Law of Nature,' and that,
from a philosophical point of view, this was mere nonsense and, from a moral point of view, terrible. But
Savinkoff could not be moved from his position." The
interests of the Battle Organization and its terrorist
activity stood higher for him than anything else.

All his concrete conclusions emanated from the same
belief. For him the party fell into two sections—the
members of the Battle Organization and all the others.
The former, his closest comrades, were to form one
compact indivisible whole joined in brotherly union for
life and death. The others, beings of lower order, had
only the right to admire them or to help them, but never
to importune them with demands or to criticize their
actions. Any criticism of the Battle Organization coming
from outsiders was considered by him as an affront
to its "honor,"—an attack which its members should

repel as one man. Savinkoff's conception of honor was purely that of an officer, and it formed an important element in that psychology of "Revolutionary Guardsmen" which Aseff cultivated within the Battle Organization and which was particularly reflected in Savinkoff's attitude. This made it easy for Aseff to use him as an instrument for putting into execution the Aseff-Gerassimoff-Stolypin plan.

Savinkoff had come back to the Battle Organization, feeling somewhat embittered by his inactivity during these critical days. Like others, he sought to explain these failures, but naturally enough he listened first of all to Aseff's version. The latter argued that the terrorist methods were out of date and that the police methods had improved. At the same time, he played upon Savinkoff's weaknesses, his conception of honor, and his irritation against the "civilian" members of the Central Committee, who dared to talk disrespectfully of the terrorists. He interpreted all criticisms of the Battle Organization as a systematic attempt to discredit its leaders and to demoralize its members. He interpreted the individual retorts of the party treasurers to Aseff's increasing demands (for Aseff, in accordance with the plan which Gerassimoff and he had worked out, had augmented the financial demands of the Battle Organization so much that the party treasurers had begun to protest) as being the result of systematic persecution and a deliberate refusal of funds for necessary expenses. Armed with these arguments, Savinkoff rushed into battle against the Central Committee.

The latter held a meeting in Finland, in September, 1906, at which the question of the Battle Organization's alleged grievances against it was raised. There were present Kraft, Natanson, Pankratoff, Sletoff, Tchernoff, and also Aseff and Savinkoff as Battle Organization representatives. Aseff, as usual, declined to talk in public and asked that Savinkoff should be invited to defend the point of view of the Battle Organization. In an eloquent and impassioned speech, Savinkoff brought forward his accusations against the Central Committee. It was a real indictment. Anticipating the reproaches against the terrorists, he charged the Central Committee with being responsible for the failures of the Battle Organization, for, he declared, "It provides neither sufficient means nor enough people for terrorist activity; it is indifferent to the terror, and not only does not feel confidence in the leaders of the Battle Organization, but is doing its best in the persons of Tchernoff and Sletoff to bring discredit on them by referring to them slightingly and with disrespect. Under such conditions the Battle Organization could not continue its work."[1] Savinkoff, with Aseff's support, demanded that the Central Committee should change its attitude, give them all their confidence and, as a guarantee, bring Tchernoff and Sletoff to trial. If this were not done, Aseff and Savinkoff threatened to give up their direction of the terror.

These accusations were as astonishing in their unexpectedness as in their lack of foundation. They not only did not answer to the real temper of the Central Committee as a whole, or of its individual members, but their fundamental assertions in most cases did not correspond with reality. It was difficult to understand how such a perversion of the facts could have arisen. The debate became very heated. Savinkoff took up a very provoking attitude, especially towards Sletoff,

---

[1] This is the account of Savinkoff's speech given in *The Conclusions of the Legal Committee of Inquiry into the Aseff Affair*, page 51, which was based upon the evidence of those present at the above meeting. In his memoirs, Savinkoff also draws upon this version of his speech.

with whom he had old scores to settle. The meeting
lasted far into the night, and the atmosphere was at
times really that of a court. On Savinkoff's demand, a
confrontation was arranged between Tchernoff and
Lapina ("Comrade Bella"), in conversation with whom
Tchernoff was alleged to have spoken insultingly of the
terrorists. With considerable difficulty the quarrel was
partly smoothed down. No mention was made of the
failures of the Battle Organization and of the necessity
of changing its working methods, for Savinkoff's
maneuver had shifted the whole ground of discussion.
A vote of confidence was passed in the Battle Organization, and Savinkoff, moreover, was elected a member of
the Central Committee.

This collision gave Aseff further confirmation of the
strength of his position in the Battle Organization and
the Central Committee, and he now prepared to execute
the final part of his plan. After this meeting he tried
particularly hard to win over Natanson and Tchernoff
to his side. In long heart-to-heart talks he enlarged
upon his point of view as to the causes of the "Battle
Organization crisis." He definitely went back upon
Savinkoff's attack on the Central Committee. He held
that the attack was an expression of a mood prevalent
among the terrorists who, conscious of the failure dog-
ging their efforts, had become nervous and were ready
to blame anybody. In its essence the matter did not lie
in the behavior of the Central Committee or in the
tactlessness of its individual members. Savinkoff had
unwisely sidetracked the discussion from its real business—that of examining the reasons for the failure of
the Battle Organization.

The real reasons were very different. The truth must
be faced courageously; the old methods of the Battle
Organization were out of date, the police had learned

them and knew how to forestall any attempts, and it was, above all, true that nothing new could be evolved from the old methods. New ways must be found. The employment of the newest technical discoveries might provide these. Aseff put particular hope at this moment in mines which, according to him, opened great possibilities for the terror. But considerable preparatory work was necessary for this, and he suggested the "logical conclusion" of dissolving the Battle Organization and of discontinuing the terror. The interruption, of course, would be only temporary and would be used for the preparation of new and more decisive blows. Aseff and Savinkoff would go abroad and study the up-to-date technique of mining, and they would in a few months' time send in a report as to what terrorist action the party might take. Aseff used all his powers of persuasion, and he was very much surprised when it became clear that even those members of the Central Committee who were habitually his closest supporters disagreed with him. The cessation of the terror, even though temporary, seemed absolutely inadmissible to most of the members.

Aseff's plan was more favorably received by the Battle Organization. Savinkoff tried to combat it by putting forward plans of his own, and Aseff let him do so, for he was sure that Gerassimoff and he would be able to thwart them. There seemed, indeed, no possibility of getting anywhere near Stolypin. After the Maximalist attempt against him, Stolypin had been invited by the Czar to take up residence in the Winter Palace, and he lived there almost without leaving the grounds except for rare visits to the Czar in Peterhoff. On these occasions he usually went by water, embarking on an official steamboat at the Winter Palace, and he was so well guarded that the terrorists could do nothing. Savinkoff had the idea of dropping bombs from one of the Neva bridges as the boat passed under it, but it was discovered that the bridges were always carefully guarded at the time, and that the steamboat raced under them at full speed. Savinkoff then proposed an attack on Stolypin at the moment of embarkation, but in view of the strong guard this plan was no more feasible than the other.

Thus, one after another, Savinkoff's projects came to nothing, and he finally went over to Aseff's side. A meeting of the Central Committee was due in October, and this was to be followed by the second session of the party Soviet. Aseff and Savinkoff decided to hand in their resignations. Aseff was convinced of the success of this maneuver and guaranteed to Gerassimoff that the Soviet would pass a resolution to stop the terror.

All the members of the Battle Organization working in St. Petersburg were recalled from their posts and ordered to go to Finland. Here, at the Battle Organization headquarters, situated in the Tourist Hotel, Imatra Falls, a meeting was held of the twenty members present. Aseff had taken care to acquaint them beforehand with the motives of his decision, while Savinkoff made a public statement of them. The terrorists were formally asked whether they would abide by this decision or whether they would continue to work independently of Aseff and Savinkoff. It was difficult to dispute the authority of this decision. The majority agreed with the conclusions put before them, and one of the members, Popova, even thought it her duty to express publicly her profound respect for the chiefs of the organization, who had "so thoroughly examined the situation and who had so generously shouldered the blame for the late failures." Though no formal decision was formulated at this meeting, it made it possible for Aseff and Savinkoff to put forward their views as those of the Battle Organization in general at the next session of the Central Committee.

This session was held in the same Tourist Hotel, and was attended by Argunoff, Kraft, Natanson, Rakitnikoff, Sletoff, as well as by Aseff and Savinkoff. The latter made a detailed report on the causes of the failures of the Battle Organization and declared that they could no longer see their way to continuing their work.

Although the Central Committee was prepared for some such attitude on the part of the terrorists, nevertheless, their brusque declaration made a startling impression. It was followed by an impassioned discussion. As the chiefs of the Battle Organization remained adamant, the Central Committee decided to summon a general meeting of all the terrorists, a really revolutionary measure, as it implied the intention on the part of the Central Committee to incite the rank and file of the Battle Organization to revolt against its acknowledged leaders. Natanson, Tchernoff, and Sletoff were chosen to parley with the terrorists, and Aseff and Savinkoff, though obviously indignant, were unable to protest formally against this.

Tchernoff was the principal spokesman at the meeting which followed, and he detailed the reasons why the Central Committee opposed the cessation of the terror. According to Tchernoff's later account, he was soon surprised to notice from individual remarks that the terrorists were far from being solidly behind Aseff and Savinkoff. As the debate proceeded it became clear that not only was there no such solidarity, but that a number of terrorists were dissatisfied with the bureaucratic centralization introduced by Aseff and Savinkoff. The first to speak in this strain was Vnorovsky, the brother of the man who perished in the attempt against Dubassoff.

He attributed the late failures to Aseff's suppression of all personal initiative on the part of the terrorists, and he insisted on the remodeling of the organization on a democratic basis. Savinkoff made a bitter attack on Vnorovsky, but the latter found some supporters. A number of other terrorists agreed that the political situation did not warrant the cessation of the terror. Thus the united front of the Battle Organization was quickly broken, and it became clear to the Central Committee that the resignations of Aseff and Savinkoff would not be followed by those of all the terrorists. As a result, the Central Committee accepted their resignations and dissolved the Battle Organization but, in its place, formed a special "Battle Organization attached to the Central Committee," with more limited powers, from those of the terrorists who were anxious to continue in the terror.

Zilberberg was appointed its chief. A former student of mathematics, gifted with considerable mathematical talents,[1] he was a fine organizer and a daring terrorist. But he had from the beginning of his terrorist work fallen under the exclusive influence of Aseff and Savinkoff and had supported them against the Central Committee. As he had been one of the first to refuse to work under the leadership of Sletoff, there can be

[1]Arrested in February, 1907, and condemned to death, Zilberberg became engrossed during his last days in the geometrical problem of trisecting an angle and wrote a short treatise on the subject which he sent from prison to the Academy of Science. The Police Department, however, confiscated the treatise, and it was kept in the police archives until the Revolution of 1917, when it was brought to light and published.

no doubt that his later change of mind and his consent to
lead the new Battle Organization was made with Aseff's
and Savinkoff's approval. Zilberberg was actuated by
motives of terrorist honor, but Aseff's motives were, of
course, very different. Now that he was no longer the
terrorist chief, Aseff's principal concern was to have at
the head of the terrorist movement somebody whose
confidence he could command and from whom he might
learn all the necessary details.

Aseff could not take part in the later stages of these
discussions, as he had fallen seriously ill; he developed
an abscess in the throat, and his condition was for a
time critical. His closest friends in the Central Committee feared that they might have made him feel that
they mistrusted him, and they now showed him every
consideration. In spite of his illness, Aseff followed with
lively interest the discussions and the sessions of the
party Soviet, which opened soon afterwards. Nor did
he conceal his irritation against those terrorists who
had helped to bring about his defeat. As an illustration
of this we have the cases of Popova and several others
to whom Aseff soon afterwards supplied "safe passports" which almost cost them their liberty, for he had
given a list of these to Gerassimoff, who himself dis-
tinctly remembers Popova's alias among them.

Such was Aseff's revenge. The Battle Organization,
too, had been dissolved, formally, at any rate. The
terror, however, was continued, and the conflict over
the Battle Organization had only helped to concentrate
the revolutionary energies on the terror. In the end,
Aseff, Gerassimoff, and Stolypin, who had planned the
big campaign against the Battle Organization, were
obliged to admit that the results obtained were purely
negative.

CHAPTER XIV

The Terror without Aseff

SOON AFTER the party Soviet had finished its work, Aseff went abroad to recuperate. "I have been in the terror since the days of Gershuni, and I have a right to rest," he said. He settled down with his wife in Alassio, on the Italian Riviera. His wife gave him every care and attention, for she thought that he was all the time going about with a "rope round his neck." He was also treated with respect by the members of the Russian colony, who were for the most part old revolutionaries. Aseff rested, regained his strength, talked much of the hardships of a terrorist's life, and only from time to time broke away to divert himself in Monte Carlo on the pretext of party business.

He did not for a moment let his interest in party matters and in the terror relax. Before leaving Russia, he had got hold of all the information he could as to the future plans of the terrorists, and he continued to receive information in Alassio, but this was limited by the dangers of using the post, and he learned the more technical details only from terrorists who chanced to visit him, very often after the plans had been put into practice.

Aseff, on his side, busied himself in fulfilling the promise, and studied the possibilities of applying the latest technical inventions to the terror. His conversations on this theme were accidentally given a more concrete form, for he was told of an inventor named Buchallo, who was working on a flying machine. This inventor was an anarchist in his opinions, and, as he thought the Czar's assassination of primary importance, he was prepared to hand his machine over to the Battle Organization for that purpose. Aseff eagerly followed this up and went specially to Munich to see the inventor, with whom he went over the technical details of his invention. His conclusions, as a specialist, were that Buchallo had theoretically solved the problem of flying, and that it only remained to get hold of funds for establishing a workshop and obtaining the necessary materials; and, if the party were to provide the money, the machine would be soon ready and the Czar's assassination easily carried out.

These declarations made an impression. They were thought feasible by many. We must not forget that this was in the winter of 1906–07, that is, at the time of the first successes of the "heavier than air" flying machines, and that the possibility of an invention which would solve the problem of flying at one blow seemed

more than likely. This explains the comparative ease
with which Aseff was able to put his plan into execution. The necessary funds, some twenty thousand
roubles, were found and, under Aseff's control, the
inventor set to work.

These activities and the extent of his general information define the contents and tone of his letters
to his police chiefs. He had given the general outline of
the terrorist plans and groups to Gerassimoff before
leaving Russia. Now he communicated only supple-
mentary details and directions. He wrote in detail
about Buchallo's invention, regarding it as a means of
exhausting the party treasury.[1] From time to time
he forwarded some information concerning the party
centers, but this was almost always too late to be of
practical value to the police. The general tone of Aseff's
letters was reassuring. "There is no need for alarm.
Nothing serious will happen!" Such was the note on
which almost all his letters ended. Gerassimoff, however, found it increasingly difficult to follow this advice,
as the new situation in the terrorist organizations was by
no means reassuring.

The Battle Organization had monopolized the terror;
all terrorist work was centralized and was entirely under
Aseff's control. No step could be taken without his
knowledge and consent. But now this monopoly had
come to an end, and terrorist work branched off on

[1]Buchallo's experiments gave no practical results; he disappeared, and
nothing is known of his ultimate fate. There is, however, no ground for
assuming that all his plans were impracticable. There is no doubt that Aseff
regarded them in a more serious light than he conveyed in his letters to Gerassimoff. After his arrest in 1915, the Berlin police found among his papers the
designs of Buchallo's machine, and explanatory notes. Making his escape
from Paris, Aseff, it would seem, did not forget to take these among his most
valued papers, and he would scarcely have done so had he thought Buchallo's
project was nonsense.

several different lines. Each terrorist group had still
to be approved of by the Central Committee, but this
sanction was easily granted to individual groups. As a
result, soon after the dissolution of the Battle Organization, three distinct terrorist groups made their appearance in St. Petersburg.

In the first place, there was a group composed of the
old members of the Battle Organization under the
leadership of Zilberberg. A second group was formed
also by members of the Battle Organization for the
special purpose of making an attempt against Von
Launitz, the St. Petersburg commandant. This group
was commanded by Lapina, who was known in the
party as "Comrade Bella."

The third group consisted of terrorists who had no
connection with the Battle Organization. Its chief was
Prauberg, known as "Karl," a Lett who had taken an
active part in the 1905 risings in the Baltic provinces. He
came to St. Petersburg in the summer of 1906 and soon
made a reputation for himself as a talented organizer
and terrorist. By November, 1906, he succeeded in form-
ing a small and independent terrorist group, which he
offered to put at the disposal of the Central Committee.

This group was sanctioned only after a heated debate.
Savinkoff in particular was strongly opposed to the
recognition of "Karl's" group, whom he regarded as
mere interlopers. In his opinion both their attitude and
their methods were contrary to those of the "aristocrats
of the terror" whom Aseff and he had educated. He
considered any approval of this group an act of sacrilege
and demanded that the Central Committee should for-
bid it to take any part in the terror.

Savinkoff's campaign failed, however. In Aseff's absence his influence in the Central Committee was very

much weakened. He was regarded as an impressionist and a very bad judge of men. Such people as Argunoff and Tchernoff had the most favorable opinions about "Karl," and the Central Committee therefore approved of this group which was now named, "The Flying Terrorist Detachment of the Northern Region."

Savinkoff, however, persisted in his hostility to "Karl," and there can be no doubt that Aseff egged him on. Aseff had good reason to do so, for "Karl's" was the only terrorist group about which he had no sources of inside information. All that he knew of it at the time was its leader's pseudonym, and of this he duly informed Gerassimoff, stressing the important rôle which "Karl" was beginning to play, and urging that every effort should be made to establish his identity and learn his plans.

On Aseff's departure, Gerassimoff at first intended to combat the terrorists by pursuing the same policy which he had so successfully applied in association with Aseff. He avoided making arrests and attempted to keep the terrorists under "control." But in this he was unsuccessful. By chance, those terrorists who had been given passports by Aseff had been obliged to change them, and they did this so quickly and so cleverly that they managed to elude police observation. These persons were the only links that Gerassimoff had for keeping the Zilberberg and Lapina groups under observation. Furthermore, the new terrorist groups had changed their methods, and there were no more cab drivers and hawkers to put the police on their trail. The terrorists now depended on useful information provided them by the party organizations, and this made them more rapid and elusive. They could be caught only by means of inside information, but this, in Aseff's absence, was far from adequate. Gerassimoff now only received information of what went on in the Central Committee, but no details at all as to the plans or members of the terrorist groups.

Very soon after Aseff's departure the Ochrana found itself completely in the dark as to the activity of the terrorists. The consequences of this were not slow in showing themselves. Beginning with December, 1906, the terrorists succeeded in carrying out a number of attempts. On December 15th a second attempt was made against Dubassoff; Von Launitz was killed on January 3d; the chief military prosecutor, General Pavloff, was killed on January 8th; and Gudima, the governor of the temporary prison in St. Petersburg, who had distinguished himself for cruelty to political prisoners, was also killed, on January 30th.

Of these attempts only that against Von Launitz was organized by Zilberberg's group, all the others being executed by "Karl's." The Ochrana was quite powerless in all these cases. The most it knew was that an attempt was to be made against such and such a person, but it had no inkling as to the means by which the attempt was to be carried out. The assassination of Von Launitz is particularly characteristic. It was organized impromptu and was intended to deal a double blow. Information had been received from a secret source that the official opening ceremony of the Institute of Experimental Medicine would take place in a few days' time and that Stolypin's presence was expected. The informers also promised to supply tickets to the terrorists. Zilberberg eagerly seized this opportunity and got the permission of the Central Committee for the deed. The attempt was to be made by Sulyatitsky, the soldier who had rescued Savinkoff from prison, and Kudryavtzeff, a former student. The former was to shoot Stolypin and the latter Von Launitz, who had previously been Governor of Tamboff, where he had crushed peasant risings with great cruelty. Kudryavytzeff had worked as an agitator in Tamboff at that time and had sworn that he would take revenge on Von Launitz. Now his chance had come.

Gerassimoff learned of the intended attempt the day before it was to take place. The agent who gave him the information knew nothing beyond the fact that the attempt was to take place within the next few days. Gerassimoff at once called on Stolypin and warned him not to leave the Winter Palace till the police were in full possession of the facts. On the further entreaty of his wife, Stolypin canceled all his public engagements for the next few days. This saved his life. Von Launitz, on the other hand, refused to follow Gerassimoff's advice. According to the latter, there had been friction between them of late in connection with the "Union of the Russian People," which was opposing Stolypin. Gerassimoff, who had helped to found this "Union," had by that time become disillusioned, and Von Launitz regarded him as an enemy.

Sulyatitsky and Kudryavtzeff arrived for the ceremony in the Institute in faultless evening dress specially ordered for the occasion. After the religious service the guests went in to lunch. By that time it was evident that Stolypin was not coming, and Sulyatitsky left, as had been arranged. Kudryavtzeff, letting Von Launitz come close to him at a corner of the staircase, killed him with three shots from his Browning, and then, not wishing to be taken alive, killed himself. His identity was not established for a considerable time, and the police, putting his head in spirit, exhibited it publicly for identification. . . .

After this assassination, Stolypin suggested to Gerassimoff that he should take extra measures for the suppression of all terrorist groups. The system of waiting in order to paralyze the activity of the terrorists had ended in complete fiasco. The terrorists had, instead, commenced to deal telling blows against the government.

From Aseff the police learned the address of the Finnish base of Zilberberg's group, which had organized the assassination of Von Launitz and had almost succeeded in attempting Stolypin's life. As it was the only group whose trail the police could follow, they decided to suppress it, and an expedition was sent to its headquarters at the Tourist Hotel, which was off the main road. The clientele led a very secretive life. The whole hotel was at their disposal, for the proprietress was a sympathizer and so were all the Finnish servants. No outsiders were admitted, and if any chance travelers happened to come that way they were told that there were no rooms vacant. But late one evening in January the manager admitted two travelers, a man and a woman, wearing ski-ing dress, who turned out to be students. They said that they had lost their way in the forest, that they were tired and cold, and asked to be put up for the night: as the weather was shockingly bad and a snowstorm was threatened, it was impossible to refuse their request. Next day it was discovered that these unexpected visitors were possessed of the most varied talents: they sang, they danced, they talked wittily, and were able to bring a smile to the gloomiest face. They were soon on the most friendly terms with all those living in the hotel, and, as no one suggested that they should depart, they stayed on for several days. They finally left, taking with them the good wishes of everybody. No one had the slightest suspicion that these "students" were Gerassimoff's agents, who had succeeded not only in obtaining the photographs of everybody in the hotel, but also in persuading two of the servants, the porter and a maid, to enter the service of the police.

The results of this visit were not long in making themselves felt. The "students," and later the hotel porter, began to keep careful watch on the trains arriving from Finland at the St. Petersburg railway station. They soon pointed out Sulyatitsky and Zilberberg to the police, who arrested them. The porter and the maid officially identified them as men who had frequently been in the company of Von Launitz's murderer, and, on the strength of this evidence, they were both condemned to death by court-martial and executed on July 29, 1907. Although the Ochrana had been informed by Aseff of all particulars regarding them, it thought it advisable not to bring these before the court lest the suggestion of provocation might be raised, and they were executed under their assumed names of Gronsky (Sulyatitsky) and Shtiftar (Zilberberg).

These arrests dealt a heavy blow to Zilberberg's group, but they did not alter the course of the terror, as even this group was not put out of action, plenty of volunteers being found to replace those arrested. Gerassimoff saw clearly that he could not cope with the terror without Aseff, and that Aseff must, at all costs, be put back in his former position. It did not take long to persuade Aseff. Gerassimoff recalls that he had a feeling even then that Aseff had already grown tired of his "rest," of his tranquil family life, and that he was looking forward to St. Petersburg, with its easy money and gay life.

CHANCE FAVORED ASEFF in finding an excuse for resuming his revolutionary activities. Gershuni had shortly before made his escape from Siberia. He had been smuggled out of the prison yard in a barrel of sauerkraut and then sent out of the country with all precautions by way of Vladivostok and Japan to America. His trip through America was a triumphal procession, and he returned to Europe in 1907 in high spirits and with a large sum of money collected in America for the needs of the Russian revolution.

Gershuni, of course, saw Aseff very soon after his arrival. He looked on Aseff as on a disciple who had even

212

outdone his teacher. Rumors of Aseff's successes against Plehve and the Grand Duke Sergei had reached him even in prison. He could not reconcile himself to his withdrawal from the terror, and he urged him to go back to the Battle Organization. Aseff pretended to be convinced and agreed to go back, if not into the Battle Organization, which was difficult in view of his former declaration, at least to active party work. He accompanied Gershuni to Finland and arrived in time for the second Congress of the Social Revolutionary party, which met in Tammerfors at the end of February, 1907. Gershuni took part under the assumed name of Kapustin.[1] But all those present were aware of his real identity, and the first session developed into an enthusiastic ovation of him.

Aseff, as the man who had helped Gershuni to lay the foundations of the party, now came in for a share of reflected sympathy. His return to active work seemed to be a guarantee of renewed solidarity cemented by Gershuni. Aseff was therefore welcomed and once more elected a member of the Central Committee. But it was only Gerassimoff who had any real cause to welcome Aseff's return, for the police had now restored to them their regular source of information. Moreover, Aseff at once supplied his chief with all those details about the terrorist groups which the police had been unable to obtain, and particularly information about the survivors of Zilberberg's group, and this permitted Gerassimoff and Stolypin to bring on the trial which was famous in its day as "The Conspiracy against the Czar."

The arrests of Zilberberg and Sulyatitsky were a severe blow to their group, but they did not break it up

---

[1]*Kapusta*—cabbage. Obviously a playful reminder of Gershuni's original escape.

or undermine its activity. This group had a reserve of volunteers and influential connections, which enabled it, before the arrest of its chief, to project such grandiose plans as an armed attack on the Winter Palace with the object of killing Stolypin and the blowing up of the Grand Duke Nicholas's train. The group's connections were so powerful that even an attempt against the Czar himself seemed feasible.

The most outstanding of this group's new volunteers was Nikitenko. A lieutenant in the Black Sea Fleet, he was not connected with the revolutionary movement until after the Sebastopol rising in November, 1905. The mine-layer *Dunai*, on which he was then serving, did not join in the revolt, and Nikitenko was obliged, though very much against his will, to support the authorities. He commanded the detachment which had orders to occupy the cruiser *Otchakoff*, one of the ships to mutiny, after it had been shelled by the land batteries and forced to surrender. Nikitenko was the first to step aboard, and he never forgot the picture which met his eyes. The deck was running with blood and was "strewn with killed and wounded, many of whose bodies had been ripped open or whose legs and arms had been torn off." Human nerves reacted much more violently to such impressions in those days than now, after the bloody nightmares of the Great War and the civil wars that followed it. Nikitenko was affected to the point of hallucination and, as a result, resigned his commission, but only to join the ranks of the active revolutionaries.

Shortly afterwards, Nikitenko chanced to meet the members of the Battle Organization, who had successfully planned Savinkoff's escape from the Sebastopol prison, and who were now trying to get him away in a sailing boat. This was the only comparatively safe way of getting him out of the town, which was surrounded by troops. An experienced sailor was required for the expedition. Nikitenko volunteered for the undertaking and carried it out with brilliant success, in spite of a storm which overtook them in the open sea. He safely reached a Rumanian port and returned without rousing the suspicion of the authorities. Savinkoff and Zilberberg had had every opportunity for judging Nikitenko, and they welcomed him when, at the end of 1906, he offered his services for terrorist work.

Nikitenko, who was living in St. Petersburg as a retired naval lieutenant and was in no way connected with the police, was a real find for the terrorists. He was able to move in circles to which the revolutionaries as a rule had no possibility of access; it is enough to say that he was a member of the English Club, which was frequently visited by the Grand Duke Nicholas, one of the prospective victims of the Battle Organization. Nikitenko could easily have assassinated the Grand Duke, and he suggested doing so. His suggestion, however, was vetoed: his daring and initiative made him a potential leader of the terrorists, and he was being reserved for this. And, as a matter of fact, Nikitenko did succeed Zilberberg in the leadership of his group after the latter's arrest, although he was not only a junior, but also one of the youngest members (he was only two or three and twenty).

The most difficult and complex of all the undertakings which had fallen on his shoulders was that of the conspiracy against the Czar. The plan had already been formulated in Zilberberg's time. Zilberberg had entered into relations with a certain Naoumoff, the son of the manager of the Palace telegraph office in New Peterhoff, and had made friends with him in order to learn the

time of Stolypin's and the Grand Duke Nicholas' visits
to the Czar. Naoumoff had also told him that he knew a
cossack in the Czar's Guard, who was sympathetic
to the revolutionaries. This suggested the possibility
of an attempt against the Czar, and Naoumoff even
sketched out several plans which seemed to promise success. All these, of course, were merely fragmentary ideas
which had to be examined and worked out in detail.

The problem raised by this information was very
complex. The question of killing the Czar had been
discussed before, but the party had so far taken no
practical steps. The decision of the party in 1902,
which had forbidden the Battle Organization to attempt the Czar's life, was to all intents and purposes
still in force. But the general situation had radically
changed in the five years following. In 1902 the Czar
had seemed to hold himself aloof from the political
struggles of the day. Very few were aware of what he
really represented. The peasant masses still believed in
a "Father Czar," who had the good of his people at
heart, and all the first manifestations of discontent were
directed exclusively against such representatives of
authority as the Ministers, who were alleged to conceal
the real truth of the sufferings of the people from the
Czar.

In their agitation work the revolutionaries had to
take this feeling into consideration and to avoid making
any direct attack on the Czar. Even during the Revolution of 1905, it frequently happened that people who
had been listening sympathetically to revolutionary
speeches would interrupt the orator if he ventured to
criticize the Czar. There was the danger that a terrorist
attempt against the Czar would not be understood by
the people and would only alienate those elements which

were still wavering. The events of 1905 and 1906, however, had involved the Czar in the political struggles of the day and had made him personally responsible in the eyes of the masses for the actions of his Ministers. Antimonarchical agitation, and that personally directed against Nicholas II, had made great strides.

The Social Revolutionary party had, in the autumn of 1904, decided to manage its agitation in such a way as to prepare the ground politically for a possible attempt against the Czar. By 1906–07, many of the party members thought that the political question of the Czar's assassination had been settled, and that only the technical question remained to be resolved on the first opportunity.

In any case, the decision did not rest with Zilberberg: he consulted Kraft, the Battle Organization representative on the Central Committee, who, in his turn, referred the matter to Tchernoff and Natanson. They came to the conclusion that, though the time was ripe for such an attempt, the moment was unfavorable, as the parties of the Left were gaining heavily in the elections for the second Duma. On this occasion the Social Revolutionary party was formally participating in the election, and it was already clear that it would be well represented in the future Duma. Under these circumstances, the Czar's assassination was inadvisable. But such a step could be appropriately taken if the Duma were dissolved. Zilberberg was therefore told to collect as much useful information for the attempt as he could, and his activity was restricted to this.

That was the state of affairs when Nikitenko assumed leadership of the group. The complexity of the problems apparently confused him; for, besides collecting information about the Czar, he was at the same time

directing attempts against Stolypin and the Grand
Duke Nicholas. It was natural, therefore, that he
eagerly seized the opportunity to consult Aseff, the old
and experienced chief of the Battle Organization, who
had just returned from abroad. They met in Finland in
February or March, 1907, and Nikitenko initiated Aseff
into all the details of his plan. He even wanted Aseff to
assume the leadership of his group. But Aseff emphati-
cally declined to do so. One of the reasons given by him
for his refusal was that he could not guarantee that
there would be no *agent provocateur* in the group, as he
was not personally acquainted with all its members.
This excuse was all the more pertinent as he intended to
betray the group himself.

This did not prevent him, however, from advising
Nikitenko; he insisted that greater energy should be
displayed in collecting information about the Czar,
and he also counseled that closer relations should be
established with the cossack indicated by Naoumoff.
Nikitenko followed this advice, although the cossack
did not inspire great confidence in him.

And, in reality, Ratimoff, as this cossack was called,
played a decisive rôle in the fate of the group as a whole
and of Nikitenko personally, for, at the orders of his
chiefs, he was acting as a secret agent. Strong and handsome, a hard drinker, Ratimoff belonged to that type of
unreliable guardsman who had been corrupted by the
temptations of life in the capital. This type was well
known to those who were engaged in revolutionary work
in the army, and they knew that such men, though they
could talk glibly on any theme and pretend to sym-
pathize with progressive ideas, had really neither faith
nor convictions, and were ready to betray all and sundry
for the sake of material gain.

That was precisely how Ratimoff acted. Seeing at once that he had to do with a revolutionary, and knowing that the authorities were ready to reward informers, Ratimoff ingratiated himself into Naoumoff's confidence, took the revolutionary proclamations given him, but soon after reported this to his superiors. This report, in the end, reached the gendarme Colonel Spiridovitch, who commanded the Palace Police. Spiridovitch was a disciple of Zubatoff and a specialist in detective work; he was also very anxious to be of signal service to the Czar. His strict duty was to have Naoumoff arrested immediately on a charge of revolutionary propaganda, but that would mean that Naoumoff would get off with a year or two in a fortress, while he, Spiridovitch, would get very little credit. Instead, he instructed Ratimoff to keep up his relations with Naoumoff and to learn all he could; and his own agents at the same time kept watch on Ratimoff. This continued for some six months without giving any particular results until, one day, the cossack's evidence was given added significance by more important information provided by Aseff.

Almost immediately following his interview with Nikitenko, Aseff had informed Gerassimoff of the composition and plans of Nikitenko's group, and had further stated that the group had "established some sort of relations with the Czar's Guard." He urged that particular attention should be paid to this information, as the Central Committee had decided upon the assassination of the Czar and had given the group orders to take action.

This made it possible for the Ochrana to set a watch on Nikitenko and the terrorists working under him. But they failed to discover the link with the Czar's Palace.

Gerassimoff relates that he was already on the point of suppressing the group by arrest and banishment, since he was afraid that the terrorists might, for lack of evidence to bring them to trial, elude his observation and take action. It was at this moment, however, that the Palace Police told Gerassimoff of its relations with the cossack informer, who was in touch with terrorists aiming at the Czar's life. The evidence now in the hands of Spiridovitch and Gerassimoff was sufficient to enable them to stage a trial of the first importance.

The evidence thus collected was brought before Stolypin, for the question had become of too great political significance to be decided by the police alone. This fell in very well with Stolypin's plans, and he grasped at the opportunity of staging a sensational trial which became known as the "Conspiracy against the Czar." The second Duma was about to meet at this time. In composition it was more Left than the first. Stolypin aimed from the beginning at a new dissolution and a change in the fundamental laws. Since it had been organized by the Social Revolutionary party, which had over thirty official representatives in the Duma, the "Conspiracy against the Czar" would help to compromise the Duma in the eyes of the Czar and the monarchical-minded section of the population.

As soon as the trial had been decided upon, Gerassimoff was instructed to carry out all the preparatory work. This was not difficult. Ratimoff had one or two more interviews with the terrorists; these were carefully watched by the police, who were to act as additional witnesses of the facts. Documentary evidence was likewise carefully collected. The terrorists had asked the cossack to send them code telegrams as to the times of the visits of Stolypin and the Grand Duke

Nicholas to the Czar, but he had only done so on the eve of the terrorists' arrest, and these telegrams figured later, at the trial, as important but patently manufactured evidence.

When the collected evidence seemed sufficient, the cossack was asked to write an official declaration, which Gerassimoff revised and made effective. The arrests were made on the night of April 14th. Some twenty-eight members of the Battle Organization, and those connected with it, were taken. Very few escaped the net spread for them; the group was entirely smashed. The preliminary investigation reserved a pleasant surprise for the authorities: Naoumoff, knowing that he was in danger of being sentenced to death, lost his nerve and made a full confession. He was, of course, a newcomer to the terror and was spiritually unprepared for the end which every terrorist must expect. His confession naturally strengthened the case for the prosecution.

According to his plan, Stolypin at once made use of these arrests for political ends. At his instigation, the reactionary members of the Duma asked the government to make a statement on the "Conspiracy against the Czar," rumors of which had disquieted them. In his reply Stolypin asserted that the Battle Organization had been preparing an attempt on the Czar's life on the direct order of the Central Committee. The Social Revolutionary deputies found themselves in an awkward predicament: if their party had really been plotting against the Czar, the *political* responsibility would fall on them as the official representatives of the party in the Duma. They were not, of course, directly in touch with the Battle Organization and were ignorant of its plans. But Tchernoff, whom they questioned, categorically denied Stolypin's assertion. On the basis of this denial, the deputy Shirsky contradicted Stolypin's assertions in the Duma, but his words did not carry conviction. Thus Stolypin had succeeded in bringing confusion into the ranks of the Moderate and Progressive parties in the Duma and in having a monarchist resolution passed.

This was undoubtedly a victory for Stolypin. But in so far as he was counting upon a wave of monarchist feeling throughout the country, he was fated to experience a bitter disappointment: the attempts of the monarchist organizations to rouse "a storm of patriotic indignation" completely failed. The manifestations organized by them with the support of the authorities bore a purely official character and evoked no response from the masses. The news of a projected attempt on the Czar's life met at the best with indifference and, in many cases, with obvious regret at its failure. The political conclusions of this were clear. There could be no doubt now that the assassination would not produce a reaction in favor of the monarchy. The ground for such an attempt had thus been prepared in the psychology of the masses.

Eighteen of the arrested terrorists were handed over to courts-martial. The trial took place at the end of August. The prosecution concentrated its attention on the attempt against the Czar. In view of the attitude taken by the Central Committee, the accused found their political position very difficult: they were obliged to make statements in harmony with the position adopted by the Central Committee, and they could not therefore defend themselves with sufficient force.

The sentence, of course, had been fixed beforehand. Naoumoff, it is true, went back on a part of his confession, but this did not help the others and proved fatal to himself, for it gave the authorities an excuse to break their promise to spare his life,[1] and, together with Nikitenko and the former student Sinyavsky, he was condemned to death. The sentences were carried out on September 3, 1907. The other terrorists were sent to penal servitude or banished.

Gerassimoff was the hero of the trial. He had refused to give evidence in court on the pretext that his life was in danger from the revolutionaries, and the Court had assembled specially at the Ochrana to hear his evidence. He was hailed as the man who had saved the Czar's life, and, a few days after the execution of the terrorists, the Czar, on his own initiative, promoted him General. The Czar, of course, knew nothing of the political intrigues which had brought about the trial, but he had always thought it necessary to encourage the chiefs of the Political Police. This was a tradition of the House of Romanoff.

[1] If there were any doubts as to the real reasons for Naoumoff's execution, they were resolved on the publication of Spiridovitch's memoirs. Their author states that Naoumoff would have been pardoned if he had agreed to help the prosecution to secure the conviction of the accused. (*Vide* General A. Spiridovitch: *Les dernières années de la Cour de Tzarskoie-Selo*, Paris, 1928,.p. 172.)

CHAPTER XVI

The Revival of the Battle Organization

EVERY STEP was taken to hide Aseff's part in the suppression of the Nikitenko group. Aseff had gradually broken off all relationship with the members of this group, and he had, shortly before the arrests, left St. Petersburg for the Crimea.[1] During the trial no information given by Aseff was made public or even disclosed to the prosecution. All the accusations were

[1]Although Aseff gave ill-health as his reason for visiting the Crimea, he profited by this to enlighten Gerassimoff as to the activity of the Crimean social revolutionaries and made arrests there possible on a large scale in the spring of 1907. The Crimean Social Revolutionaries were planning an attempt against the Grand Duke Nicholas and were in touch with the Nikitenko group. This explains Gerassimoff's particular interest in the Crimea.

based exclusively on the statements of the cossack and those of the detectives who had acted on his information. Thanks to these measures, no suspicion fell upon Aseff, but nevertheless the clouds were gathering over his head, and the threat of exposure was becoming a real danger.

The events of 1905–06, which had shaken the foundations of the old régime, also brought disorder into the machinery of the Political Police. Like rats escaping from a sinking ship, the number of police officials ready to betray official secrets increased. More definite indications now began to appear as to the part played by a mysterious *agent provocateur* who had penetrated to the heart of the Social Revolutionary party. Menstchikoff, the author of the letter exposing Aseff and Tataroff, had, on seeing how his accusations had been received by the party, thought any further warnings useless. But evidence was now arriving from many other sources. Most of it, however, was addressed to the Central Committee, whose members had the fullest confidence in Aseff and paid no attention to it. Savinkoff later said, "My confidence in Aseff was so great that I should not have believed his guilt even if I had seen it stated in his own handwriting. I should have considered it a forgery." And this was the general opinion of the members of the Central Committee.

But not all of those who volunteered information addressed themselves to the Central Committee. One of them, a certain Bakay, approached Burtzeff, the editor of the historical journal *Byloye*, which was then published in St. Petersburg. Bakay's past was far from irreproachable. A few years previously he had been a member of a revolutionary group in Ekaterinoslav and had, on being arrested, betrayed all his friends and become a secret agent of the police; when this was discovered by the revolutionaries, he openly entered the service of the Political Police. The authorities were satisfied with his work; he had been promoted several times and, at the moment of his first visit to Burtzeff, he occupied a responsible position in the Warsaw Ochrana. He at once declared that he sought no material gain and that his only motive was to help the revolutionaries, for what he had seen during his police work filled him with hatred for the government.

Burtzeff did not at first place very great faith in his protestations, but careful examination showed all his stories to be correct. Some of his information was of great political significance. Thus, for example, he got hold of the secret report which officially established the fact that the police had organized an anti-Jewish pogrom in Siedlce. He also brought to light the story of the tortures and shootings without trial practised by the Warsaw Ochrana. He likewise provided a full list of police agents working inside the Polish revolutionary organizations. All this information was perfectly accurate. Everything pointed to the fact that Bakay was sincerely breaking away from his past, and this indeed later proved to be the case. On Burtzeff's advice, he handed in his resignation and devoted himself to compiling his memoirs and making his exposures. Betrayed by Aseff, he was arrested and sent to Siberia, whence he escaped abroad and once more provided Burtzeff with material for the exposure of police secrets. Later he took a university degree and is at present working as an engineer in the French Congo.

In view of this, credit had to be given to his story of a police agent in the heart of the Social Revolutionary party. Bakay not only knew of him under his police name of "Raskin," but he was in possession of various details of his activity, which he now laid before Burtzeff. If Bakay's information were correct, the *agent provocateur* could only be one of the leaders of the party. Burtzeff, who was in close touch with the party and who knew all its leaders, had some difficulty in fixing on the culprit. On the one hand, it seemed impossible that there should be a traitor in the small band of devoted revolutionaries, but, on the other, Burtzeff now *knew* that such a traitor did exist.

Chance, however, aided him. One day, as he was walking in the streets of St. Petersburg, he caught sight of Aseff driving by in an open cab. This was in the late autumn of 1906. The police were then making widespread arrests, and all leading revolutionaries were obliged to show every discretion. And here was Aseff, whose position in the Battle Organization Burtzeff knew, dispensing with the most elementary precautions. This at once excited Burtzeff's suspicions. But he did not at first suspect Aseff, refusing to credit that the whole of the terrorist activity was being directed by a police agent, and he thought rather that the traitor might be some person close to Aseff, who used the latter as a screen and for that reason shielded him from the police. Burtzeff therefore went over in his mind all he knew about Aseff and his closest friends. "And unexpectedly to myself even," he recalls in his Memoirs, "I asked myself whether 'Raskin' and Aseff were not one and the same person." This thought appeared monstrous, but Burtzeff could not rid himself of it and, almost involuntarily, he began to examine all he knew of Aseff and the Battle Organization in the light of this idea. "And I was forced," he says, "to admit that the more I weighed this suggestion the more plausible did it become."

Thus Burtzeff was the first revolutionary to believe in Aseff's treachery, and he began his fight to expose him. For Aseff this was the beginning of the end.

Aseff soon got to hear of Burtzeff's suspicions, and with Gerassimoff's help he tried to deprive him of his source of information. He also used these suspicions for another end. It is indisputable that about this time, that is, following the suppression of Nikitenko's group, Aseff ceased to be perfectly frank with Gerassimoff and began to conceal a great deal from him. He pleaded ignorance more and more frequently to Gerassimoff's questions and definitely refused to carry out certain inquiries, excusing himself on the ground that Burtzeff's campaign had aroused suspicions against him and that any questions on his part would be fatal to him.

Gerassimoff found this excuse plausible. Aseff's services in the terrorist campaign against Stolypin and in the conspiracy against the Czar had raised his value so much in his chief's eyes that "Aseff's safety" became one of the cardinal problems of the Ochrana policy. Gerassimoff would, therefore, not allow Aseff to take any unnecessary risk, reserving him only for the most important tasks. And this was all the more advisable as the possibility of such "important tasks" became more likely every day.

On resuming his party activity on his return to Russia in February, 1907, Aseff concentrated his attention principally on general organizational tasks such as controlling the printing presses, setting up storehouses for party literature and arranging for its distribution in the provinces. After all, he was unfitted for work of another kind: he had no literary or theoretical interests, and, as his manner of late had become very dictatorial, he was unable to deal with those people of secondary importance whose support was necessary to the party.

Aseff's choice of work was also dictated by the fact that the greater part of the party funds went on printing, and that it was to his interest to control large sums of money. This consideration made him take a lively interest in the various sources of party income. It was about this time, too, that he suggested the idea of forging banknotes, but this did not meet with general approval, though not through any lack of insistence on his part.[1] Although Aseff devoted himself with great energy to this work, it was evident that it was but a temporary occupation and that he hoped to resume his terrorist activity.

The general political situation was becoming more gloomy every day. The reactionaries seemed completely victorious. The "Conspiracy against the Czar" had been followed by the "Conspiracy of the Social Democrats," who were accused of plotting an armed rebellion. This was admitted as a sufficient reason for the dissolution of the Duma on June 16, 1907. At the same time, the electoral law was modified to the prejudice of the democratic element. Repressive measures increased.

Gershuni, who had been agitating for a revival of the terror, met with growing sympathy. He maintained that the time had come for an attack at the very heart of absolutism, at the Czar himself, whose personal rôle was now patent to everybody. The question of his assassination was brought before the Central Committee

---

[1] Aseff had discussed this question with Turba (who was shot with other social revolutionaries by the Bolshevists in 1918), who was then in charge of the party's legal printing press.

immediately after the dissolution of the second Duma.

This meeting took place in Finland and was sparsely attended. There were present, very likely, Natanson, Gershuni, Tchernoff, Aseff, and, perhaps, even Rakitnikoff and Avksentieff. Natanson, who presided, and who had generally argued in favor of the Czar's assassination, now opposed this suggestion in the interests of the party. The meeting developed into an argument between him and Gershuni. Natanson relied on all the old arguments against the Czar's assassination, such as its effect upon the peasantry and the dangerous weapon it would be for the reactionaries, but Gershuni parried these with a series of facts which showed that these arguments had lost all weight. Everything now pointed in favor of the Czar's assassination. Tchernoff and the others supported Gershuni. Aseff did not take any leading part in the discussion. His deep conviction in the necessity of such an assassination was generally known.

Aseff's position was difficult. He knew that, when there was talk of a "hunt against the Czar," people looked upon him as the natural leader of it. Gershuni in particular urged him to take on the leadership of this enterprise, and he argued that its success would once and for all put an end to all suspicion against him. Aseff, of course, could not fail to see the danger of such a course to him. He saw that his game would be up: if he allowed the Czar to be killed, the police would make short work of him; if the attempt failed, the doubts of the revolutionaries would turn to certainty. He stood at a fork in his road, with Gershuni urging him forward in one direction and Gerassimoff in the other.

Gerassimoff, according to his own account, was fully informed of the projects against the Czar. His instructions to Aseff on the eve of the Central Committee meeting were that he should attempt, if that did not jeopardize his position in the party, to prevent any final decision being arrived at, but, if such a decision were made, he should take the matter into his own hands in order to paralyze the work of the Battle Organization from the inside.

The Central Committee unanimously decided that the time was ripe for the Czar's assassination, and that the party should immediately proceed to organize this. But as the Battle Organization had to be put on its feet again, and as this necessitated a deal of preparatory work, the execution of the decision was postponed till the autumn. Soon afterwards, at the beginning of July, Aseff and Gershuni went abroad. They set to work to reorganize the Battle Organization. Their parleys with Savinkoff, which took place at the end of August in Switzerland, were of particular importance. Aseff did most of the negotiating, as Gershuni did not have a very high opinion of Savinkoff. Aseff, too, was well aware of Savinkoff's unfitness to play any leading rôle in the terror. "Savinkoff," he had said in private conversation, "is too much of an impressionist and too unreliable for such a delicate business as directing the terror." And yet it was Aseff who insisted on bringing Savinkoff in. His reasons undoubtedly were that he wished to have a collaborator whose perspicacity he need not fear but on whose devotion he could rely.

The negotiations with Savinkoff were dreary and not very successful. Savinkoff still argued, on the basis of the ideas instilled into him by Aseff a year before, that it was impossible to pursue the terror by means of the old methods, and he accused Aseff of inconsistency. Unable to combat successfully his old opinions, Aseff fell back upon arguments of a "moral" nature, and maintained that it was "the terrorist's duty to do his work under any conditions," and that this duty was particularly imperative at a time like the present, when the reaction was at its height in Russia and when even an unsuccessful attempt would have the moral effect of showing the country that all spirit of protest had not been crushed.

These conclusions were far from convincing, and Savinkoff very justly retorted that he had no moral right to incite people to deeds which had no chance of success, and where there was reason to suppose that their lives would be thrown away for nothing. He was in favor, however, of combating the reaction by means of attacks by armed bands without any preparations of the old type. The old Battle Organization was to be restored, but reorganized on absolutely different lines, and its membership was to be largely increased. Neither Aseff nor Gershuni agreed with these suggestions. They stood for the old type of Battle Organization. But Savinkoff refused to join it: for, though he did "understand" the real reasons for the failure of his terrorist work in the past few years, he rightly "felt" that he had been beating his head against a wall, and he was not inclined to continue such a hopeless game.

Aseff returned to Russia in late September or early October. The headquarters of the Central Committee were now in Viborg. A special session was devoted to the reorganization of the Battle Organization. Savinkoff, who arrived expressly to defend his own plan of terrorist work, was received very coldly by Aseff and Gershuni. An overwhelming majority voted against his proposals. It was decided to revive the Battle Organization in its old form. Aseff and Gershuni promised all their energies to its direction. As many did not wish Gershuni to give up his party organizational work, it was resolved that Aseff should, at the beginning, be its sole chief. But all knew that Gershuni, as Rakitnikoff, then present, wrote, "would devote himself wholly to the terror as soon as Aseff had prepared the ground." As it was, Gershuni at once became Aseff's closest adviser. The latter took no step without first consulting him and getting his approval. Until his illness compelled Gershuni to go abroad, Aseff and he between them directed all the party's terrorist work.

The Czar's assassination at once became the principal, if not the only, task of the Battle Organization. All its energies were to be devoted to this end. If the Central Committee at the same time judged the moment suitable for a far-reaching campaign of terror and gave instructions to this end, it decided nevertheless to entrust the execution of all these other terrorist acts to "Karl's Flying Detachment," which immediately passed under the control of the Central Committee. The latter in its turn placed this detachment under the control of Aseff and Gershuni.

CHAPTER XVII

The End of "Karl's Flying Detachment"

IT WAS AT THIS TIME that Aseff established direct and close relations with "Karl's Flying Detachment," which was fated to bring to an end the tragic chapter of the Russian terrorists' heroic struggle—and the last pages of this are all the more tragic in the light of later revelations.

The autumn of 1907 was a bleak and somber one in Russian history. The triumph of the reaction overshadowed every activity, whether political, social, or literary. The mass movement had been crushed. The villages groaned under the heel of repression. City workers were silent and sullen. There were no more political demonstrations, no more strikes. The old régime had obviously, even if only temporarily, triumphed.

The effect of this was to weaken the unity and damp the ardor of the representatives of the revolutionary organizations, whose minds became more and more preoccupied with their own personal problems. This was typical of all grades of revolutionaries. Many of the most active workers, who had not long before thought only of working for the collective good and the interests of their class, now devoted all their energies to the improvement of their personal conditions. Many of the revolutionary peasants now turned their backs upon the collective plans for solving the agrarian problems and profited by the new laws to abandon the "community" and set up as individual farmers.

This withdrawal was particularly noticeable among the revolutionary intelligentsia. Self-denial had always played an important part in the life of these intellectuals, who had usually opportunities for their personal advancement; but if they took no advantage of this, it was because they did not wish to do so. But now the desire was there, and most of them ceded to it. Only very few remained at their posts. The withdrawal was usually accompanied by a change in ideas, for the justification of the retirement led them to defend the "rights of the individual" against those of society. Thus, like weeds, all sorts of "individualisms" sprang up. Another result of this change of atmosphere was the replacement of the old rigorous revolutionary morale by pleasure-seeking. It seemed as if people were trying to make up for lost time. This was reflected in the literature of the time by a wave of pornography. . . .

Such was the general mood of the day. But there were

still men and women who were not carried away by this wave. Stronger willed and more sincere than the others, they refused to desert, and seeing that they could not rely upon the masses in this atmosphere of general apathy, they took the logical course of deciding to struggle on as best they could by themselves. Acting with fatalism and despair, they went into the terror moved by a feeling of revenge rather than faith in the possibility of victory. This was quite logical. In the days when the masses were still inactive, individual terrorists had begun the struggle in the vanguard, but now, when the masses had already ceased to be active, these individual terrorists were the last to leave the field of battle, covering the retreat of the revolutionary army by a rearguard action.

"Karl's Detachment" was formed out of such individual terrorists. They were a closely knit and united family, whose members led an almost ascetic life. In this respect they were the antipodes of many of the leaders of Aseff's Battle Organization. The latter had inculcated into his followers the idea that it was essential for a terrorist to live on a grand scale and not to be sparing of the party treasury. "When it is a question of human lives," he often used to say, "it is not the moment to count the pence." "Karl's Detachment," on the contrary, took every care of the "party pence." Many of its members not only lived independent of its funds, but even subscribed to them. Argunoff, who, as the Central Committee treasurer, was accustomed to Aseff's demands, recalls his astonishment at this attitude. This economy at times was harmful to the interests of the conspiracy, but it was highly characteristic of the temper of these terrorists.

In its work, this detachment relied upon sudden

blows. Its base was in Finland, whose constitution made it impossible for the Russian police to get at the revolutionaries. All preparatory work was done by sympathizers who collected the required information. All of its work was directed by "Karl," but the democratic nature of its constitution allowed every member to show personal initiative. The terrorists chosen for the attempts came forward only when all the preparatory work had been done: they would appear in St. Petersburg, make their attempt, and, if not arrested, return again to Finland.

A typical example of such work was the assassination of the chief military prosecutor, General Pavloff. Pavloff was aware that he was the object of almost universal hatred, and he took exceptional measures for his safety, never leaving the building of the Military Tribunal where he had his private apartments. The attempt was only made possible by the fact that sympathizers were found among the army clerks, who not only supplied details of Pavloff's daily routine but also gave a prearranged signal when Pavloff took his walk in the grounds. At this signal, a terrorist, Igoroff, one of the leaders of a Kronstadt mutiny which had been suppressed with great cruelty, penetrated into the grounds disguised as a courier and shot Pavloff dead with his revolver.

Not all of the detachment's plans were as successful as this. But in spite of occasional failures, the detachment's activity was developing satisfactorily until Aseff took control of it. The detachment devoted a great deal of attention to the struggle against those representatives of the prison administration who had made a name for themselves for their cruelty to political prisoners. This "prison terror" was very characteristic of the years immediately following 1907, when the victorious reaction was systematically venting its rage on its prisoners. But as the closest ties still bound the prisoners with the revolutionaries outside, these latter replied to the violence of the authorities by acts of terror.

Several such reprisals can be attributed to "Karl's Detachment," among them the organizing of the assassination of Borodulin, the governor of the Algatchinsky prison, who was the first to apply corporal punishment to political prisoners. A like attempt was being planned when the detachment passed under the control of Aseff and Gershuni. Its victims were to be Stcheglovitoff, the Minister of Justice, who had inspired the system of prison persecution, Maximovsky, the chief of the central prison administration, and Dratchevsky, the military governor of St. Petersburg. It was also planned to blow up the Cabinet during the session of the State Council. A specially chosen group was to prepare an attempt against General Gershelman, military commander of the Moscow Region. All these plans were submitted to Aseff and Gershuni for their approval, which they gave. The first attempts to be made were those against Stcheglovitoff, Maximovsky, and Dratchevsky on the one hand, and against Gershelman on the other. The two attempts were made, but the former was only partly successful, since only Maximovsky was killed.

Aseff was in a position to thwart both of these attempts, but he did not wish to do so. Gerassimoff gives the following account of Aseff's attitude at that time. Aseff had told him of the Central Committee's resolution to revive the Battle Organization with a view to the Czar's assassination, and that he was again becoming

its chief; he also said that all the other terrorist undertakings had been handed over to "Karl," but he did not
mention the fact that "Karl" had been put under his
and Gershuni's control. On the contrary, he pointed out
that he had no connection with "Karl's Detachment,"
and that any such connection would not be in the interests of his safety. The one task he assumed was to paralyze the attempt against the Czar. He did mention
vaguely that there was talk in the Central Committee of
important attempts to be made by "Karl," and he counseled the taking of precautionary measures, but he
did not name the intended victims. As Gerassimoff also
thought the attempt against the Czar of paramount importance, he approved of Aseff's measures of self-protec-
tion, and it was only after Maximovsky's assassination
that he began to insist on Aseff giving him some clues
for running "Karl's Detachment" to earth.

"Karl" at that time was giving all his attention to
blowing up the State Council. The originator of this
plan was Lebedintzeff, one of the most talented of the
intellectuals who had entered the terror. A man of good
family, a brilliant linguist, a specialist in astronomy and
mathematics, and by nature a gifted musician and
artist, he evolved this plan entirely on his own. Having
spent a number of years in Italy, where he lived in the
closest contact with the people, he had managed to obtain an Italian passport in the name of Mario Calvino,
under which name he achieved European notoriety,
and he was appointed correspondent to an important
Italian paper. In this capacity he came to St. Petersburg and had entry into the press gallery of the State
Council and the Duma. As he was unable to carry out
his plan unaided, he asked "Karl's Detachment" to
help him.

Aseff, who for reasons of his own had not interfered with some of "Karl's" minor attempts, now systematically put obstacles in the way of the realization of Lebedintzeff's grandiose plan. He was obviously afraid that its success would damage his prestige with the police, but as direct betrayal was fraught with dangers from the other side, he had recourse to obstruction from the inside. At first he gave his consent to this attempt, but then, under various pretexts, delayed it; and when all the preparations had been finally completed, he raised the principal objections, pointing out that the elected members of the State Council, including many Liberal politicians, might lose their lives in the attempt.

This produced a very acrimonious passage between Aseff and the leaders of the detachment—which may have been partly due to the fact that Burtzeff had confided his suspicions about Aseff to "Karl." Members of the detachment even talked of disobeying the Central Committee and of making the attempt at their own risk. It was at this stage that Aseff apparently resorted to direct betrayal. At least, so Gerassimoff's account would lead us to suppose. According to him, Aseff, on being pressed, told him that he had had an interview with "Karl." Even so Aseff gave but scant information, contenting himself with saying that "Karl's" headquarters were somewhere in Finland; but, on the other hand, he gave a detailed description of "Karl." He spoke of him as a most talented and enterprising organizer, and advised his immediate arrest. "You will never have any peace while he is at liberty," he said to Gerassimoff.

Aseff also told Gerassimoff of the plan to blow up the State Council, but again without giving him any useful facts. According to him, the idea had only been discussed in a general way by the Central Committee, it had been opposed by some members including himself, and he hoped that it would come to nothing; but he feared that "Karl's Detachment" would not accept the Central Committee's ruling and would take independent action. He therefore advised Gerassimoff to take immediate measures of precaution. Aseff gave no further information beyond hinting that the terrorists had got into the State Council by the use of press cards and that they intended to bring their bombs in their portfolios.

This information, of course, had its effect: precautionary measures were taken in the State Council, journalists' portfolios were carefully examined and their press cards verified. But chief attention was directed towards catching "Karl." All detective resources were mobilized to trace his detachment, and to that end a strict watch was kept on all Finnish railway stations. This synchronized work on the part of the police soon resulted in the discovery of two suspicious flats near the Kelomyak station, and information received from another agent, who had been watching a suspect, led them in the same direction. On the night of December 5, 1907, in violation of the laws governing the right of search on Finnish territory, a raid was made with the approval of Stolypin himself on these flats. A rich treasure was found in one of them—the archives of "Karl's Detachment" and a number of other compromising documents. Two women and a man, whose identity could not at once be established, were arrested. It was only two or three weeks later that Aseff remarked to Gerassimoff, not without malice, "You are still looking for 'Karl,' but you have had him in your hands for a long time already. You got him in Kelomyak. . . ."

Among the captured documents was an annotated plan of the State Council, and this made it possible for the police to state publicly that it had thwarted the blowing up of the State Council. Lebedintzeff still consoled himself with the hope that he might put his plan into execution, but it was clear that the plan was no longer feasible. The remaining members of the detachment kept together and appointed Lebedintzeff as their chief, and he set to work feverishly to organize attempts against the Grand Duke Nicholas and the Minister of Justice, Stcheglovitoff. It was proposed to carry these out on New Year's Day, when both of them were due to attend the Czar's levee. The terrorists were to throw bombs at them on their way. These attempts, however, were frustrated by treachery, but not on Aseff's part this time. Gerassimoff heard of this on New Year's Eve from another agent, who informed him of the time of the attempt and the intended victims, but gave no details as to the perpetrators.

Gerassimoff resorted to the same device by which he had saved Stolypin from the attempt engineered against him at the Institute of Experimental Medicine. Early on New Year's Day he called on the Grand Duke Nicholas and on Stcheglovitoff, warned them of the intended attempt, and asked them not to leave their houses for a few days. In any case, all measures of precaution had already been taken. Every available detective had been ordered to look out for suspects along the route. Gerassimoff himself came on the scene and directed the detectives from a café in the Mikhailovsky Square, in the vicinity of the Grand Duke's Palace. . . . But it was all in vain, for no suspicious signs were noticed. And only later did it become known that Lydia Sture, one of the members of the detachment, had sat in that café, at the next table to Gerassimoff, with a live bomb in a neatly tied parcel. She recounted this fact herself when examined by Gerassimoff after her arrest. She interrupted Gerassimoff, saying, "But, General, we have already met somewhere." Gerassimoff, she says, was astonished and could not remember. Then she explained, "Don't you remember on New Year's Day we sat next to each other in the Mikhailovsky café? What a pity I did not know who my neighbor was. . . . You would not have got away. . . ."

In the next six weeks the terrorists renewed their attempts. Their nerves were strung to a breaking point: they went out almost daily with bombs in their hands, convinced that that would be their last day, but returned home cursing the fate which accorded them another day to live. . . . All the terrorist forces were mobilized and concentrated in St. Petersburg. The terrorists were eager to attack at any cost and were ready to sacrifice their lives. The Ochrana, in the meantime, had taken every measure of precaution to guard the houses of Stcheglovitoff and the Grand Duke Nicholas. Both of them chafed at the régime prescribed by Gerassimoff. But in spite of all his efforts, the latter could not get on the track of the detachment, for his agent had been unable to supply him with any further details and had declared that he was not in possession of any additional information. "Though I insisted on his giving me some clue," Gerassimoff relates, "he declined, assuring me that he knew nothing more, nor could he make any inquiries as such questions might compromise him."

As a matter of fact, Aseff was aware of all the details of the plot, and was also in constant touch with the terrorists. The exposure of the detachment, however, would have put him in a very awkward position. But

he finally had pity on Gerassimoff and, four or five days
before the arrest of the terrorists, told him that, from a
discussion which had taken place in the Central Committee about the attempt, he had understood that
Anna Rasputina, a former political prisoner, was connected with the detachment. Aseff gave no further details, but hinted that Rasputina was probably living
under an assumed name. This information was, however, sufficient to lead to the downfall of the detachment.

On returning from his interview with Aseff, Gerassimoff immediately stirred the Ochrana into action. Rasputina's past was at once gone into. The addresses of
all the Rasputins living in St. Petersburg were obtained.
"I did this," writes Gerassimoff, "fully convinced that
it would lead to no results, as I had no doubt either
that Rasputina would not be living under her own
name. What was my astonishment when I assured myself that Rasputina was actually living in St. Petersburg, on the Nevsky Prospect, under her own name. ..."

The police machine was set in motion early next
morning. A preliminary investigation established that
Rasputina was living in a furnished room, and that the
room next to hers was now vacant. Gerassimoff went to
examine it personally. Passing himself off as a book-
keeper in search of a room, he was able to examine the
whole apartment. At first, he thought of taking the room
himself in order to overhear what was being said next
door, for the walls turned out to be very thin. But the
room was too shabby for such a respectable "book-
keeper" and instead, two young detectives who gave
themselves out to be students were installed. Rasputina
was now kept under the most careful observation. The
terrorists took every measure of precaution when meet-

ing each other. Thus, for example, they usually met in churches during the service, knelt side by side in front of the icons and talked while pretending to pray. But the prolonged tension had made them less careful, whereas the police watch, on the other hand, was intensified. The result was that within three days Rasputina's principal connections were discovered, and, on February 20, 1908, when the terrorists, who were under police observation, took up their watch near the houses of the Grand Duke Nicholas and Stcheglovitoff, they were arrested. Nine in all were arrested, three of them with bombs in their possession; three others, armed with revolvers, offered resistance; and explosives were also found in the rooms of another of them.

The trial was brief and merciless. Seven terrorists, including three women, were condemned to death. The sentence was immediately carried out. Soon after, "Karl" and several other members of his detachment, who had been arrested at different times, were likewise tried. They also were sentenced to death. . . . The "Flying Detachment" had been annihilated.

CHAPTER XVIII

Aseff's Last Game

IN CONVERSATIONS in party circles Aseff usually spoke in a slightly contemptuous manner of "Karl's Detachment," which he looked down upon as being "provincial." He defended with increasing insistence his own point of view that the assassination of the representatives of authority, of ministers even, was now bereft of all political significance. The only terrorist act which had any significance in his eyes was that of the Czar's assassination, and he proposed the concentration of all the party's energies to this end. He did not conceal the difficulty of this undertaking, nor the fact that it would demand of the party tremendous sacrifices in both lives and money, nor that its preparation, too, would take considerable time. But he was deeply convinced that, as Rakitnikoff recalls, "by methods of systematic siege and the penetration of defences, they could hope to bring this matter to a successful conclusion in a year or two." Such a success would be well worth all their sacrifices. And with that flow of sentimentality which Aseff loved to display in intimate conversation, he would say that he regarded this as his last revolutionary act—the one that would crown his revolutionary career.

A great deal in Aseff's statements was deliberately intended to deflect attention from his betrayal of "Karl's Detachment," but it would have been a mistake to look on *all* this as hypocrisy. From what we know of him, Aseff was, at this time, preparing to enter on a new phase of his prolonged double game, and he was about to play his last card. . . . And as he never gambled unless he knew his opponent's cards beforehand, he was now particularly careful in preparing the setting for his last game.

Very many of the members of the Central Committee agreed in principle with Aseff's plan for the assassination of the Czar. His views were very logical from the point of view of the terror, and it is not surprising that the Central Committee continued to support the Battle Organization with every means in its power. The party treasury was always at Aseff's disposal. It need only be said that when, later, the three hundred thousand roubles taken in a raid on the Charjui government treasury were added to the funds of the Central Committee, on Aseff's insistence a third was handed over to the Battle Organization, that is, for all practical purposes, to Aseff himself.

Aseff was also given a free hand in choosing recruits for the Battle Organization. Karpovitch, who had to his credit a number of terrorist acts, including the assassination of Bogolepoff, the Minister of Education, in February, 1901, now became his right-hand man. He had spent some years in prison after the assassination and had now just escaped and was anxious to resume terrorist work. Tchernavsky, another old revolutionary, who had first been sentenced to penal servitude some thirty years before, now also played a leading part in the Battle Organization. Aseff likewise tried to enroll a number of other old revolutionaries. . . . The theory has been put forward that Aseff's conduct can be attributed to sadism, that he got pleasure from endangering the lives of those who had already suffered enough. But this theory will not stand examination. It would be nearer the truth to say that membership of the Battle Organization was at this time a guarantee against arrest. Aseff's conduct can be explained much more simply: he realized that the support of tried revolutionaries would be the best protection against the growing suspicions assailing him.

His preliminary work was to feel the ground very carefully. He sought for means of approaching the Czar and examined every possibility. He broke his usual reserve as to the work of the Battle Organization, and spoke of his plans at length in the Central Committee in order to ascertain his comrades' view of them. He explained his change of attitude by the complex nature of the work in hand and by his own isolated position, for Gershuni had died on leaving Russia at the end of 1907.

All were convinced that he was doing everything in his power to organize a successful attempt against the Czar. He was full of plans. According to him, watch was being kept on the Czar's comings and goings in St.

Petersburg, and there was a project to attack him in the street. Argunoff also speaks of a plan to gain entry into the Palace as members of one of the innumerable deputations staged by the reactionaries to demonstrate the "loyalty of the masses." Aseff also welcomed eagerly the suggestion of a young Social Revolutionary, who had just taken orders and who hoped with his family influence to be appointed priest somewhere in the vicinity of Tsarskoye Selo. He thought that in this way he might have the opportunity to get within striking distance of the Czar and thus to execute the party's sentence. A priest assassinating the Czar—this was obviously a combination which appealed to Aseff, and he urged the youth to abandon all other revolutionary work and to devote himself entirely to this plan.[1] There was also a whole series of other plans and projects.

But there were two plans to which Aseff gave really serious attention. The first was an attempt to be made on the Czar while he was hunting, and the second while he was on a journey to Reval. For the execution of the first, the terrorists opened a tea shop in one of the villages in the hunting district, near Tsarskoye Selo. Tchernavsky was to play the part of proprietor, representing himself to be an old monarchist and a member of the "Union of the Russian People." The second plan contemplated either blowing up the Czar's train, or a bomb attack in the streets of Reval.

For all these plans Aseff was merely playing with both the revolutionaries and the police; he had no intention of allowing such an attempt to take place, as the police would never have forgiven him. He therefore readily in-

---

[1]This plan has not so far been mentioned in the literature on Aseff. The author of this book first heard of it from the lips of the originator of the plan. It must be added that it failed through no fault of Aseff's.

formed the police of most of the details of the plots against the Czar, but, as we can establish, he did withhold a certain amount of information such as his connection with the young priest, reserving this for future use. He was still on the best of terms with Gerassimoff. The latter's confidence in him was equaled only by that of the Central Committee. Since their common object was the frustration of the Czar's assassination, Gerassimoff took every care to "safeguard Aseff." No attempt was made to arrest the members of either the Central Committee or the Battle Organization; and if any of them were arrested by chance without his knowledge, he took every pains to arrange for their escape without rousing their suspicions. He made no demands on Aseff to betray the terrorists, and the incident of Lebedintzeff's Detachment was the only exception.

Aseff was so sure that no arrests would be made without his sanction that he allowed himself the luxury of telling Gerassimoff that the party treasury was shortly going to be enriched by the proceeds of the Charjui raid, a large share of which was going into his own pocket. Gerassimoff did not even press Aseff for information which might lead to the recapture of this money, and this in spite of the fact that this raid had particularly angered Stolypin, who had given orders that *the raiders should be arrested at any cost* and the money restored.[1] "I knew," says Gerassimoff, not without humor, when relating this episode, "that a good part of this money would return to us, as it would pass under the control of our agent." Reassured by Gerassimoff's "loyalty," Aseff now took the risk of organizing the transfer of the sum in question from Turkestan, and

[1]According to Tchernavsky, Aseff would seem to have given the police some help in this matter. But, in any case, he did not restore the money.

this was successfully done by the terrorists under him.

In view of this, it is not surprising that Aseff never importuned Gerassimoff with requests for an increase of salary or for bonuses and seemed content with his thousand roubles a month. The department was no longer his chief source of income. That Gerassimoff had unbounded confidence in him is shown by the fact that Aseff was aware of his private address. For Gerassimoff was at that time living, like a conspirator, under an assumed name and concealed his place of residence even from the most responsible officials in the Ochrana. Aseff was the only "secret agent" who knew his address and who had the right, in case of necessity, to call there at any hour of the day or night, after previously telephoning.

There can be no doubt that Aseff also made use of Gerassimoff to find out the extent of the police knowledge as to what was taking place within the party. In this way he had opportunities for discovering the identity of other secret agents against whom he had to be on his guard when betraying the police. He was thus pursuing the same methods that he had used in his dealings with Ratayeff, but, of course, with much greater circumspection.

It was at this moment, too, that Aseff's personal affairs began to intrude and to play a more conspicuous part in his life. The double game which Aseff had been playing for many years in the political world had its counterpart in his private life. Here he was as skillful as in politics. In party circles he had made a reputation for himself as an exemplary husband and family man who was devoted to his wife and children. And there were, indeed, the elements of such an attachment in his character. He was fond of his children, and it is not for nothing that he has been called "fond Judas." But Aseff could easily reconcile this genuine attachment to his family with a passion for all sorts of casual love affairs. This propensity had already been remarked by some in his student days, and the detective reports of his later years are full of references to the nights he spent in brothels and such places. Discreet in his home life, which could be observed by his party comrades, he gave way to his real inclinations when traveling in Russia or abroad on party business. And it was this mode of life which accounted for his heavy expenses, and put him in constant need of such large sums of money. . . .

The winter of 1907–08 was a critical one for Aseff in this respect. He was getting on toward forty, the age at which the habitués of such places of amusement begin to grow more staid. And Aseff had other reasons impelling him in this direction: the fear of exposure as an *agent provocateur* was daily becoming more real, and threatened him among other things with the break-up of his home. His wife had remained an idealistically minded revolutionary, and she knew nothing of Aseff's relations with the police. She sincerely believed that her husband was a hero of the Revolution and that he lived in daily fear of arrest and execution, and Aseff had no doubt that his wife would break with him if she learned the truth. The prospect of remaining alone by no means appealed to him. The old and much experienced Jewish God had said that it was not good for man to be alone. . . . So now, when preparing to stake his last card, he was not averse to enter into a "more permanent liaison," which might in case of need prove a substitute for his family happiness.

Such a liaison commenced when he met Madame N——, a cabaret singer. The date of their meeting,

December 26, 1907, is given by Aseff himself in one of his last letters to Madame N——; it took place in the then famous St. Petersburg *café chantant*, the Aquarium. Their "romance" began at their first meeting, when they dined together and went afterwards to Madame N——'s flat. "From that time we have never separated," wrote Aseff nine years later to Madame N—— from the cell of a Berlin prison. Madame N—— entered so deeply into Aseff's life and brought to it so many characteristic and colorful traits that she deserves our special attention.

When she first met Aseff, Madame N—— was already a star in the St. Petersburg *cafés chantants*. By birth she was a German of petty bourgeois family. She has still in her possession a family photograph taken when she was a child. There can be no doubt that hers was a respectable middle-class family which had inculcated into their daughter the four K's essential to all good German women: *Kaiser, Kirche, Kinder,* and *Küche.* Madame N—— remained at heart faithful to this teaching, and when the author of this book met her in 1924–25, her only regret was that it had been legally impossible for Aseff to realize her dearest wish by marrying her before he died. Her principles had not prevented her, however, from embarking on an adventurous career in Russia almost on leaving school. Judging from her account, it was by no means unusual for girls in her station in life to seek their fortunes in that way, just as a century earlier the younger sons of impoverished families used to do. If one of these girls returned to her native town with her fortune made, no questions were asked—even by a prospective bridegroom.

Madame N—— was one of the more successful. She had come to St. Petersburg shortly before the Russo-Japanese War, at the very height of the Far Eastern boom, when the nation's gold was pouring into the pockets of the Bezobrazoffs, the Vonliarliarskys and other financial opportunists, and when both the "gilded" and the "golden" youth were setting St. Petersburg agog with their riotous debaucheries. Madame N—— had not a very fine voice, but this was not essential in her profession, and she had no difficulty in getting an engagement in one of the best known St. Petersburg *cafés chantants*. She soon attracted the attention of the very cream of gay society, even that of the Grand Dukes, who set the tone for this mode of life. During the war her success was at its height. Her accounts of this period are somewhat vague, as if much had been lost in the drunken fumes. There is no doubt that she lived on the very Olympus of the riotous rearguard of the Russian army, and she has the most tender recollections of her travels in the train of the Grand Duke Cyril, who with his brother Boris "adorned" the army with his presence.

It is well known that their orgies became so scandalous that General Kuropatkin was obliged to beg for their removal, as they were demoralizing the troops. Madame N——'s only recollection, however, is that "it was a very gay life"! And not unprofitable, let us add, for we learn from documents in her possession that as early as 1906 she was able to invest fifty thousand roubles in a scheme, proposed to her by an officer, for exploiting some gold mine in Siberia. The succeeding stages of her career are what one might expect but of less interest. She made a tour of all the principal cities of Russia, Moscow, Kharkov, and Kiev, appearing everywhere at the best *cafés chantants* and enjoying considerable success. Among Aseff's papers there is preserved a picture postcard of her in which she is represented as

MADAME N—— OR "LA BELLA HEDDY DE HERO."

one of those "luxuriant women," which the old novels liked to depict; this postcard, which bore the facsimile signature, "La bella Heddy de Hero," had undoubtedly been printed for sale.

When Madame N—— met Aseff she was already looking out for "substantial friends." She had been in Russia for four years, but she had not saved enough for a triumphal return to her home town. The investment in the Siberian gold mine had been anything but successful, for the gold-prospecting officer had mysteriously disappeared, and thus most of the money she had so easily earned at the expense of the suffering Russian army had melted away. After such a bitter experience she had had enough of "romanticism," and she thought now only of these "substantial friends" who could make good her losses.

Aseff fitted this rôle ideally. He gave himself out to be a prosperous merchant, who had a family but wished to form a liaison. His appearance and behavior inspired every confidence in his credit. He did not throw his money about, but on occasion he would pay large bills without demur. His presents, too, spoke of financial stability. He was also less coarse than most of the habitués of the Aquarium. This liaison rapidly grew stronger. Soon Aseff began to pass all his spare time with her. They were seen together in theaters and other places of amusement and in the street. Aseff had apparently been genuinely carried away by her, and he threw his customary discretion to the winds. His behavior did not pass unnoticed in party circles; he had been seen on various occasions either in an expensive box at the latest musical comedy, or dining at a first-class restaurant, invariably accompanied by Madame N——, whose reputation was well known. Also, he had been seen buying expensive jewelry. All this became a matter for talk amongst the revolutionaries. For a time, however, Aseff stopped this talk by telling his comrades in the Central Committee that he had made acquaintances in the *café chantant* world who would be useful to him in preparing his plot against the Czar. There was an element of truth in this, for Aseff could scarcely help getting some useful information from acquaintanceships of this kind, and Madame N—— tells us that he liked to question her about the life and habits of the Grand Dukes and their friends.

But such evasions could not satisfy people indefinitely. Rumors about Aseff's unusual conduct gained ground, and, at the same time, reports about him began to reach Gerassimoff from other agents in the Social Revolutionary party. One of these was particularly insistent that the police should profit by the situation and arrest Aseff, a member of the Central Committee and head of the Battle Organization. Gerassimoff's evasive replies perplexed this zealous agent, and it was only some time later that he reported with relief the suspicions that existed about Aseff's loyalty to the party. Gerassimoff recalls that he had warned Aseff more than once of the dangers involved in his mode of life. But Aseff did not feel inclined to change the latter. He realized the danger, but he sought another solution, and with growing conviction told Gerassimoff that it was time for him to stop the game and retire. Nor did Gerassimoff put great objections in his way, for he thought Aseff had a right to this after fifteen years of such work. He only made one stipulation, that Aseff should successfully frustrate the attempt against the Czar which was projected for that spring, and to this Aseff agreed.

At this time, too, there occurred an episode—the

accidental arrest, upon a denunciation, of Karpovitch,
Aseff's right-hand man in the Battle Organization—
which had some influence on Aseff and caused him to
hurry forward to the final dénouement. Argunoff, who
saw Aseff the moment when he heard the news of this
arrest, says that Aseff was "unusually perturbed" by
it. According to Gerassimoff, Aseff called on him at once
and made an almost hysterical scene. He said that this
arrest would irrevocably compromise him in the eyes
of the revolutionaries, and he threatened to throw up
everything and go abroad. Gerassimoff was entirely of
his opinion, for the arrest had been made without his
knowledge. He was therefore ready to do everything in
his power to appease Aseff, who demanded that Karpovitch should be immediately released without his suspicions being roused. Gerassimoff acceded to this, and
Karpovitch made his "escape." Everything was thus
satisfactorily arranged, although Karpovitch himself
very nearly spoiled it.

While he was being taken in a cab, his guard went into
a tobacconist's on the pretext of getting cigarettes. "I
was sure," the latter told Gerassimoff afterwards, "that
the cab would be empty on my return, but to my surprise Karpovitch was quietly sitting there." The guard
then suggested that they should go .to a restaurant
and have something to eat. Karpovitch consented, and
they ordered dinner. The guard then excused himself
again to wash his hands but watched Karpovitch
through the door. For a long time Karpovitch hesitated,
apparently fearing that a trap was being set for him.
"I got tired of him," said the guard. "I thought he
would never escape! What could I do if he simply did
not want to take his chance?"

It was this that made Aseff hasten his preparations

for going abroad. According to Madame N——'s account, Aseff suddenly announced in March, 1908, without giving any reasons, that they must go abroad, and advised her to get rid of her flat at once. As there was no time to sell the furniture, it was stored, and Aseff, like the practical man he was, pawned the receipt for seven hundred roubles. Aseff suggested that they should take as few things as possible with them, and insisted only on the inclusion of a samovar, so that they might be able to drink tea in the Russian way. On this occasion, Aseff and Madame N—— spent about a month abroad, sometimes together in Germany and sometimes apart. It is possible that Aseff may have visited Paris, where Gershuni was then dying.

At Easter, Aseff returned to St. Petersburg with Madame N——. They stopped at one of the best hotels in St. Petersburg and registered as man and wife. Here Aseff spent very little time with Madame N——; he was very busy and often absented himself for the whole day. Once he was away for several days on end. He explained his conduct by his difficulties in winding up his commercial affairs. In reality, of course, he had "commercial" affairs of another sort to attend to, for, besides his general work on the Central Committee, he was directing two important operations, the transfer of the Charjui money from Turkestan and the attempt against the Czar in Reval.

Aseff represented this latter to Gerassimoff as an affair of great importance, and said that a special group of ten to fifteen terrorists had been appointed to carry it out. There was a great deal of exaggeration in Aseff's statement, for he seems to have been trying to make his last service appear of much greater value than it really was. The account of this attempt given by Tchernavsky, the only member of the Battle Organization of the time to have published his memoirs, does not point to its having been arranged with any great thoroughness. According to the understanding between Aseff and Gerassimoff, this attempt was to be frustrated without any arrests being made. Gerassimoff was all the more ready to agree with Aseff's insistence on this point, as the Czar's trip to Reval was connected with international politics, for there he was to meet the King of England, and therefore the government was anxious to avoid the public discussions which would have inevitably been roused by arrests. It was of the first importance that the trip should take place without any incidents. And it was for this reason that Stolypin gave his approval to the plan agreed upon by Aseff and Gerassimoff.

According to Aseff, the Battle Organization had several schemes for attempting the Czar's life, depending on what route he was to take and where he was to stay. The problem before Aseff and Gerassimoff was to arrange the Czar's itinerary in such a way as to thwart all these plans, and yet to leave the terrorists firmly convinced that their failure was due to accidental circumstances. This they succeeded in doing without great difficulty: thus on one occasion a prearranged telegram arrived late, and on another a terrorist missed his train. Furthermore, the Czar did not, as had been arranged, visit a certain Esthonian baron, and it was on this that the Battle Organization had placed their chief hopes. Thus the various schemes were thwarted one after another. . . .

Gerassimoff recalls that he was particularly struck at the time with the extraordinary fullness of Aseff's information as to all the Czar's intended movements.

Any proposed changes in the Czar's itinerary, however secretly they were kept, were immediately known to him. He even boasted of this to Gerassimoff, who, in fact, usually got news of these changes later than Aseff. On one occasion they had a dispute over this: while discussing their plan of campaign, Aseff pointed to the necessity of attending to a small detail in the Czar's proposed itinerary. Gerassimoff objected that there was no such detail in the itinerary and referred to the official documents in support of his views. Aseff, however, stuck to his point.

"This new change has evidently not yet reached you," he declared authoritatively. "You will probably hear of it tomorrow or the day after."

And however much Gerassimoff tried to convince him of the improbability of such a change, Aseff remained unmoved.

"Our information is perfectly reliable!"

What was Gerassimoff's astonishment when, on the following day, he received a "strictly confidential" envelope, which informed him of the proposed change in the Czar's itinerary of which Aseff had spoken.

When they next met, Gerassimoff naturally enough tried to find out the source from which Aseff obtained such full and accurate information, but the latter definitely refused to satisfy the curiosity of his police chief.

"You know that I am taking every means to thwart this attempt and that I guarantee to be successful. But I am unable to give you the name of my informant because he is very highly placed, and only two or three people know of our relations. If he should notice that his rôle was becoming known, his suspicions would fall upon me, and I should be lost. . . . Please don't press it: I must have some regard for my own safety."

He did not fail, however, to emphasize the fact that he had been right.

"You see, I was right, after all. Where would you be if there was someone else at the head of the Battle Organization?"

Gerassimoff did not think it advisable to press this question. Aseff's right to "look after his safety" had long been recognized, and it was also clear that insistence would lead nowhere. But later, when the excitement of the Reval trip was over, Gerassimoff instituted a strictly secret investigation to find out Aseff's informant. As the number of those initiated into the details of the Czar's itinerary was very limited, and as Aseff had unwittingly let fall a few hints, there were some clues to work upon. The results of this investigation made Gerassimoff doubt his own senses: everything pointed to the fact that this informer was no minor official, as Gerassimoff had hoped would be the case, but a very highly placed personage. Gerassimoff was not in a position to take any measures against him on his own responsibility, and he therefore decided to make a confidential report on the matter to Stolypin. The latter for a long time refused to believe the facts put before him, and he insisted on further verification of them being made. This only confirmed the results of the first investigation. The highly placed personage, judging by all the evidence, would really seem to have been deliberately coöperating with the terrorists in their attempt against the Czar. . . . The government, it might seem, had no right to connive at such a state of affairs, but nevertheless, after long reflection, Stolypin decided that no further action was to be taken in the matter.

"The scandal would be too great; we cannot allow ourselves this luxury at the moment. . . . Later, perhaps.

... We would be obliged also to expose Aseff's rôle in the affair, and he is essential to us. ... We had better leave the matter alone. ... We must look after *him*. ..."

Stolypin, as it can be seen, was also very much concerned with "Aseff's safety," and the highly placed personage was left untouched. After Aseff's exposure, it became absolutely impossible to make public that a personage of almost Cabinet rank had actively helped in a plot organized against the Czar's life by the Battle Organization, whose very chief was a police agent acting under the orders of the president of the Cabinet himself. The name of this personage still remains a mystery, for Gerassimoff considers it impossible to publish it even now. This incident, however, gives us an idea of the connections now at the disposal of the Battle Organization, and which might, if necessary, have been put to serious use instead of being wasted in Aseff's game.

The Reval celebrations passed off without a hitch. All were content: the Czar and Stolypin with the political results of their interview with the King of England; Gerassimoff with his rewards; and Aseff chiefly with the one hundred thousand roubles which he had just lodged safely in the Battle Organization's treasury.

Reval was not Aseff's last card. Immediately after the "Reval campaign," Aseff again hastened to go abroad with Gerassimoff's permission, for he had news of another possibility of attempting the Czar's life with a greater chance of success. On hearing of this, Aseff sent his assistant, Karpovitch, to get full particulars. Karpovitch's reports were exceedingly hopeful, and Aseff now hastened to the spot himself.

Aseff took leave of Gerassimoff as if he was destined never to see him again. He said that he had grown weary

and wished to retire and that he would soon give up any
active participation in party affairs, but that he would
like to be able to refute the accusations brought against
him by Burtzeff in order that he might be able to end his
days in peace, without the fear of vengeance on the
part of the revolutionaries. He was now finally giving
up his work as a police agent, but he promised as a personal favor to Gerassimoff to inform him from time to
time of the more important events taking place in the
Central Committee, which would serve as material for
reports to Stolypin, for whom Aseff felt something akin
to personal sympathy. Gerassimoff promised that his
salary would be paid as long as it was possible to do so,
and he regarded this in the light of a pension for his past
work. It is hardly necessary to add that Aseff did not
even hint to Gerassimoff of the existence of a new plot
against the Czar.

In June, 1908, Aseff left Russia with the idea of never
returning (he returned only once for a short visit in
November, 1908, to see Lopuhin). Leaving Madame
N——, who had of course accompanied him, in Germany, he himself hurried on to Paris, and then to Scot-
land, where in Glasgow an attempt was being prepared
against the Czar.

The new plan was as follows: There was being built
in Vickers' Glasgow shipyard a new Russian cruiser,
Rurik, one of those intended to replace the old Russian
fleet which had met with such a disastrous end in the
Yellow Sea. A skeleton crew had been sent over to
Glasgow to watch the work and to acquaint themselves
with the ship. The revolutionaries had approached its
members, and both the Social Democrats and Social
Revolutionaries were conducting propaganda work
among them. The work of the latter party was directed

by Kostenko, a naval engineer, who was a member of
the central group of the party's officer organization,
and who was in direct touch with the Central Committee. It was his idea to have the Czar assassinated during
the ceremonial review which would be held on the arrival of the cruiser in a Russian port.

Such an attempt might be successfully carried out in
one of two ways: either by a member of the crew, who
would shoot the Czar during the review or the inspection of the ship; or, if there was no volunteer from the
crew, by a member of the Battle Organization who was
to be smuggled aboard and hidden until the inspection
took place.

As there was no volunteer from the crew at the beginning, all attention was concentrated on the second
plan. There was no difficulty in smuggling a revolutionary on board the cruiser while she was in Glasgow.
Kostenko helped to find a hiding place where a man
might remain concealed without fear of discovery.
The place was small and uncomfortable. The volunteer
would have to remain in a cramped position, unable to
stretch his limbs. It had, however, this advantage:
from it one could get quite easily into the central venti-
lating shaft, and, by the ladder inside it, reach the
admiral's quarters and blow them up while the Czar was
breakfasting there.

This plan was open to several objections. It was not
known in advance when the review would take place,
and it might happen that the terrorist would have to
spend not days but whole weeks in his hiding place (in
fact, the review did not take place till two months after
the cruiser had left Glasgow), and no man could hope to
withstand such a trial. Still, it was thought worth while
to take this risk.

Aseff arrived in Glasgow in the middle of July. Through Kostenko's influence he obtained permission, under an assumed name, of course, to look round the cruiser, and he explored it thoroughly, inspecting possible hiding places, the ventilation shaft, and so on. As a result, he reported unfavorably on the plan, considering it impracticable, and it was therefore abandoned. All hopes were now centered on finding a volunteer among the crew. After some time, two volunteers, the sailor Gerassim Avdeyeff and the signaler Kaptelovitch, were found. Particular hope was laid on the first, a very daring, energetic, and most revolutionary-minded man. Both Savinkoff and Karpovitch knew him, and Aseff was to meet him later. They were provided with revolvers by the Battle Organization, and they wrote farewell letters in which they explained the motives for their action. These letters, together with photographs, were taken by Aseff, and they were to be published after the attempt had taken place.

In the middle of August, 1908, the cruiser sailed for Russia. On the way, Avdeyeff wrote in a personal letter to Savinkoff: "Only now do I begin to understand myself. I shall never be a propagandist. . . . After serious reflection I can now realize the significance of the task entrusted to me. . . . One minute will decide more than whole months."

The Czar's review took place on October 7th. "Both Avdeyeff and Kaptelovitch met the Czar face to face," wrote Savinkoff at the time. According to Kostenko's account, Avdeyeff was even asked by the Czar to bring him a glass of champagne and was therefore as close as possible to him for a few moments. Although the attempt could easily have taken place, it was not made. Savinkoff explains this by the fact that both Avdeyeff

and Kaptelovitch lost their nerve at the critical moment. But Kostenko, who was better informed, tells quite
a different story. It would seem that the crew was plotting a mutiny: the number gained over by propaganda
was large, and the plotters hoped for success. Avdeyeff
and Kaptelovitch were members of the organization
which was plotting this mutiny, but they had not informed it of their own plan. Its other members, however, guessed by their conduct that they had a plot of
their own and insisted on an explanation. They confessed the truth, and it became clear that the plan to
assassinate the Czar would upset the plan for the
mutiny; such an attempt would lead to arrests and inquiries on board and could not fail to put the police on
the track of the plotters and of their plan to seize Kronstadt. The result was that the plotters forced Avdeyeff
and Kaptelovitch to renounce their plan.

There are good reasons for believing that Kostenko's
version is the correct one. If this is so, Aseff's last move,
on which his safety depended, was thwarted by the supporters of the mass movement in which he never believed and against which he always struggled. One
thing is clear, the attempt failed through no fault of
Aseff's. He had done everything in his power to bring
this attempt to a successful conclusion. Gerassimoff
knew nothing of what was to take place on the *Rurik*.
Avdeyeff's farewell letter, together with his photograph, which might have cost him his life, remained in
Aseff,'s possession until his exposure. When leaving his
Paris apartment on January 6, 1909, Aseff deliberately
put this letter on his writing table for all the world to
see, as a proof that he was no traitor, since he had not
betrayed Avdeyeff when he could very well have
done so. . . . In reality, the significance of this document

was quite different: it merely showed that, at that stage
of his game, Aseff thought it more profitable to betray
not the revolutionaries, but rather the other side. . . .

Later, in 1912, when he met Burtzeff in Frankfort-
on-the-Main, Aseff said to him reproachfully:
"If you had not exposed me then, I would have killed
the Czar."

Aseff's life as we now know it compels us to think that
on this occasion he was speaking the truth: he would
have really organized the assassination of the Czar.
We must believe it not because of any particular initiative and invention on Aseff's part, since, in fact, he had
no creative initiative and had not brought anything of
his own to the Battle Organization. But he became by
the will of fate the collective center of the initiative of
all those whose minds worked solely for the terror. The
majority of these perished, for Aseff sold them to the
police. But when it was advantageous to him, he knew
how to choose the most *practically* expedient of the mass
of talented and original plans as any business man will
choose only the most profitable of the inventions of
genius. And he could always realize such a practical plan
when it was of advantage to him.

The plan to assassinate the Czar organized by Aseff
in this way could not be considered a terrorist act in the
sense that this is understood in Russia. Taking his inner
motives into consideration, it would have been nothing
more than an ordinary premeditated murder for the
purposes of gain. These motives would have been of no
great interest to the student of history. But the student
of history would have had to consider the fact that the
dynasty of the Romanoffs would at least not have
ended with Nicholas II. . . .

CHAPTER XIX

Aseff's Exposure

BURTZEFF'S CAMPAIGN against Aseff was in the meantime making good progress. He was steadily collecting incriminating evidence, and he had ceased to make a secret of his accusations. He was now no longer alone. The systematic failures of the Battle Organization in all its principal undertakings had sown dark thoughts in the minds of many, and in those of the outstanding members of the party in particular. It became indisputable that there was a traitor in the very heart of the party, and by process of elimination suspicion came to be centered on Aseff. This suspicion had not yet affected Aseff's party position. The party leaders steadily refused to believe these accusations, regarding them

as "idle chatter." Aseff continued to direct the party's
terrorist activities and to participate in the work of the
Central Committee. As a member of the latter, he attended, in August, 1908, the party conference, which
was held in London.

This forced Burtzeff to more drastic action. Learning
of Aseff's presence at the London conference, he sent
to his old friend Teploff, also a member of that conference, a letter in which he made a direct accusation
of treachery against Aseff. This letter came to the
knowledge of the Central Committee, which decided to
abandon its passive attitude and to arraign Burtzeff
for trial. It was not a question so much of investigating
the grounds for Burtzeff's accusation as of trying him
for "libeling" Aseff. And as it was, the decision of the
Central Committee met with strong opposition on the
part of leading members, and particularly of those who
had anything to do with the Battle Organization. These
latter, with Savinkoff at their head, offered the most
decided opposition to the trial, considering the very idea
of such a trial an insult to the honor of the Battle Organization.

Regarding Burtzeff as a sincere man who was laboring under a profound delusion only because he was
ignorant of the real story of Aseff's life, Savinkoff gave
Burtzeff a detailed account of Aseff's relations with the
Battle Organization. In this there was a deal which was
absolutely new to Burtzeff. He learned for the first time
of the attempt that was to take place on the cruiser
Rurik, for his conversation with Savinkoff took place
in September, when the *Rurik* was still on her way to
Kronstadt, and when the terrorists were waiting daily
for the telegrams which would announce the Czar's
assassination during the review. We can easily imagine

the impression this account made on Burtzeff. He had the firm *conviction* that the accusations which he had brought against Aseff were true, but he had neither absolute *certitude* nor documentary *proof*. Savinkoff's information made his position all the more embarrassing and trying. And it was then that he decided to draw Lopuhin into a frank conversation. This attempt, as we have seen in the first chapter, was fully successful.

"I know nobody of the name of 'Raskin,' but I have seen the engineer, Ievno Aseff, several times," had said in an agitated tone the former chief of the Police Department, who had permitted Aseff to enter the Battle Organization, but who had not until that conversation the slightest conception of how far his assistant had traveled along the path on which he had set him.

That conversation gave Burtzeff what he had hitherto lacked—the *certitude* of the correctness of his accusation. It did not matter now that Aseff had killed Plehve and might any day kill the Czar himself. The motives of his action were unknown, but it was known now that he was in the pay of the police, and if he was not betraying the terrorists at the moment, he had certainly betrayed them in the past. It was impossible to accept such a situation. If Aseff's closest friends still refused to open their eyes, there would be nothing left but to make the accusation public.

In this mood, Burtzeff, immediately after his conversation with Lopuhin, wrote an open letter to the members of the Social Revolutionary party and had it set up in type. In it he repeated his accusations against Aseff and explained the reasons which led him to make these public. This letter was sent in proof to the members of the Central Committee. And only after this was the decision to try Burtzeff, arrived at a month earlier,

put into execution. Among the judges it was decided
to include three of the oldest and most popular revolutionaries, Figner, Lopatin, and Krapotkin. "We must
take measures to pacify Burtzeff, who is spreading
right and left the rumor that Aseff is an *agent provocateur*," said Natanson, a member of the Central Committee, when inviting Figner to officiate at the trial.
Everybody was still convinced that it was merely a
question of "pacifying" Burtzeff.

The Court of Honor sat in Paris, for the most part in
Savinkoff's apartment, in a small unpretentious room
almost bare of furniture. The proceedings were conducted entirely without ceremonial; all sat together,
the judges, the accused, and the representatives of the
prosecution; Lopatin was the official chairman, but, in
fact, the inquiry was conducted principally by Tchernoff, who, together with Natanson and Savinkoff, as delegates of the Central Committee, represented the prosecution. The atmosphere, which was easy enough at the
beginning, became more and more tense as the proceedings went on.

Burtzeff, who had promised not to reveal Lopuhin's
name, confined himself at first to the facts which he had
learned from Bakay. But all this was indirect evidence,
based chiefly on rumors current in police circles. They
would carry conviction if the hearers had complete faith
in Bakay. But this, of course, was not the case. Burtzeff
himself, too, was in a difficulty, for he was one against
three, and each of these was a much more experienced
and clever orator. He was particularly violently attacked by Tchernoff, who, according to Figner, "like a
skilful cross-examiner, pounced on every statement he
made." Burtzeff astonished everybody by his complete
inability to parry the thrusts of his opponent.

Some of the judges wavered. Krapotkin, who had had great experience with *agents provocateurs* among the French anarchists of the 'eighties and 'nineties, remembered that history knew no case of suspicions roused in different circles and spread over a number of years against any definite person not being justified in the end. Nevertheless, the scales seemed to be weighed against Burtzeff. The prosecution's strongest card was Aseff's revolutionary services. Unfolding these in a long and eloquent speech, Savinkoff turned to Burtzeff and asked him with emotion:

"I turn to you, Vladimir Lvovitch, as a historian of the Russian Revolutionary movement, and I beg you, now that we have told you of Aseff's achievements, to tell us absolutely frankly whether there exists in the history of the Russian Revolutionary movement, already famous for its Zhelyaboffs, Gershunis and Sazonoffs, or in that of other countries, a more brilliant name than that of Aseff."

"Do you know," said Figner to Burtzeff, "what you will have to do if your accusations are proved groundless? You will have nothing left but to shoot yourself for all the harm that you have done to the Revolution. . . ."

Finding himself in such a terrible position, Burtzeff at the last moment decided to break his promise to Lopuhin.

"I have the evidence of one more witness," he began, and demanding from those present a solemn promise not to let it go beyond the room, he told them in detail of his meeting with Lopuhin.

His account made a tremendous impression. "Never in my life," Burtzeff recalls, "have I talked to such an attentive audience. . . . When I repeated Lopuhin's words—'I know nobody of the name of "Raskin," but I have seen the engineer, Ievno Aseff, several times'— everybody jumped up and began talking at once. Lopatin, agitated and with tears in his eyes, came up to me, put his hands on my shoulders and said, 'Give me your word of honor as a revolutionary that you heard these words from Lopuhin....' I wanted to answer him, but he turned away and said with a hopeless gesture, 'But, what's the use of talking? ... It's all clear now!'"

The situation had completely changed. "All those present were absolutely dumbfounded," confesses Figner, who had up till then been entirely on Aseff's side. The Central Committee delegates tried to combat the general feeling. Natanson said that Lopuhin was a disgraced director of the Police Department, and that he was deliberately slandering a "dangerous" revolutionary, hoping in this way to regain favor with the government, but this explanation sounded artificial to all. After a brief consultation Krapotkin announced in the name of the judges that the party must verify Lopuhin's story. The trial of Burtzeff had come to an end; and now, for the first time, began the investigation into Aseff's activities.

The trial had lasted over a month, and Aseff was out of Paris most of the time. He had spent the greater part of the summer, after his visit to Glasgow, with Madame N——, first in Ostend and then in Paris. Then he had gone with her to London to take part in the Conference. Argunoff states that Aseff was often absent from its sessions, and this, according to Madame N——, was due to the fact that their London stay was one long picnic. But there was one question to which Aseff gave serious attention; he put forward new and increased demands for money for the needs of the Battle Organization after the Central Committee had worked out its budget of expenditure. The Central Committee, as usual, gave way, and the budget was readjusted. . . . His life in Paris with Madame N——, after their return from London, was as much of a picnic. Even his outward appearance had changed so much that it began to attract the attention of his party comrades. Always carefully shaven, wearing an elegant, well-cut suit, he looked a regular dandy. And it was at this time that Madame N—— received from Aseff her most valuable presents, one of which, a pair of diamond earrings bought in Paris, cost him twenty-five thousand francs. . . .

Aseff had attended the meetings of the Central Committee previous to the summoning of the court and had helped to draw up the program for the court's procedure. He had refused, however, to appear before the court, as he was "too disgusted to wallow in the mud which Burtzeff was stirring up," and he entrusted the defense of his "honor" to his closest party friends. These latter sympathized with an attitude which they themselves would have taken up in similar circumstances. And they not only readily undertook his defense, but they also urged him to leave Paris in order to rest and think things over quietly.

Aseff did go away to a small resort in the Pyrenees, not far from Biarritz, where his wife and children were living at the time. He separated for the moment from Madame N——; he had to live up to the rôle of one suffering from a deep insult, and a gay life might have provoked comment. In spite of the threat hanging over him, Aseff's thoughts turned constantly to Madame N——, and family life appeared very boring to him now. His letters to Madame N—— are full of reproaches for not writing and of hopes of seeing her again as soon as

possible. Fairly soon he found an opportunity of putting
an end to the separation. His children's summer holi-
days were over, and Aseff persuaded his wife to take
them back to school in Paris. Madame N——, summoned by telegram, soon arrived, and while his friends
were defending his "honor," he once more resumed his
gay life in Biarritz. At the end of October, when the
weather got colder, Aseff and Madame N—— went on
a tour through Spain; they saw bullfights in San Sebastian, and wandered about Madrid. . . .

He was not particularly worried about the trial at
first. Letters from Paris sounded very optimistic, and
he hoped that this "dirty business of judicial inquiry"
would come to a speedy and satisfactory end. It is
possible, too, that he was hoping to receive a telegram
any day announcing that Avdeyeff had made his attempt against the Czar, in which case he need fear nothing from Burtzeff, for no revolutionary court would
dare to decide against the organizer of the Czar's assassination. But this telegram did not arrive, the trial
dragged on, and Aseff grew more and more irritable in
his letters to his friends in Paris. "It is time to have done
with this farce," he exclaims in one of his letters to
Savinkoff from San Sebastian. But there was no putting
an end to this "farce." On the contrary, it forced him to
interrupt his promenade through the land of toreadors.
Madame N—— recalls that Aseff, on receiving some
letters, announced to her that they must separate for
the time being, and that he had to return to Paris on
important "commercial business."

There can be no doubt that these were the letters
written after Burtzeff's revelation of his meeting with
Lopuhin. The latter's name and the details of the interview were kept secret, but the sudden change of direc-

tion taken by the trial was no longer a secret among the revolutionaries in general. The news of a "mysterious sensation" which had compelled the Central Committee to undertake a special investigation in St. Petersburg passed from mouth to mouth. In any case, Aseff must have been informed of this by those of his friends who still considered him innocent. Among these was Argunoff, whom the Central Committee was sending to St. Petersburg to collect information about Lopuhin. Before leaving Paris he felt himself obliged not only to bid good-bye to Aseff's wife but to write to Aseff himself: "I wrote him a brief postcard in which, taking leave of him, I asked him not to alarm or upset himself and to be courageous," he recalls in his memoirs.

It may have been this very card which filled Aseff with alarm, and forced him to hurry to Paris in an attempt to save the position as far as he could. But in Paris he learned that the position was much worse than he expected. And Aseff did not improve matters by making mistake after mistake. "When God wishes to punish anyone," he wrote later about his conduct at that time, "He takes away his reason."

Though it is not known who did so, there is documentary evidence to show that somebody broke his word and told Aseff about Lopuhin and gave him the details of his interview with Burtzeff. Aseff now took a desperate step. Unknown to his comrades he hurried to St. Petersburg and, together with Gerassimoff, took every step to try to persuade Lopuhin to repudiate his statements. First Aseff and then Gerassimoff called on Lopuhin with this object in view. These visits, however, had a directly opposite effect. Lopuhin decided to burn his boats and agreed to meet Argunoff, who was in St. Petersburg collecting information about Lopuhin from the latter's

Liberal friends. In this interview, Lopuhin went further
than he had with Burtzeff and told all he knew about
Aseff. "I listened in silence without interrupting
Lopuhin," recalls Argunoff, who had gone to the interview still full of faith in Aseff. "The tale unfolded of
Aseff's activity pressed with its crushing weight upon
my brain. I wished to find but one weak spot in the tale
and so tear asunder this ingeniously contrived mesh of
evidence. But I failed to find a single false note or con-
tradiction in his account. It breathed of truth."

Lopuhin went even further: he agreed to go to London
and there repeat his story before three of the party representatives, Argunoff, Savinkoff, and Tchernoff. And
his account impressed them, too, as being entirely
true. In the meantime, other more objective evidence
against Aseff had become available. Lopuhin had given
the exact date of Aseff's visit to him, and when the latter
was asked where he had been during those days, he
tried to establish an alibi by bringing forward various
Berlin hotel bills. But on investigation these were not
only proved to be forgeries, but there were indications
also that they had been prepared with the help of the
police. The chain of accusation was now almost complete.

On January 5, 1909, the Central Committee called a
meeting of the leading party members and, putting the
case before them, asked them to decide upon a course of
action. The splendor of Aseff's past was still so dazzling
that of the fifteen or eighteen members present only
four, Zenzinoff, Prokofieff, Savinkoff, and Sletoff, voted
for immediate death. The others hesitated, though
Natanson was the only one who still hoped that Aseff
might justify himself. But the former were finally
stopped short by the fear that Aseff's immediate execu-

tion might provoke fratricidal conflict within the party, for Karpovitch had just written from St. Petersburg to say that he would "shoot the whole of the Central Committee" if they dared to lay their hands on Aseff. It was known that this mood was also shared by several other members of the Battle Organization. And it was also feared that Aseff's execution would lead to reprisals against the *émigrés*.

A compromise was reached. It was decided to try to entice Aseff, under the pretext of a trial, to an isolated villa taken specially for the purpose, and there to make an end of him quietly. This at least would reduce to a minimum the danger of reprisals on the part of the French police. In the meantime three delegates were sent to question Aseff, and the condition was made that they should go unarmed, as it was feared that otherwise one of them might not be able to resist the temptation to kill him.

These delegates, Tchernoff, Savinkoff, and Panoff ("Nicolai," as he was known in the Battle Organization), called on Aseff late on the evening of the same day. From their first words Aseff realized that the verdict had gone against him. His self-control now deserted him. He became confused and contradicted himself, but seeing that they were not going to shoot him, he soon recovered some of his equanimity and endeavored to turn his confusion to profit. He said that he could not now give a satisfactory explanation, as circumstances were against him and he felt himself in a hostile camp, and he was also put out by the fact that his closest friends were now turning against him. He made an attempt to play upon the past. Facing Tchernoff and looking him straight in the eyes, he said in a trembling voice:

"Victor, we have been such good friends for so many years. We worked together. You know me. . . . How could you come to me with such loathsome suspicions?"

But this availed him nothing. Instead, he was asked to give a frank account of his relations with the police. Aseff evidently hesitated for a moment. It can be said with certainty that, if he had been looking down the barrel of a revolver, he would have acquiesced and bought his life at any cost. But there was no revolver; and after a moment's hesitation he persisted in a complete denial. The delegates eventually left, having made Aseff promise that he would come at midday on the following day to Tchernoff's flat. Aseff promised, but, of course, had not the slightest intention of keeping his word.

As soon as the door had shut upon the delegates, Aseff began to prepare hurriedly for flight. To his wife, who still believed in him, he explained that he must go away for a time in order to be able to collect at peace the proofs of his innocence. He said that he could not defend himself now, as "they" had decided to kill him. But he would soon return with proofs and vindicate his honor. He was worried most by the thought that the revolutionaries might be keeping watch on his house. He looked out of the window of a dark room several times, but the streets were deserted. No revolutionaries were to be seen.

Aseff took practically nothing in the way of luggage with him. However, he went carefully through his papers, destroyed some of them, and, before leaving, put the sailor Avdeyeff's farewell letter in a prominent place on his writing desk. He took with him the rest of his papers, letters from party friends, documents, and such relics as Sazonoff's letters from Schlüsselberg. It is hard to believe that the delegates had made no effort to examine his papers.

It was half-past three in the morning of January 6, 1909, when Aseff left his apartment. His wife accompanied him to the station, and put him on the first train going to Germany. Aseff gave her a Vienna address to which letters were to be forwarded for the moment; but he did not go direct to Vienna, stopping first in Madame N——'s native town in Central Germany, where she had been staying with her mother since her return from Spain.

On the following day, his wife sent him a letter full of sadness, fears and doubts, and of urgent prayers that he should establish his innocence as soon as possible: the situation was becoming unbearable, and even their most devoted friends were beginning to look on her with mistrust and even suspicion. And as it happened, Aseff was that very day writing his last report to Gerassimoff, in which he drew the latter's attention to the part played by Lopuhin in his exposure as he had understood it from the delegates who had questioned him.

Aseff's police career was now at an end. He could no longer be of service to either Gerassimoff or Stolypin. For this they could not forgive Lopuhin. Stolypin determined to make an example of him by bringing him to trial and thus demonstrating the measures which the government was prepared to take against those of its officials who had betrayed their trust. As the trial would be very sensational, Stolypin consulted the Czar beforehand and acquainted him with Aseff's services. Nicholas II now learned for the first time who had betrayed Nikitenko and who had frustrated the Reval attempt.

The Czar sanctioned the trial all the more readily because he had disliked Lopuhin for his exposure of the secret of the printing of the pogrom manifestos; Nicholas himself regarded these manifestos with great favor. The trial was carried through in record time. On Stolypin's special instructions, Lopuhin was prevented both at the preliminary inquiry and in court from making his most important statement, which would have accused his opponents in the Police Department, and in particular Stolypin himself, of being chiefly responsible for Aseff's double game. Lopuhin was only able to make this statement in 1917, before the Extraordinary Commission of Inquiry set up by the provisional government. His account is not entirely dependable, for he undoubtedly did not speak the whole truth before this commission, concealing a great deal in the hope of whitewashing his own police past. Still, it is of great interest and deserves to be given here:

". . . Once in the spring of 1906 my former associate in the Police Department, Makaroff, told me, on my questioning him about Aseff, that he was still working for Ratchkovsky and Gerassimoff, and that his informative rôle was greater than ever. Soon after, my old school friend, Stolypin, with whom I had renewed acquaintance only two years previously, became Minister of the Interior. I immediately told him about Aseff, and gave him the details of the police printing press which had been used for printing pogrom manifestos discovered by me in January, 1906. Stolypin, it seemed to me, was equally indignant at Aseff's rôle as an *agent provocateur* and at the department's pogrom policy, and he expressed his determination to put an end to both of them. I went abroad a few days later and there read the report of the Duma session at which Stolypin replied to questions about the activities of this printing

press. His explanation was such a perversion of the facts
that I was forced to conclude either that Stolypin was
deliberately lying to the Duma or that he had been deceived by his subordinates. As I had no grounds for
suspecting him of the first, I wrote an official letter to
him in which I warned him of the deception and set
before him the evidence which I had told him orally.
The explanations which took place between us on my
return from abroad left no doubt that Stolypin was
deliberately perverting the truth in his statements to the
Duma.

"Our relations after this were almost broken off, and
soon they did, in fact, come to an end. In our conversation about the Jewish pogroms in Siedlce in September,
1906, Stolypin angrily accused me of being a manifest
revolutionary, and, as Minister of the Interior, warned
me to regulate my conduct accordingly. I replied that,
after his false statements in the Duma, I no longer
trusted him in anything, and that I thought him
capable of making use of Aseff's services; and I also
warned him that, if it came to my knowledge that Aseff
was acting as a police agent, I would make every effort
to expose him and put an end to the matter. Learning
from Burtzeff, in September, 1908, that Aseff was still
acting as an *agent provocateur*, I told Burtzeff all I knew
about Aseff, and afterwards confirmed this to the representatives of the Social Revolutionary party. When
I was brought to trial I was asked why I had informed
Burtzeff rather than any personage in the government of
these facts about Aseff. I replied that I had, in the first
place, turned to such a personage, but before I had time
to name Stolypin the assistant prosecutor interrupted
me by asking me if I could prove this by producing any
witness of the interview. As my reply was in the nega-

tive, the assistant prosecutor warned me that if I
named this personage without bringing evidence in support of my statement I would only prejudice my case
still more.

"I had no witness of my interview with Stolypin, and
therefore did not mention his name during the preliminary inquiry. I wished to do so in court, but the president deprived me of the right to address the court. I
am sure that one of the chief reasons for my arrest and
trial was to prevent me from naming Stolypin as Aseff's
protector. This was thought worth the scandal which
my arrest and trial cost Stolypin and the government. . . ."

The historian is forced to admit that Lopuhin was
right in at least one thing: that Stolypin was Aseff's
immediate protector. Gerassimoff's account referred to
above removes all doubt about this. Lopuhin was far
from realizing the whole truth!

The court condemned him to penal servitude, finding
him guilty, in the face of all logic and evidence to the
contrary, of belonging to the Social Revolutionary
party, solely on the ground that he had talked about
Aseff to some of its members. Only on appeal to a higher
court was this sentence mitigated, but Lopuhin was
nevertheless exiled to Siberia.

Stolypin might well regard this as a victory, but it
brought him little joy. The trial had excited the attention not only of the Russian, but of the world press. The
Aseff affair and the "mysteries of the Russian police"
were for a long time the favorite theme of the world's
sensational journalism, and the Russian government
came in for severe criticism. Wide currency was given
to theories that Aseff, the terrorist, was but a tool in
the hands of his police chiefs, and that only those of

his attempts were successful which were organized on the direct instructions of Ratchkovsky and then Gerassimoff. These theories, though fundamentally untrue, received credence even in Russian governmental circles. They poisoned Ratchkovsky's last years, and, as if he had not enough on his own conscience, he had to pay for Aseff, with whom he had had fewer dealings than had any other police chief. In connection with this affair he was put under observation and his house was searched. Gerassimoff paid still more dearly. He who had boasted that the Revolution of 1905 had been crushed thanks to him barely escaped being court-martialed.

After Aseff's exposure, Gerassimoff had gone on long leave. In the four years that he had been chief of the St. Petersburg Ochrana, he had not once taken a holiday, and he now intended to take a rest. He was at that moment at the height of his fame. Stolypin had entirely supported his view of the Aseff affair, and had undertaken the latter's defense in the Duma. Gerassimoff was promised on his return the post of Assistant to the Minister of the Interior, with the special task of directing the police throughout the Empire. But by the time he had returned a radical change had taken place in the situation. To the suspicions aroused by the Aseff affair were now added those of the Petroff affair.

Petroff was a young Social Revolutionary who was in prison at the moment of Aseff's exposure: he was threatened with penal servitude. Inspired by the Aseff affair, he decided, in order to save himself and his friends, to pretend to be anxious to enter the police service. He was believed, and the police helped him to escape, releasing at the same time several of his friends who were to help to consolidate his position in the party.

On arriving abroad, Petroff told his party friends of his relations with the police, with romantic exaggerations, it is true, and offered his services to the party in expiation of his error. His offer was accepted, and he was detailed to organize the assassination of Gerassimoff, with whom he was in negotiation, about his entry into the police. With this object, Petroff and his friends set out for St. Petersburg, but he did not succeed in seeing Gerassimoff, as the latter had just been suspended from his police work on account of the suspicions against him over the Aseff affair. Instead, he came into touch with Gerassimoff's successor, Colonel Karpoff. Petroff organized his assassination, and, when questioned after his arrest, declared that he had carried out the assassination on Gerassimoff's instructions. This he did to compromise Gerassimoff in the eyes of the government. Petroff obviously was unable to prove his statement, but in the atmosphere of distrust which followed Aseff's exposure there were found many to believe this. Petroff himself was speedily executed, but a special secret commission long puzzled over the question of what to do with Gerassimoff. The majority were in favor of handing him over to a court-martial, and only Stolypin's personal intervention stopped another sensational trial.

But the very possibility of such a suggestion is a clear indication of the changes that had taken place in the positions of the police chiefs after the Aseff affair. Disintegration and complete mistrust on the one hand, and, on the other, an evil reputation throughout the world: such was the vengeance taken by Aseff, the *agent provocateur*, against the system which had made his existence possible.

Aseff's vengeance did not stop with the police. When

all doubt as to his treachery had vanished, the *émigré* terrorists began to agitate for the necessity of "rehabilitating the honor of the terror." Savinkoff was a particularly warm advocate of this. He recognized only one mode of action—to resurrect the Battle Organization and to prove by deeds that terrorists still existed and that terror was still possible. He said that this was the only way of washing out the stain on its honor left by Aseff. His appeals were heard by many, and he carefully chose twelve terrorists to form his detachment. Among them were some who, like Prokofieff, Klimoff, Sletoff, and Tchernavsky, had already made reputations for themselves in revolutionary work. There was not one of them who had not already behind him a record of imprisonment, exile, and penal servitude. There was something in their campaign which was reminiscent of the last attack made by Napoleon's Old Guard. It seemed that nothing could stop these veterans or turn them from their purpose. But, in fact, this last attack turned out to be worse than useless.

Not only did three of these twelve prove to be traitors, whereas the old Battle Organization had known no traitor except Aseff himself, but Savinkoff, the author of the campaign, could not summon up enough courage to risk his head: he traveled aimlessly abroad, spending large sums of party money, but never ventured to cross the Russian frontier. Aseff's treachery would seem to have undermined all belief and purity of motive. "The terror was not begun by Aseff and will not end with him," wrote Tchernoff in one of his articles on the Aseff affair, at the time when Savinkoff was organizing the last campaign. The student of history is, alas, forced to admit that only the first half of this sentence is true: the terror was not begun by Aseff, but it came to an end with him. A year or two later, while traveling secretly in Russia, Sletoff found everywhere in party circles either indifference to the terror or prejudice against it. "My impression was," he said, "that even if the party had succeeded in assassinating the Czar himself, most of its members would have suspected this to be the result of provocation." In these circumstances, the terror as a method of fighting became both politically and psychologically impossible.

CHAPTER XX

The Traitor in Retirement

AFTER HIS FLIGHT from Paris Aseff began a new life, one which he had long dreamed of and for which he had been systematically preparing.

He did not stay long with Madame N—— in her provincial home. On receiving his last month's salary from Gerassimoff (his last month, as officially recorded, is December, 1908: in all, he had been fifteen years and seven months in the police service) and a small additional bonus and, what was of the greatest importance to him, a few safe passports, he at once set out on a voyage with Madame N——. This was a real "honeymoon," stretching over many months. They spent the

first half of 1909 in the south, in Italy, Greece, and
Egypt, wandering among the ruins of the Coliseum,
visiting Ægean islands, and climbing the pyramid of
Cheops. Later, when it grew hot, they went northward
and toured Sweden, Norway, and Denmark. They
spent money freely, traveling first class and stopping
at the best hotels. They did not stay long anywhere,
their most protracted visits being to Luxor, and Vester-
felde on the North Sea. Aseff was, of course, afraid of
being recognized.

At that time the newspapers were full of articles about
him and photographs of him, and Aseff always looked
carefully around him for fear of meeting anybody who
knew him. On arriving at a new hotel he carefully
examined the list of other guests, and he refused to
remain there if any Russians were among them. There
were times, too, when he would return home agitated
after some meeting or another and give orders for their
immediate departure. He constantly changed his passport, and Madame N—— recalls that she often found
it difficult for the moment to remember her name.

It was only towards autumn that Aseff to a certain
extent recovered his equanimity. It was time to think
of settling down. He chose Berlin as his permanent
place of residence and had himself registered as Alexander Neumayer, a merchant, and his wife. They took a
large six-room apartment in one of the best quarters
of Berlin, in Wilmersdorf, 21 Leopoldstrasse. They did
not stint money in their furnishing. They bought a
grand piano, cut glass and silver for their table service.
Later Aseff insured these things for twenty thousand
marks, although they were worth more. He had evidently settled down "seriously and permanently."

He took up the profession of a stockbroker. It would

seem that he was already interested in the Stock
Exchange and had been buying shares during the last
few years. From 1911 his name figures on the official
register of traders in Berlin, and he had an annual
membership card for the Stock Exchange (his card
bore the number 765 in 1915). He did business on a
fairly large scale, and it was not without pride that he
wrote later from his Berlin prison that his name was
known, not only in Berlin, but also in the New York
and London exchanges. It is difficult to estimate the
amount of money he invested, but certainly it was not
small, for we know that the loss of some fourteen
thousand marks in 1913 did not upset him much. We
may assume that the sum was not less than one hundred
thousand marks. As he had at this time set aside thirty
thousand marks in the name of Madame N——, and
spent at least twenty-five thousand on furnishing his
apartment, and no less than fifty thousand at Madame
N——'s valuation on jewelry for her, and as his
"picnics" of 1908–09 must also have cost him a good
sum, we cannot put the total amount saved by Aseff in
the course of his "highly respectable" work for the
police at less than two hundred fifty thousand marks.

Life now flowed in a measured and peaceful way. He
made influential friends in German circles and was fond
of entertaining. The life seemed to satisfy Aseff fully.
A photograph of the time shows him as a tranquil and
good-natured citizen, and his letters of the time breathe
bourgeois happiness. Aseff displayed, too, a fondness for
gambling. This helped, perhaps, to make the transition
easier from his former life of nervous tension to the
more tranquil existence of a stockbroker. In any case,
his passion for gambling often took him to the South
of France, where he frequently indulged it to such an

ASEFF AND MADAME N—— AT THE SEASIDE.

extent that he would often be left without a penny and be obliged to telegraph for money to pay his bills and bring him home.

Aseff did not keep in touch with the Political Police, nor could he do so any longer, for, after 1910, the Police Department began to have an inkling of the double game he had been playing, and it published secret instructions to its agents to try to discover his whereabouts and put under close observation all those police officials who had come into contact with him. All possibility of regaining favor in that quarter was closed to Aseff, but he had nothing to fear from it, for any attempt on the part of the government to call him to account would have provoked too great a scandal. But from discussions about him which found an occasional echo in the newspapers, it was clear that the revolutionaries were still on his trail. And Aseff understood perfectly well that he always ran the risk of being accidentally discovered by them.

We know now that Aseff's fears were more than justified. News of his residence in Berlin had come to the ears of the revolutionaries, and a small group of Russian and German Social Democrats under the leadership of Karl Liebknecht began a systematic hunt for him; and they had got very near to him. It was no secret what would happen to him if he were discovered: Alexander Neumayer, the merchant, would not have long enjoyed his bourgeois happiness. In these circumstances Aseff must inevitably have thought of ways in which he might obtain an amnesty from the revolutionaries. He remembered well that Tchernoff had suggested to him during the inquiry that he should save his life by revealing the whole truth of his relations with the police. He had no particular incentive to preserve police secrets, for he had never shared any sympathy of ideas with the police, and at the moment it was the question of his personal advantage that weighed most with him.

With this object in view Aseff, as early as 1910–11, began to make overtures to his former party colleagues. In letters to his wife he spoke of his readiness to appear before a party court, to which he would tell the whole truth, and whose decision he would accept, even if it were a death penalty. But his letters remained unanswered. He did, however, get the opportunity of parleying with the revolutionaries and of telling the world at large that he had broken his relations with the police.

This happened in 1912. Aseff was spending July of that year in Neinar, near Nauheim, which was a center of treatment for acute neurasthenia and slight disorders of the heart. He liked this resort very much, but its one drawback in his eyes was that there were too many Russians there. It is evident from his letters that he scanned the list of the new arrivals every morning with great trepidation for fear of running up against some old acquaintance. His anxiety was not without foundation, for the revolutionaries did discover his address and informed Burtzeff of it. The latter had long sought the opportunity of meeting Aseff, being convinced that he would learn much that was of interest to him as a historian, and he therefore immediately wrote suggesting an appointment. Burtzeff assured him that there was no question of a trap, and that he was eager to meet him simply as a historian, but he let it be known that if Aseff would not agree to this meeting he might make different use of his knowledge of his address.

This letter could scarcely fail to frighten Aseff. Realizing the justice of Burtzeff's remarks, he hastened to agree. "Your suggestion that we should meet," he wrote, "coincides with my own long-standing desire that the truth about me should be told." But he put off the meeting for a week in order to arrange his personal affairs. These were none other than the disposal of the flat taken in the name of Neumayer, which was no longer safe. Madame N—— went off to her mother in the provinces, while all the furniture was stored. Aseff also took the precaution of making a will, in which he left everything to Madame N——.

His meeting with Burtzeff took place on August 15, 1912, in the Café Bristol in Frankfort. For two days Aseff spoke of his past, trying to make himself out to be a revolutionary who had in his youth committed the error of establishing relations with the police and who, not having enough courage to confess the fact to his comrades, had used his connections with the police to benefit the revolutionary cause.

From his account it would appear that he had wished to make his services to the revolution so indisputable as to be able to confess freely to his relations with the police. It was with this object in view that he had organized various terrorist acts. But on each occasion he had doubted whether he had made sufficient atonement for his mistake. He had hoped to be able to bring about the Czar's assassination and then to tell the whole truth. But it was he, Burtzeff, who had prevented him from achieving this.

"If it had not been for you," said Aseff reproachfully, "I would have killed him. . . ."

And then Aseff tried to show that his activities had on the whole benefited the revolutionaries much more than the police. He harped continually on this theme, in illustration holding his hands in front of him as if they were scales on which the good he had done to the revolutionary cause outweighed whatever services he had done to the police.

"Do you think the two can be compared?" he said in a persuasive voice. "What did I do? I organized the assassination of Plehve, that of the Grand Duke Sergei . . ."—and with every new name his right hand dropped lower and lower like a scale when new weights are added to it—"And whom did I give up to the police? Only Sletoff, Lomoff, Vedenyapin . . ."—and as he mentioned these names he did not lower his left hand, but, on the contrary, raised it as if in illustration of the insignificance of his services to the police in comparison with those to the Revolution.

Burtzeff had no desire to debate this point. He had not come to discuss revolutionary ethics. But in reply to these arguments he could not help remarking:

"But it's not a question merely of that. . . . It is one of principles at bottom. . . ." But he pulled up short, for Aseff was staring with large, astonished eyes, which reflected such complete lack of comprehension that all desire to discuss the question disappeared.

Aseff talked a great deal about his relations with the police and gave characteristic descriptions of all those of its chiefs with whom he had come in contact. He spoke with respect of only one of them, Gerassimoff. But even here he boasted that he had got round Gerassimoff so well that he was sure that the latter still fully trusted him, which as we know was true. . . . Of the other police chiefs Aseff talked with unconcealed contempt as of brainless people whom he had no difficulty in twisting round his little finger. He even put on the air of being offended at the idea that he could feel any sympathy for them, while, on the other hand, he spoke of the affection he felt towards many of his colleagues in the Battle Organization.

Aseff was particularly eager to show that he had had no connection with the police for some time past, and that all suggestions of this in the Russian and foreign newspapers were entirely untrue, and that, furthermore, the supposition that he could continue to be of harm to the Revolution was entirely without foundation, for he had neither the opportunity nor the wish to do so. On the contrary, he would be glad if his account of his relations with the police could be of use to the Revolution, and he therefore asked Burtzeff to take it upon himself to organize his trial, and was especially anxious that a notice of the coming trial should be published in the papers, French and German as well as Russian.

The impression Burtzeff carried away with him was by no means definite. He believed that Aseff "really wished to be tried by his old comrades," but he was not clear as to Aseff's motives. He also felt that Aseff had not given him an absolutely frank account. This made him anxious to have Aseff tried, so as to be able to question him in greater detail instead of killing him off like a mad dog, as many of the revolutionaries felt inclined to do at the time. It was in this frame of mind that Burtzeff wrote his account of his meeting with Aseff, an account which was printed in papers all over the world.

The idea of the trial came to nothing, for Aseff's "old comrades" had a spiritual aversion to meeting him and refused to have anything to do with it. We shall never know what Aseff would have done if the court had sentenced him to death. Our knowledge of Aseff leads us to doubt whether he would have submitted to it and put an end to his life as he had promised to do. But Aseff had gained at least one point by his conversation with Burtzeff: he had made the latter believe, and through him the whole world, that he was no longer connected with the police. This could not but have the effect of making the revolutionaries slacken in their hunt for him. This was what Aseff wanted most.

Burtzeff had promised not to put the revolutionaries on his track. Aseff believed this promise, but nevertheless he took measures of precaution. He at once left Frankfort for Deauville, to "refresh" himself at the green tables. On this occasion luck went against him to begin with, and he had already lost nearly all his money and had sent a telegram to Madame N—— for a thousand francs, when at the last moment fortune turned, and he left a winner. Aseff returned to Germany from Deauville, but he at first avoided Berlin, going down the Rhine and the Moselle, stopping at a sanatorium at Wildungen and also staying with Madame N——'s mother. The Balkan crisis forced Aseff to return to Berlin in the interests of his Stock Exchange affairs, but he lived alone in hotels, using different passports. It was only in the autumn of 1913 that he risked establishing himself again in a more permanent way.

The war dealt Aseff his cruellest blow. He had had the imprudence to keep most of his money in Russian bonds, and the interdiction to quote Russian bonds on the Berlin Stock Exchange after the outbreak of war was a real financial disaster for him. He lost almost all his fortune. His "picnic" days were over, and he was now faced with the problem of earning his daily bread. But Aseff made a fight for it. Gathering all that remained, and even selling part of Madame N——'s jewelry, he opened a fashionable corset shop in her name. Mobilizing all his practical abilities, he conducted the whole of the commercial side of the business himself. Later he even tried to direct the business from prison, advising Madame N—— as to the quality and quantity of things to buy, and so forth. His prison letters make curious reading: in them we find almost philosophic arguments in favor of increasing the production of smaller sized corsets; he argued that the war threatened to be prolonged and the scanty diet would be bound in the long run to tell on women's figures. His shop, at any rate, caught on and made existence possible.

But the blow of August, 1914, was only a prelude to that of June, 1915. Madame N—— recalls that, returning home one summer day in the second year of the war, Aseff was angry with himself because some evil chance had sent him into a café in Friedrichstrasse, where he had met somebody who had known him by his real name. Aseff was absolutely crushed and said:

"He recognized me, and now I am in for it. . . ."

He spent the evening going through his papers, many of which he burned.

His fears were justified. The following day (from documents we can establish that this was June 12, 1915) they were approached on their way home by a respectably dressed man, who warningly turned back the lapel of his coat displaying a police badge. . . . That was enough. Aseff submissively followed him. Thus began the days of his prison trials.

The prison conditions were hard. Aseff was kept in solitary confinement in a damp, cold cell and had no light until the end of October, 1915. He was then given a gas lamp, but he could only use it up to eight o'clock in the evening. He was not allowed to see anyone.

From outside came the disquieting news that the remnants of his material fortune were rapidly disappearing; creditors were pressing, and debtors refused to pay.

Still more disquieting was his uncertainty as to his fate. At first he had some hope of an early release, but time passed, summer and autumn had gone by, and winter was at hand, but still nothing had happened. Aseff bombarded the police with petitions. Thinking that he had been arrested for his former connection with the Russian police, he repeatedly declared that he had long since broken all relations with them, and on November 22, 1915, in "utter despair," he sent in a petition to the police president, requesting that "his case should be investigated and that he should be set at liberty as an innocent man." From the answer to this petition he learned to his surprise that he was being held in prison not as an agent of the Russian government, but as a dangerous revolutionary, anarchist, and terrorist, who, according to the international police conventions, was to be handed over to the Russian authorities at the end of the war.

Aseff protested against this accusation with all the energy of his affronted innocence; first by oral statement and then in writing he declared that he had always been only a faithful agent of the government, acting on the instructions of his police chief, and that Stolypin himself had given him a certificate of his irreproachable police service. These pleas did not convince the German police, who replied, at the end of 1916, to an inquiry made by the Spanish consul that Aseff was "undoubtedly an anarchist, and moreover an upholder of the terror." Aseff succeeded, however, in having his prison conditions improved. There was even question at one time of transferring him to a civilian concentration camp, but Aseff himself was the cause of this not being done: he had asked to be placed in a camp composed of non-Russians, but the police absolutely refused to accede to this request, and they stated, moreover, that he would be registered under his real name, and that they would accept no responsibility for his safety. This prospect was so unpromising that Aseff preferred to remain in prison, and even signed a document to the effect that he was doing this of his own free will. But now he obtained certain privileges. He was allowed to see people, to read newspapers, and he was even permitted to go into town for two hours a day for walks and to make purchases.

That was the best period of his imprisonment, but it did not last very long, for soon after Aseff fell ill and was transferred to the hospital in the Moabite Prison. Here he was kept in strict solitary confinement, and there was now no question of visits to town. "I cannot exchange a word with anybody for weeks on end," Aseff complained, and he was even prepared to go to the civilian camp. But this was refused him on the ground of the paper he had signed himself. Aseff was thus obliged to live on in the prison hospital until the end of 1917, when he was released.

All this affected Aseff's spirits, and we can see this in his many letters to Madame N———. In these he always showed himself worried and depressed, but at the beginning he still had the strength to place himself in a favorable light to impress his readers. The readers were, of course, Madame N——— and the police official whose duty it was to read his letters. In writing Aseff kept both of them in mind.

At first he was more preoccupied with Madame N———. Her letters to him were full of bitter complaints.

She was not at all used to such trials; and it is possible
that Aseff was afraid that she would abandon him, for
he was no longer able to support her, and, indeed,
Madame N——'s jewelry was of late their only source
of income. It was a matter of the utmost importance
for Aseff to hold her, for not only was he sincerely
attached to her, but she was also the one person in the
world left to him. Therefore his early prison letters
show that he was chiefly preoccupied in retaining his
hold on Madame N——. All his letters emphasize his
love for her and his anxiety about her. He took the
deepest interest in every trifle, gave her advice and
the benefit of his worldly experience. As he could not
make any concrete suggestion, he counseled Christian
patience. His letters of the time are full of "God":
"with God's help" and such expressions are to be met
with in almost every line. "God" in Aseff's letters was
no mere phraseology, but began to become an integral
part of a wider Christian philosophy. He gave himself
out to be a man who had faith, who accepted with
humility the misfortunes which had befallen him, and
who was prepared to thank God for enlightening and
purifying his soul by these misfortunes.

Aseff played this part only while he was still anxious
about Madame N—— and uncertain as to his own fate.
Later, he allowed the mask to drop and thought more
and more of himself and his hard lot, forgetting her
trials. He took it as his due when she handed over her
ration of butter and cheese, and herself went to eat
in a communal dining room. His letters entirely lost
their religious tone. There was no more talk of attaining
bliss through suffering. But his views on his solitary
confinement now had a sincerer note. "I have already
been two years without you," he writes in an undated

note which had been delivered to Madame N—— without the knowledge of the authorities. "It's too disgusting for anything."

At the same time he exaggerated his sufferings. He was firmly convinced that his was the most trying lot of all those who had suffered through the war; for even though others died, they at least knew what they had fought for, whereas he was suffering for no known cause and through no fault of his own. "The greatest misfortune that could befall anybody has come upon me," he wrote not without humility. "A misfortune which can only be compared with that of Dreyfus." Thus Aseff remained an egotist to the last.

Aseff's release from prison came only after the conclusion of the Armistice which followed the October Revolution. On the basis of the agreement of December, 1917, as to the exchange of civilian prisoners, he was freed just before Christmas of that year. Madame N—— recounts that, on regaining his liberty, Aseff raged against the German authorities who had kept him in prison for two and a half years for no valid reason, and his one thought was to go as soon as possible to Switzerland. But it was not easy to leave Germany. The Armistice had been concluded only in the East; elsewhere restrictions still remained in full force, and, besides, his material position was very difficult. He had to think of earning a living, and, as Madame N—— tells us, he finally obtained a position in one of the departments of the German Ministry of Foreign Affairs. How he managed to secure this position, and what the nature of his work was, it has not yet been possible to establish. . . .

Aseff was not, however, fated to walk freely about the streets of Berlin for long. His imprisonment had seriously undermined his health, and he was now frequently unwell. About the middle of April, 1918, he had trouble with his kidneys and went to a hospital. On April 17th he wrote to Madame N—— saying that he was feeling very bad and that he had difficulty in writing even a short note. He rapidly grew worse, and on April 24th, about four o'clock in the afternoon, he died. He was buried on the 26th in the Wilmersdorf cemetery. Madame N—— was the only mourner. . . .

THE END

INDEX